The Great Houdini

The Great Houdini

His British Tours

Derek Tait

PEN & SWORD
HISTORY

First published in Great Britain in 2017 by
Pen & Sword History
an imprint of
Pen & Sword Books Ltd
47 Church Street
Barnsley
South Yorkshire
S70 2AS

ISBN 978 1 47386 794 9

A CIP catalogue record for this book is available from the British Library

Typeset in Minion by
Mac Style Ltd, Bridlington, East Yorkshire
Printed and bound in the UK by CPI Group (UK) Ltd,
Croydon, CR0 4YY

Pen & Sword Books Ltd incorporates the imprints of Pen & Sword
Archaeology, Atlas, Aviation, Battleground, Discovery, Family History,
History, Maritime, Military, Naval, Politics, Railways, Select, Transport, True
Crime, Fiction, Frontline Books, Leo Cooper, Praetorian Press, Seaforth
Publishing and Wharncliffe.

For a complete list of Pen & Sword titles please contact
PEN & SWORD BOOKS LIMITED
47 Church Street, Barnsley, South Yorkshire, S70 2AS, England
E-mail: enquiries@pen-and-sword.co.uk
Website: www.pen-and-sword.co.uk

Contents

Introduction

Harry Houdini was born Erik Weisz in Hungary on 24 March 1874, however, he claimed that he had been born in Appleton, Wisconsin on 6 April 1874. He was the son of Rabbi Mayer Samuel Weiss and his wife, Cecilia. He had a very close bond with his mother all his life.

Erik was one of seven children and had five brothers and one sister. One of his brothers, Herman, died at a young age.

On 3 July 1878, he travelled to the United States sailing on the SS *Fresia* with his mother and brothers and they settled in Appleton, Wisconsin where Erik's father served as a Rabbi. They changed the spelling of their surname to Weiss and Erik's name became Ehrich. His friends called him 'Ehrie' or 'Harry'.

At the age of 9, Ehrich gave his first public appearance when he performed as a trapeze artist and was billed as the 'Prince of the Air'. When he became a magician, he changed his name to Harry Houdini as he greatly admired the French magician, Jean Eugene Robert-Houdin.

Houdini started performing magic in 1891 and entertained with card tricks at sideshows and dime museums. At the time, he called himself 'The King of Cards'.

He later became interested in escape acts and appeared with his brother, Theo (Hardeen) whom Houdini also called 'Dash'. In 1893, while performing at Coney Island with Theo, he met Wilhelmina Beatrice Rahner (Bess). Houdini married Bess and she replaced Theo in his act.

In 1899 Houdini met his future manager, Martin Beck in Woodstock, Illinois. Beck was impressed by Houdini's stage act and booked him to appear on the Orpheum vaudeville circuit. The following year Beck arranged for Houdini to tour Europe. His first interviews in London were unsuccessful until he escaped from handcuffs at Scotland Yard, baffling his captives. Then he was booked at the Alhambra Theatre for six months by its manager, C. Dundas Slater and so began a series of tours around Great Britain that would continue for the next twenty years.

I have always been fascinated by Houdini and the more I've read about him, the more I've discovered about all the many venues that he played at all over Great Britain. There have been many books written about Houdini but none cover his tours of Britain in their entirety. In this book I have tried to collect together as many stories, newspaper cuttings, posters, adverts and photos of his visits to the UK.

A theatre poster advertising Harry Houdini King of Cards.

Houdini visited many theatres and music halls between 1900 and 1920. This book contains all his known venues during those years. There are probably more and, as they are discovered, they will be added to the book when it's revised in future editions. Amazingly, many libraries have no information that Houdini ever appeared in their towns and cities. This seems strange but perhaps newspaper articles and photos were lost during the heavy bombing of the Second World War.

Where possible, I have tried to include the complete account of the show as it was reported at the time in the local newspaper. This not only gives a good impression of what Houdini's act was like but also gives a feel of the time by including other performers who appeared on the bill with weird and wonderful acts such as performing dogs, contortionists, jugglers, illusionists, trapeze acts and comedians.

I hope that the book will not only provide a good reference for people interested in the life of Houdini, but will also prove interesting to those who had no knowledge that Houdini ever appeared in their town or city.

Chapter One

1900 – The First Tour

In a time when there were no cinemas, television or radio, theatres attracted audiences in their thousands and music hall artists were the film stars of the day. Top acts could pack out theatres and many people were turned away. Typical acts in 1900 included comedians, acrobats, military displays, bicycle acts, gymnasts and, of course, magicians. Well-known illusionists included Chung Ling Soo, the Great Lafayette, the Great Raymond, David Devant and many more. All would have a great influence on one man, who, at the beginning of 1900, hardly anyone in Great Britain had heard of. That man was, of course, Harry Houdini and, at the beginning of the twentieth century, with music hall at its peak, all was about to change for Houdini. Over the next twenty years, he appeared in theatres all over Great Britain performing escape acts, illusions, card tricks and outdoor stunts which would lead to his becoming one of the world's highest paid entertainers.

Houdini's tours of Britain began in the summer of 1900. He had heard that American magicians and vaudeville acts were doing well in Britain so he decided to travel to London with his wife, Bess. They sailed for England on 30 May 1900. Houdini was seasick for much of the journey and always suffered the same when travelling across the ocean. Arriving with no future engagements or work lined up, they visited several London agents but little interest was shown. At the same

The Alhambra
Theatre in the
early 1900s.

time, they met Harry Day, who was new to the business. He liked Houdini and promised to get him an audition at the Alhambra Theatre.

The Alhambra had formerly been the Royal Panopticon of Science and Art which had been built in the early 1850s to display scientific exhibitions and discoveries in art and manufacturing. It had limited success and was sold in 1857 so that it could be converted into the Alhambra Palace and a circus ring was installed. By 1860, a stage was added and the venue was converted into the Alhambra Palace Music Hall which opened its doors in December of that year. A new licence was issued in 1871 and the theatre was allowed to stage drama productions. The theatre was destroyed by fire in 1882 before being re-opened the following year and renamed the Alhambra Theatre of Varieties. All the big names of the day appeared there and it proved to be a major attraction in London.

Houdini visited the Alhambra Theatre in Leicester Square, shortly after meeting Harry Day, where he met with the manager, C. Dundas Slater, who told him that handcuff artists were 'a dime a dozen'. To prove his worth, Houdini arranged to have a Superintendent Melville cuff him to a pillar at Scotland Yard using British regulation handcuffs. Melville showed Dundas to the door saying that they would return and free Houdini when he had exhausted himself. Before they could turn the doorknob, they

Photo by Ellis and Walery,

MR. C. DUNDAS SLATER.

A portrait of C. Dundas Slater, the manager of the Alhambra Theatre.

Leicester Square, London.

A view of Leicester Square showing the Alhambra Theatre in the background.

An early publicity photo showing Houdini, complete in dress suit, with his hands cuffed.

Houdini displaying the manacles and handcuffs which he has managed to escape from.

Houdini manacled and chained before his miraculous escape.

heard a shout and Houdini was free. On the strength of his miraculous escape, Houdini was signed up to open at the Alhambra in July.

On Wednesday 27 June, Houdini put on a private rehearsal for members of the press at the theatre. Some had come prepared with their own handcuffs and these were put on Houdini who then retired into a crimson tent, which took up centre stage, before emerging a minute later with his hands free. Afterwards, an ancient uncomfortable pair of cuffs, which had rusty locks, were placed on his wrists. They were quite tight and produced blue rings where they encircled his arms. After two minutes of seclusion in his tent, he succeeded in opening them. Although spectators were told that they could freely examine the tent, many looked upon it suspiciously. It was suggested that an ordinary screen should be used and Mr Slater, the manager, happily produced one.

Houdini then had his hands manacled behind his back and irons were placed on his ankles; a further pair of handcuffs fastened his hands to his feet. He remained in a kneeling position at the front of the stage, facing the auditorium. The screen was then placed behind him so it did not block the view of the spectators, but prevented the committee on the stage from watching the proceedings. He quickly freed himself from all his bonds and threw his shackles on the floor one by one,

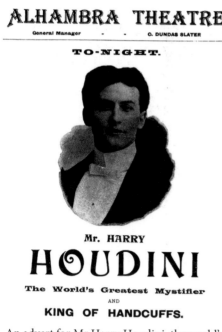

An advert for Mr Harry Houdini, the world's greatest mystifier and handcuff king.

A poster promoting the Houdinis' famous box trick, Metamorphosis.

all opened and undamaged. Houdini announced to the audience that he didn't slip the handcuffs but always unlocked them.

Afterwards, he performed the box trick and some clever feats with playing cards.

Working together, the Houdinis' act at the Alhambra soon became very popular. It combined sleight of hand tricks, singing, a clairvoyance routine and the infamous trunk trick. Their first show was on 2 July 1900 and the poster from 6 July had him tenth on the bill and listed as 'The Handcuff King'.

Part of Houdini's act was the Metamorphosis trick. His hands were fastened behind his back by his wife, Bess, his assistant, before he was placed in a large sack which was tied at the top. Both Houdini and the sack were then placed inside a strong, large box which was both padlocked and strapped. The box was placed inside a cabinet and curtains were drawn in front of it by Mrs Houdini, herself behind the curtains. She clapped three times and on the third clap, Houdini would draw open the curtain to reveal himself free of the box. However, Mrs Houdini was gone and when the box was opened and the sack untied, she was found to be inside it with her hands bound in the same manner as Houdini's had been a few seconds earlier. The trick was very popular with audiences and received huge applause.

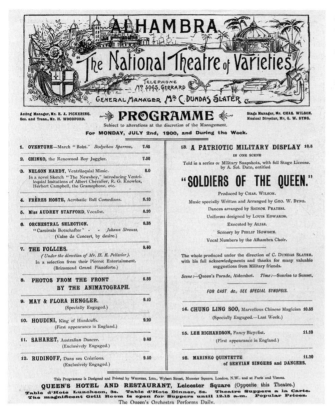

A programme showing the acts appearing at the Alhambra during July 1900. Houdini is tenth on the bill.

Also on the bill were Chinko, the renowned boy juggler; Nelson Hardy, ventriloquist; Freres Hoste, acrobatic ball comedians; Miss Audrey Stafford, vocalist; the Follies, Pierott entertainment; May and Flora Hengler, American duettists and dancers; Saharet, Australian dancer; Rudinoff; Chung Ling Soo, magician; Lee Richardson, fancy bicyclist and the Marinko Quintette, Servian singers and dancers. Also featured were an orchestral selection, photos from the front on the Animatograph and a patriotic military display. All were huge acts at the time and crowd-pullers,

An early photo of Bess and Harry Houdini on stage with the roped box used in the illusion, Metamorphosis. The crimson curtained area used during the trick can be seen in the background. Houdini called this his 'ghost house'.

Chung Ling Soo (left) who appeared on the bill with Houdini at the Alhambra during 1900.

An advert from the *London Evening Standard* of Wednesday, 4 July 1900 announcing Houdini's appearance at the Alhambra. Gentlemen are invited to bring handcuffs or manacles of any description to test Houdini.

but the best known today, apart from Houdini, was Chung Ling Soo, who was billed as Chinese but was actually an American whose real name was William Ellsworth Robinson. Houdini and Chung Ling Soo were to become great friends.

On the first night, a magician known as the Great Cirnoc shouted from the audience during Houdini's act stating that he, not Houdini, was the true Handcuff King and that Houdini was a fake. Houdini challenged Cirnoc to escape from a large pair of handcuffs called the 'Bean Giant'. The handcuffs had been built by Captain Bean of Boston who had challenged anyone to escape from them. Houdini succeeded and continued to use the cuffs in his act. Cirnoc refused the challenge and Houdini put the cuffs on himself, disappeared behind a screen before re-emerging a few seconds later with the cuffs undone. Not to lose face, Cirnoc allowed himself to be locked in the cuffs. An extension rod was needed to unlock them and Houdini gave Cirnoc the key, knowing that he would be unable to escape. He had to admit defeat and Houdini freed him. The whole act enthralled the audience and reports of the incident in local newspapers drew in huge crowds to the Alhambra.

While in London, Houdini visited various locksmiths and took apart their locks to see how they worked. By doing so, he was able to manufacture a key which could free him from the many locks he would later encounter in the British Isles.

His popularity grew through newspaper stories of his spectacular escapes. He issued a challenge which he called the '£1,000 Challenge Open to the World'. The challenge read:

An early poster advertising the Houdinis' illusion, Metamorphosis.

I, HARRY HOUDINI, known as the King of Handcuffs, at last becoming tired of so-called FAKE EXPOSURES AND MEDIOCRE MAGICIANS, who claim to DO MY ACT because they possess a lot of false keys and springs, DO HEARBY CHALLENGE any person in the world to duplicate my release from cuffs, irons and straitjackets.

A detective had a special pair of handcuffs made and challenged Houdini to escape from them. After examining the handcuffs for a short time, Houdini allowed them to be put on his wrists. He very quickly managed to escape.

While appearing at the Alhambra, Houdini and his wife stayed at theatrical lodgings at 10 Keppel Street in Bloomsbury.

The *London Evening Standard* of Tuesday, 3 July 1900 reported on the great success of Houdini's performance:

A novel feature in the programme at the Alhambra is the exhibition of skill by Mr Harry Houdini in releasing himself from handcuffs and other fetters. He made his first public appearance in London last night and his dexterity in escaping from handcuffs handed to him from the audience elicited the heartiest applause. Mr Houdini does not simply slip the shackles from his arms and legs but absolutely unlocks them without the aid of keys or springs. A member of the audience, who said that up to that time he had always claimed the title which had been given to Mr Houdini of 'King of Handcuffs', placed a pair of these instruments on the wrists of the performer who speedily freed himself from their grip much to the astonishment of the owner. At the conclusion of the severe tests, Mr Houdini was recalled and applauded again and again.

The *London Evening Standard* of Tuesday 10 July reported that two sailors of Her Majesty's ship *Powerful* had secured Houdini with a pair of ship's irons, placing him in what was called the cockfighting position with his arms on each side of his knees. His hands were locked in front of his legs and then a broom handle was inserted between his legs and arms so that he could not move. Houdini was lifted into a cabinet but was soon free. Several of his challenges over the next few years were remarkably similar leading to some suggesting that the trials were arranged by Houdini's entourage.

On Saturday 21 July, *The Era* reported:

A remarkable performance is that given by Houdini, who comes from America. He challenges anyone present to secure his wrists with handcuffs in such a manner that he cannot in a few minutes free himself. A committee of investigation is formed and on the night of our visit amongst the gentlemen who went on the stage was ex-Inspector Moore, of the Metropolitan Police, who, it was announced, has had eighteen years' experience in the handcuffing of criminals. Two pairs of handcuffs were placed on Houdini's wrists and were closely examined and thoroughly tested by the ex-police inspector and others. He then retired behind a screen and, at the expiration of a few minutes, reappeared having freed himself from the handcuffs. Again secured in a similar fashion but with his hands behind him, he liberated himself while facing the audience.

Another astonishing trick is performed. Houdini, handcuffed as before, and wearing a coat belonging to one of the committee men, envelops himself in a sack which is securely tied and sealed. He is then placed in a strong box which is locked and corded. A few seconds and it is found that the young lady assistant has changed places with the prisoner and that she is wearing the borrowed coat.

By Saturday 18 August, *The Era* was reporting:

How Houdini, 'the king of handcuffs', manages to release himself from his iron bonds is inexplicable. Many experts in the 'darby' line go on the stage and endeavour to fetter Houdini with their appliances; but the result is always the same – the production of the handcuffs and the reappearance of the 'king' free and smiling. The variation on the well-known box trick with which Houdini concludes his show is decidedly neat and smart.

MATINEE EVERY WEDNESDAY and SATURDAY. at 3.

A LHAMBRA.—Military Ballet, SOLDIERS OF THE
QUEEN. at 10.15. Varieties by Senorita Tortajada, Brothers
Schwarz, Corty Bros, Saharet, War Pictures, Werner and Reider, and
Houdini. Doors open at 7.40.

An advert from the *Morning Post* of 20 August 1900 announcing Houdini's appearance at the Alhambra.

Houdini's first appearance in Great Britain ended at the Alhambra on the night of Saturday 1 September. Houdini's booking at the theatre had been a resounding success and found him much fame and adulation. On the following day, the Houdinis left for Germany to begin a tour of Europe, his first engagement being at the Central Theatre in Dresden.

By now, he had become such a draw in London that a further booking was a must and so he was booked again at the Alhambra for the Christmas period.

In an interview with Mr C. Dundas Slater in *The Era* on Saturday 10 November, he announced:

Houdini is coming back to us with practically a new show and will do his business in a more convincing way. He will dispense with the cabinet and will do all his tricks with a small table only.

However, Dundas Slater's description of Houdini's act wasn't entirely accurate and Houdini continued to escape from handcuffs, boxes and issued challenges to the general public.

Prior to appearing again at the Alhambra, Houdini's tour of Europe, had finished with an appearance at the Circus Variete in Magdeburg. The manager of the venue was so pleased with Houdini's sell-out show that he wanted to retain him. However, Houdini was already booked at the Alhambra. Manager Jacobson, of the Circus Variete, offered C. Dundas Slater the equivalent of Houdini's wages for two weeks if he would delay the opening in London. This was refused and Houdini was soon back in England.

A studio portrait of Harry Houdini in chains and padlocks.

An advert from *The Era* of Saturday 29 December 1900 showing Houdini on the bill of the Christmas show.

ALHAMBRA.—

New Programme.

Every Evening, the New Vocal Christmas Ballet Divertissement,

THE GAY CITY ;

also,

the Nautical Ballet,

THE HANDY MAN.

Varieties by Kaufmann Family, the Marvellous Craggs, Delmore and Lee, Ian Colquhoun, Braatz Brothers, Houdini, Stanfield and Clement, Miss Lina Pantzer, Fukushima Royal Japanese Troupe, and Arras and Alice Rolf.

Doors open 7·30.

In December, to advertise his appearance, twelve men wearing sandwich-boards paced up and down outside the theatre announcing Houdini's return. His first show during the festive season was on 2 December.

For the Metamorphosis trick, Houdini had previously used a large cabinet. Now, he used a smaller box, about three feet square and four feet high, to dispel the myth that there was an assistant hidden inside, ready to help him with an assortment of keys. For many of his escapes, he no longer closed the small curtains on the front of the box. This meant that once his hands were handcuffed behind his back, he knelt directly facing the audience and they could now see all his facial expressions, twists and turns as he made his escape. This added to the excitement.

The Era of Saturday 15 December reported:

Houdini continues to puzzle all by his extraordinary expertness in releasing himself from handcuffs. On the occasion of our visit, a novel feature was the appearance on the stage of a working locksmith who came prepared with an elaborate contrivance of his own manufacture. At first, Houdini refused to

Houdini with his mother, Cecilia, and his wife, Bess.

experiment with this as being outside his scope, which he expressly limits to handcuffs used by some body of police. Eventually, however, he submitted to the trial; and the working locksmith fastened a belt around Houdini's waist and locked the handcuffs on his wrists, his hands being tied behind him. A period of suspense ensued while the 'world's great mystifier' was concealed from view under a square scarlet canopy; but after a while he emerged free, untrammelled and triumphant.

In December, Houdini accompanied a writer from the *Black and White Budget* to a shop which sold manacles. He wanted to prove that he could escape from any handcuffs and other restraints just as easily offstage as he could while performing in front of an audience. The shopkeeper produced two pairs of cuffs and happily clamped them on Houdini's wrists while dropping the keys into his own pocket. Houdini turned his back, walked across the shop floor and then turned around completely free with the cuffs open. The shopkeeper couldn't believe what he was seeing and Houdini soon revealed his true identity much to the shopkeeper's relief.

The Houdinis continued their show at the Alhambra until 2 February the following year.

Chapter Two

1901 – Bradford

At the beginning of 1901, Houdini was still appearing at the Alhambra Theatre in London. Far from being the star of the show at the theatre, Houdini was part of a far bigger Christmas attraction comprising many acts. The production was written about in *The Graphic* of Saturday 5 January:

As everyone knows, the bill of the Alhambra is a vast and varied programme. Beginning with the romantic nautical drama of The Handy Man, which is not over-burdened with patriotic sentiment, but is bright and lively, this programme includes several novel items. Balancing feats by Delmore and Lee, 'the sensation of the century', brought over from America, are performed on a glittering trapeze, before a background of black silk, which throws the grand figures of the athletes into high relief. Mr Ian Colquhoun, vocalist, fills all the vast place with his powerful bass voice. Houdini, 'King of Handcuffs' and master of mysteries, does, with the assistance of a damsel, one of the cleverest box tricks ever seen, while of the new vocal ballet divertissement, The Gay City, a good deal has been written in well-merited praise. In lively and spirited fashion it gives pictures of the Paris of fiction if not of reality and the gay uniforms and animated dances afford a series of pictures very pleasant to watch.

It has been remarked, by the way, that one of the most curious incidents in the ballet is that in a procession of groups representing various nations, that of our nearest neighbours, the French, comes in for more applause than any other, showing how magnanimous we have become. Among many other features, the Royal Japanese Troupe should be seen in their costumes of Oriental silks and also those clever equilibrists Rolf, Aires and Alice.

An advert for the show in *The Era* also features, on the variety section of the bill, Sharp and Flat; Delmore and Lee, sensational gymnasts; the Braatz Brothers, acrobats; Miss Lina Pantzer, wire dancer and the Fukushima Troupe.

While in London, Houdini bought a dress that he'd seen in a shop window. The dress had been made for Queen Victoria but she had died before it was finished. He asked the price and was told that it was £30. He purchased it for his mother, Cecilia, knowing that she would be pleased to be wearing a dress designed for

A studio portrait of Houdini and his wife, Bess, taken in 1901.

An early publicity shot showing Houdini handcuffed and manacled.

Houdini in leg-irons and handcuffs.

Cecilia, Houdini's beloved mother.

the Queen of England. Houdini and Bess arranged to have the dress altered before giving it as a surprise to his pleased mother.

Houdini played his final show at the Alhambra on Saturday 2 February.

There is only one other well-recorded appearance in another city during 1901 and that was at the People's Palace in Bradford from Monday 4 February to Saturday 9 February.

Bradford in 1901 was one of the biggest cities in the country with a higher than usual proportion of well-paid workers. The reason for this was wool and the city was involved in combing, scouring, spinning, weaving and the dyeing of wool and was, at the time, the wool capital of the world. The People's Palace was able to accommodate up to 2,100 people and was one of the oldest theatres in the provinces having been opened in 1875.

A newspaper photo showing Houdini with his sleeves turned up ready to escape from handcuffs.

The local newspaper carried the news of Houdini's appearance:

The 'star' attraction at the People's Palace this week is Harry Houdini, the Handcuff King, who for the past six months has been mystifying audiences in the metropolis, and who is now baffling Bradford audiences, even the vigilant

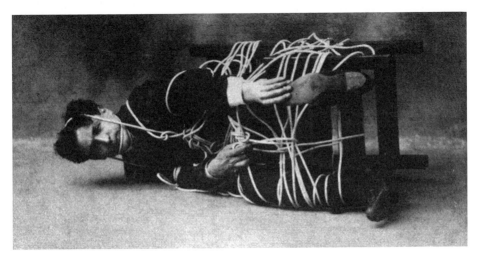

Houdini securely tied to a chair.

police force. Six pairs of handcuffs and a pair of leg irons, securely locked, cannot hold him, and in a very short space of time, he walks out of his small tent a free man. To give him the name of 'King of Handcuffs' is indeed fitting, for however fastened or screwed up, he is able to release himself with ease and alacrity. Perhaps the most marvellous of his expositions is where he is securely sealed up in a flannel sack with his hands tied behind him, put into a strong box and locked up. A lady who assists in tying the box up with ropes goes behind the screen, and two minutes after the curtain is drawn, Houdini emerges from his gaol free, but the lady has disappeared. The box is pulled to the front, the ropes unfastened, and she is found to be sealed up inside the sack in the place which had previously been occupied by Houdini. Last night, policemen galore stepped on to the platform to try their powers at securely fastening him with their cuffs, but their hopes were shattered each time.

In addition to Houdini's excellent turn, an admirable programme of 'stars' go through their various turns. The Three Auroras contribute some excellent dances, first as a double mirror, and then under an umbrella. 'The Interviewer'

An early photo of Houdini in handcuffs.

A portrait shot of Bess Houdini in the early 1900s.

is a small sketch, and gives opportunity for several small interludes, which Booker and Narbis make the most of. Harry Barker is a clever descriptive vocalist, and received loud applause for his song on the fall of Nelson at the 'Battle of Trafalgar' and also for the rendering of 'Love's Labour Lost'. Orme and Orme, in a novel comedy act, make plenty of fun, and Wilfred, described as a flexible marvel, is very good in a contortionist act. Good turns are also given by Daisy Davenport, serio and dancer; F. Cary, character comedian; and Charles Stevens, comedian.

So popular was his show that on Friday 8 February, people who couldn't get seats paid 10 shillings to stand in the aisles and watch. Extra seats were also placed at the end of the stage.

The Era of Saturday 9 February reported:

We have had no sensational performances here to equal that which is being given to crowded audiences nightly by Houdini, king of handcuffs. His marvellous box trick defies committees of experts and elicits great applause.

Jim Moffitt of 123 Dudley Hill Road, Bradford was a constable in the city police force in Bradford when he went on stage to test Houdini's abilities as a handcuff breaker. They became friends and Moffitt always helped out during performances in the north of England. He told of their friendship after Houdini's death: 'There was always the chance that no member of an audience would respond to the usual invitation to step up to the platform and form a committee of inspection so I therefore, always attended the performances to lead the way, and my response induced others to follow my example.'

Moffitt continued: 'Houdini was not a "faker". All his tricks were genuinely performed, as a host of incidents will testify. How they were done remains a mystery, and one can only hint that Houdini was possessed not only of a

Houdini with his brother Theo (Hardeen) in 1901. (*Image courtesy of John Cox http://www. wildabouthoudini.com/*)

wonderful mentality but also of remarkable physical powers, and amazing nerve control. I never appreciated the risks which Houdini ran, and imagined that his talk of danger was only showmanship until I assisted in a performance at Sheffield. The "Handcuff King" was tightly "laced" in a straitjacket. He managed, as usual, to escape from it, but he was completely exhausted and laid on the floor in a semi-conscious state for sometime afterwards. Houdini told me later, "I was nearly beaten there."

Moffitt went on to say: 'The Bradford Police were naturally vastly intrigued by Houdini's tricks, and in those early days they tested him again and again. Placed in the prison cells, he escaped with ease. Handcuffed, and naked, he liberated himself in the presence of the Chief Constable and a number of police in the old police premises behind the site of the present Bradford Town Hall. His feats aroused tremendous interest in the district, and crowds of people, eager to test him, attended his performance, only to go away dumbfounded and talking about supernatural powers.

At Leeds he was once confronted on the platform with a man who carried a pair of manacles which must have weighed a stone, and were like two big mantraps. The man adjusted them on Houdini's wrists. He was very excited and kept shouting "I'll fasten thee with these if tha's nivver bin fastened afore." Houdini simply pulled out a piece of string from his pocket, made a loop with it, and, inserting this in the lock, he drew the bolt. This feat was child's play to him.

The Krystall Palast (Crystal Palast) in Leipzig where Houdini played in February 1900 after his performance at the Alhambra.

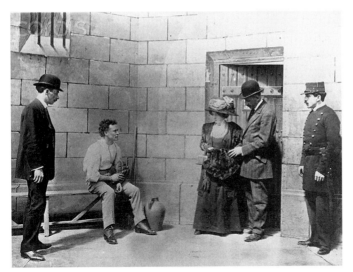

Houdini filming his first motion picture *Merveilleux Exploits du Célébre Houdini à Paris* which was made for Pathé and included some of his famous escapes.

He was never beaten, although thousands of people pitted their wits and ingenuity against him. The last time I saw him, he said to me "Jim, if ever I'm beaten with any feat, I'll wire you straightaway?" That wire never came.'

It's unlikely that Houdini played at any other venues in the UK in 1901 as, shortly afterwards, he returned to Germany where he played at the Krystallpalast and the Apollo in Düsseldorf.

Houdini made his first silent film in 1901 entitled 'Merveilleux Exploits du Célébre Houdini à Paris'. The film was made for Pathé and included some of his famous escapes. In October, Houdini was still in Germany appearing at Essen.

A year after crossing the Atlantic to try his luck in Europe, Houdini was now the biggest music hall attraction there. His bank balance had swelled greatly and offers of work came pouring in.

Chapter Three

1902 – Houdini Returns

An early studio shot showing Houdini in white shorts engulfed in leg-irons and heavy balls and chains.

Houdini did not return to Great Britain until October 1902. The previous year, a newspaper in Cologne, Germany, *Rheinische Zeitung*, reported that the chief of police, Schutzmann Werner Graff, had accused Houdini of trying to bribe him to rig an escape from one of the city's jails. The newspaper also accused Houdini of paying a Herr Lott, to help him with a fake performance. Houdini knew his reputation was at stake and so hired Cologne's top lawyer, Herr Rechtsanwalt Dr Schreiber, and began slander proceedings.

At the first trial on 26 February, Graff testified that Houdini had paid him 20 marks for a handcrafted lock and a duplicate key. Graff also stated that Houdini paid Herr Lott to supply him with a duplicate chain to display while he used a chain that had already been sawn through. Houdini denied the charges and after witnesses were called and demonstrations were given by Houdini in court, he won the case.

However, Graff wasn't happy with this and sought a second trial at a higher court. This trial began on 26 July. Witnesses were called and, again, Houdini won the case.

Graff was still not happy and the case was taken to the highest court and a hearing was held on 26 September. Houdini again proved his case and Graff was found guilty of slander. He was fined 30 marks. All expenses were awarded to Houdini as well as an amount for lost bookings due to the length of the trial. Graff had to pay all this expense as well as publicly advertising an 'honorary apology'.

With his bookings in Europe, as well as the long drawn out case, it's unlikely that Houdini would have had time to travel to the UK to perform and his next recorded booking there was in October 1902.

While Houdini toured Europe, his rival, 'The Great Cirnoc' was travelling the theatres of the UK with a similar act.

The Era of Saturday 15 February reported:

Mr Harry Lundy has secured for his next week's programme the Two Cirnocs, father and son, who are known as the 'Kings of Locks'. They give an entertainment similar in its essence to that sponsored by Houdini, Hardeen and others, but the elder Mr Cirnoc, who claims Bethnal Green as his birthplace, was a handcuff manipulator as far back as 1872, so that the show – an excellent one of its kind – can justly be termed original. The younger of the two was the principal performer at the private press view of Thursday afternoon and he is wonderfully smart. He rid himself quite easily of about half a dozen 'regulation bracelets' used by the police of various continental nations. But this feat was a mere preliminary to the special features of the show, which is termed 'the escape from the gallows'. Cirnoc was secured in an iron neckband, waistband and leg-irons; chained and doubly-chained together, back and front, and then his hands were fastened. Manacled as he was, he succeeded in astonishing a popular agent, who, blindfolded, went with him behind the screen, by taking off his coat, turning the sleeves inside-out, and putting it on again. When the curtain was again drawn, not one of the fastenings had been removed from the 'man in chains'. The box trick, too, is a wonderful piece of trickery, the imprisoned man's place being taken by his partner in the space of about five seconds. The Cirnocs will change their show frequently and should be a great attraction.

Besides the Great Cirnoc, other artists toured the UK with similar acts and gained much popularity. It would have been easy for the public to, perhaps, forget all about Houdini but his fame continued abroad and by the end of 1902, he was back on the shores of Great Britain.

Houdini's earliest recorded tours for 1902 start in October with an appearance at the People's Palace Theatre in Halifax. The theatre was described as a dingy and badly equipped variety theatre at the Oddfellows Hall. The *Halifax Daily Courier* noted, '*Halifax people had fought shy of the theatre, however this hesitancy broke down under the desire to see the stars.*'

From there, he went on to appear at Blackburn, Bradford, Halifax again, Leicester, Manchester, Blackburn for a second time, Leeds, Burnley and a return visit just before Christmas, to Leeds.

The Palace Theatre, Halifax, where Houdini appeared during October 1902.

When Houdini returned to England, he was uncertain how popular he would be after an absence of twenty-one months. He needn't have worried, his ticket sales far exceeded those of his previous visit. When he performed jailbreaks in Halifax, Blackburn and Bradford, people rioted to buy tickets. Houdini wrote that the London Police requested that he didn't reveal how long it took to escape from their cells as it made them look too easy to break out of. Houdini offered a £25 reward in every city that he visited to anyone who could produce a regulation pair of handcuffs from which he couldn't escape.

Most of Houdini's shows in Great Britain, outside London, ran for a week, commencing on Monday and finishing on Saturday. Many theatres used Sunday as a day for rehearsal.

As mentioned, his first engagement in the UK in 1902 was at the People's Palace Theatre in Halifax where he appeared between Monday, 13 October and Saturday, 18 October 1902.

Halifax's wealth came from the wool, cotton and carpet industries and, like many of Yorkshire's towns, had a large number of weaving mills.

An advert for Houdini's show appeared in the *Halifax Guardian* and read:

> *The People's Palace, St James Road.*
> *Important and very expensive engagement of Houdini –*
> *world famous jail breaker and handcuff king.*

Houdini played to packed audiences every night. He had several challengers including one from a local basket maker, T.M. Culpan, who challenged him to escape from one of their own wicker baskets. Houdini managed to make his escape within three minutes.

During the same week, he was stripped, handcuffed and locked in a local police cell. He managed to escape within two minutes.

His next appearance was at the Palace Theatre of Varieties in Blackburn between 20 and 25 October. Blackburn was also a mill town and textiles had been produced there since the thirteenth century. The Palace Theatre was described as being handsome, spacious, well equipped and one of the best in the provinces.

On 18 October 1902, an advert appeared in the *Blackburn Standard* which read:

> *MONDAY NEXT, Oct 20th, 1902 and every evening during the week:*
> *Special Expensive Engagement of*
> *HOUDINI*
> *World-famous Jail Breaker and Handcuff King.*
> *He is the originator of this Act.*
> *JOSIE JONGHMANS. Soprano Vocalist,*
> *TOM LLOYD, Exponent of Quaint Comedy.*
> *FLORENCE and LILLIAN, in Artistic Musical Act.*
> *PASSMORE BROS. Comedians, Vocalists & Dancers.*
> *Prof. A. DICKINSON and Miss MAUD JOHNSON*
> *(of the Celebrated Johnson Family) Swimmers.*
> *The Gentle Bros. LANG*
> *DOT McCARTHY, Vocalist and Step Dancer.*
> *Starring Engagement of one of the Century's Marvels*
> *CHINKO, the astounding Boy Juggler.*
> *DAY PERFORMANCE Every THURSDAY at 2.30.*
> *USUAL TIMES. PALACE POPULAR PRICES.*

The *Northern Daily Telegraph* of 21 October 1902 carried the story of Houdini's appearance at the Palace Theatre of Varieties, Blackburn:

> *The excellent programme billed at the Palace Theatre of Varieties, Blackburn, this week, attracted two unusually large houses to that place of amusement last evening. A great amount of interest was centred in the exhibition of Houdini, described on the programme as the famous gaol breaker and handcuff king. Last night, he gave a wonderful exhibition of his powers to defy 'locks, bolts and*

bars'. In response to his invitation, some half dozen members of the audience in turn locked him in various patterns of handcuffs, but in each case he was freed again in a very short time. He concluded his turn with an exhibition of the famous 'box trick'.

Houdini, however is not the only 'star' at the Palace this week, for Chinko, who is probably the cleverest juggler now on the stage, gave a display which quite maintained the reputation gained at his previous visit. A special feature of the turn is the juggling with nine billiard balls – a feat which he says, no other juggler has achieved. The Passmore Brothers, the Brothers Lang, and Tom Lloyd, all render excellent turns, and ably sustain the lighter side of the evening's entertainment. Josie Jonghman's singing elicited considerable applause, which was also gained by Florence and Lillian for a capital musical act; Dot McCarthy, vocalist and dancer; and Dickinson and Johnson, scientific swimmers.

This morning, Houdini gave a 'private sitting' on the stage of the Palace Theatre to a number of Blackburn townsmen. Divested of every article of clothing, he was

manacled with three sets of handcuffs of different patterns, the keys being retained by various spectators, and a pair of massive leg irons were locked around his ankles. Thus secured hand and foot, he moved behind a curtain which the audience satisfied themselves concealed no confederate, and in about five minutes had freed himself from his fetters, throwing down each pair, unlocked, as he took them off. The demonstration was satisfactory in all but one particular – how is it done. This is Houdini's secret, and is worth to him something like a Prime Minister's salary per annum. As a preliminary to this performance, the artist swallowed in four doses, a packet of needles, and produced them again, apparently from his throat, nicely strung on a piece of sewing cotton.

It's interesting to note that besides Houdini, the next biggest star on the

Chinko, the boy juggler. (*Image courtesy of Kevin Connolly http://houdinihimself.com/*)

bill was Chinko, the boy juggler. He performed an act which was very popular at the time but, today, Chinko is almost forgotten. However, as Teddy Knox, he later found music hall fame as part of the comedy duo Nervo and Knox who formed a key part of the Crazy Gang of the 1930s which included Bud Flanagan, Chesney Allen, Charlie Naughton and Jimmy Gold.

By 24 October, Houdini had received a challenge from W. Hope Hodgson which was published in the *Northern Daily Telegraph*. It read:

PALACE THEATRE, BLACKBURN.
To-Night and every evening during the week,
HOUDINI,
FAMOUS JAIL BREAKER AND HANDCUFF KING.

Do not confuse Houdini with any other so–called Handcuff king. He is the originator of this Act, all others are very poor imitators. Must be seen to be believed. Jorde Jonghmans, Tom Lloyd Florence and Lillian, Passmore Bros., Prof. A. Dickinson and Miss Maud, Johnson Bros., Dot McCarthy and Chinko, Boy Juggler.

TWICE NIGHTLY, at 7 and 9.
IMPORTANT NOTICE – GRAND DAY PERFORMANCE EVERY THURSDAY at 2.30.
CHALLENGE TO THE 'HANDCUFF KING' AT BLACKBURN.
HODGSON V HOUDINI.
Interest in the visit of Houdini, the handcuff magician, to the Palace Theatre, Blackburn this week is intensified by the acceptance of his challenge by Mr W.H Hodgson, of the School of Physical Culture, Blackburn. Letters have passed between the parties to the following effect:
    The School of Physical Culture,
    Ainsworth–Street, Blackburn.
    Mr Harry Houdini.
    Sir –
    Being interested in your apparently anatomically impossible handcuff test, I have decided to take up your challenge to-night (Friday) on the following conditions:
    1st I bring and use my own irons (so look out).
    2nd I iron you myself.
    3rd If you are unable to free yourself, the £25 is to be given to the Blackburn Infirmary.

Should you succeed, I shall be the first to offer congratulations. If not, then the Infirmary will benefit.

W. Hope Hodgson
(Principal).

P.S. Naturally, if your challenge is bona-fide, I shall expect the money to be deposited.

Houdini replied:

I, Harry Houdini, accept the above challenge, and will deposit the £25 at the 'Telegraph' office. Match to take place to-night (Friday).

H. Houdini.

Houdini's challenge was mentioned in the *Blackburn Standard* of 25 October 1902:

Never in the history of the Blackburn Palace Theatre, if not in the history of music hall life, has there been witnessed so remarkable a scene as that which took place in the local hall last night, when Houdini, the Handcuff King, who has been performing at the theatre during the week, set himself the task of justifying his challenge to free himself from any irons that could be brought to fasten him, the challenge having been taken up by Mr. W. H. Hodgson, of the School of Physical Culture. Houdini deposited £25, which, had he failed to accomplish the task, would have been handed over to the infirmary.

Needless to say, with such a tit-bit offered them, the Blackburn public turned up in large numbers, and the theatre was literally packed from pit to gallery. Shortly before half-past ten when Houdini appeared, he was met on the stage by Mr. Hodgson, who proceeded to produce quite an armoury of cuffs and irons. Houdini at the outset raised a protest against the irons which were to make him a prisoner, as he urged that the locks had been tampered with and had been wrapped with twine, which was against the spirit of his challenge and its conditions, which stipulated that regulation irons be used. Mr Hodgson, however, replied that he had said he would bring his own irons and use them himself.

Houdini, thereupon allowed the contest to go on, and Mr. Hodgson proceeded with the work of fastening up his challenger. He handcuffed his wrists which he bound across his chest: and then by the aid of an assistant, forced his elbows backwards to his side and pinioned them, after which he coupled them up in a very tight manner to leg irons, and Houdini looked for all the world like a trussed fowl. Some objections were taken by the audience to Mr. Hodgson receiving assistance, which was in direct violation of the terms of the challenge, but Houdini signified his readiness to allow the battle to proceed. The artiste was then placed in his cabinet and the struggle commenced. After about a quarter of an hour had elapsed it was found that Houdini had fallen on his side, and it was thought that he had fainted. But such was not the case, and after another three-quarters of an hour had elapsed, Houdini asked that his wrists might be free for a few seconds as his hands were numbed. Mr. Hodgson, however refused this concession, although Dr. Bradley, who was in attendance said it was cruel for the performance to continue. Shortly afterwards Houdini announced that he had got his legs free and he would take a short rest before proceeding further.

There were encouraging cheers raised by the audience, but there were several hostile voices raised which caused Houdini to ejaculate; 'You must remember, ladies and gentlemen, I did not state the time it would take me to take them off. These handcuffs have been plugged.'

It was evident that Houdini had the sympathies of the audience, who waited very patiently, the orchestra gallantly enlivening the tedium of waiting by supplying up-to-date musical selections.

As time went on the huge crowd began to get impatient, and in the hearts of most people it was felt that Houdini had more than met his match. But again out popped Houdini's head and he announced that he had got his hands free, and it would not be long before he had got his hands free altogether.

The crowd, however, was fast losing patience, and they loudly hooted as Hardeen, brother of Houdini, approached the cabinet to give a word of cheer, or maybe advice, to his imprisoned relative. On receiving a refreshing drink Houdini, after again calling upon the people to have a little more patience, exclaimed that every lock had been changed, and that made it all the more difficult for him to get free.

At ten minutes to twelve a huge shout went up when it was seen that Houdini was free, and as he staggered from his cabinet and appeared panting and weak before the audience, the cheers that went up were most deafening.

The cheers were renewed again and again and Houdini, whose shirt had been torn from cuff to shoulder, and whose wrists and biceps were raw in places, thus addressed the audience: 'Ladies and gentlemen, I have been in the handcuff business for fourteen years but never have I been so brutally and cruelly ill treated. I would just like to say that the locks have been plugged.'

A voice: 'Where's Hodgson? Why is he not here to offer his congratulations?'

Mr Hodgson had some time before left the theatre, and after another rousing cheer had been given to Houdini, the crowd rapidly dispersed, eagerly commenting on the performance that is certainly unique in the experience of local play-goers.

It was reported in the *Blackburn Star* that when Mr Hodgson left the theatre, he ran to the police station for protection, fearing the wrath of the thoroughly enraged audience. He showed good judgement as he would have fared badly had he fallen into their hands.

The trial was one that Houdini would never forget and he referred to it often throughout his career. It was stated that Hodgson had previously been mistreated by crew members when he was a cabin boy during the 1890s. This led him to take up body building as a means of defence and when he left the sea in 1902, he set up a school of physical culture teaching body building and weight training. After his cruelty to Houdini, he found himself just as unpopular as he had been at sea.

From Blackburn, Houdini next travelled to Bradford to appear at the Palace Theatre between 27 October and 1 November.

The local newspaper carried the story of his appearance:

Large audiences were present at both performances at this house last night, the chief attraction no doubt being the presence of the 'handcuff king', Harry Houdini, whose remarkable skill from getting free from 'the darbies' and breaking out of prison cells, approaches the marvellous. Houdini is not a stranger to Bradford, but his performance is such that come as often as he likes he is certain to draw crowded audiences.

In addition to the handcuff king, Mr Will Murray has a splendid diversified programme, made up of quite a host of good turns. Zaro and Arno, comedy bar performers, give a pleasing show, and the Steinway Glee Singers were also welcomed, their rendering of old plantation songs proving very acceptable to the audience. Lily Marny deserved the very flattering attention paid her, for her songs were not only good but were well rendered. Moretti and Alice are a duet of speciality artistes, who give a pretty entertainment, and Maudie Vera, who comes as the 'Infant Vesta Tilley' was very taking. Other turns were given by E.L. Sheldon, Pastede and Olio.

Houdini had nothing very difficult (for him) to do, for though handcuffed and tied up by local gentlemen, he had himself free in the course of a few minutes, a second test being treated to a similar fate, in front of the audience. The Palace show this week is one of the best presented to patrons of this house for some time past. Last night's booking was a record for Monday, the house being filled by the early doors.

Houdini was proving to be a huge draw and theatre takings were greatly increased when he appeared. It's interesting to note the other acts appearing with him at Bradford, including comedy bar performers, singers and various other artists who all fitted in well with music hall entertainment at the time, making a complete and entertaining show.

Houdini next performed at the People's Palace Theatre in Halifax again between 3 and 8 November. The crowds were so large that the management of the Palace Theatre hired the Victoria Hall so that they could run further matinees.

The *Halifax Courier* of Saturday 8 November stated: *Complying with numerous requests from better-class people, Mr. Harrison (theatre manager) has engaged the Victoria Hall for this afternoon. Mr. Houdini will appear with some new tricks, and there should be a big audience.*

The People's Palace was small and would only accommodate about two hundred people and was considered only suitable for the working classes of the area which is why the Victoria Hall was booked. This was Houdini's second appearance in Halifax, having just played there in October. It seems that he was so popular that there were calls from the public to have him back. Houdini wasn't bothered by the state of the theatre and was equally comfortable there as he was at the Victoria Hall.

Lewis Crossley, the manager of T. Gaines and Sons issued him with a challenge to escape from a box which then had its lid nailed down and was secured by ropes. He took twenty-two minutes to free himself.

While at Halifax, an audience member drew a sketch of Houdini performing on stage. He is shown surrounded by discarded handcuffs while sitting on a box belonging to Gaines and Sons.

After Houdini's appearance, the dingy People's Palace closed and became the Friendly and Traders Club. A new theatre was built and the *Halifax Daily Courier* reported:

A sketch by an audience member of Houdini's act at the Palace Theatre in Halifax during October 1909.

Of the success of Houdini there is no doubt. Contributed by the curiosity of his demonstrations, exerted as a drawing force, Halifax people are indebted to bringing into being the new theatre Wards End House of Entertainment, now such a favourite rendezvous.

This later became known as the Palace and Hippodrome.

Houdini's next venue was at the Pavilion Theatre in Leicester between 10 and 15 November. Leicester was a hosiery, textile and footwear city and its population had risen greatly from 1861 to 1901 from 68,000 to 212,000. The city had many large mills as well as factories including the Co-operative Boot and Shoe Company. In 1900, the Great Central Railway had provided a direct link to London.

During his appearance there, Houdini was challenged by Francis John Walker of the Windmill Inn at 7 Church Gate. He had a lock which he thought Houdini wouldn't be able to pick. The lock, which was over five hundred years old, originally came from Leicester's Old East Gates. In 1896, the lock was sent to Chubb in London and a key was made for it. Walker and other interested parties put up £25 and asked Houdini to do the same. He did and the wager was deposited with the *Sporting News*. The men were asked to bring the lock to his first performance on Friday 14 November and the challenge drew a large crowd.

The Era reported:

Houdini's visit to the Leicester Pavilion established a record both in attendance and money taken. On the Friday evening, the building was densely packed, when a wager of £25 a-side was made that Houdini could not undo and escape from a lock that fastened the old Eastgate, Leicester, the lock being over five hundred years old. It was thought that this would prove Houdini's masterpiece, as it took four days to make the key. The gentlemen who made the wager consisted of persons who are considered very shrewd but their hopes were doomed to disappointment, as after twenty minutes Houdini succeeded in his task and was rewarded with a reception that must have been most gratifying to him. This was Houdini's first visit to Leicester and the frequenters of the vaudeville halls owe a debt of gratitude to Mr Frank Macnaghten and his lieutenant, Mr C.A. Wordworth, for the enterprise displayed in booking such a turn.

Houdini's next appearance was at St James' Hall in Manchester between 17 and 22 November.

Manchester was known worldwide for its cotton industry and many members of the audience would have worked at local mills and factories. There was also great poverty in the city and visitors were greeted by billowing smoke from the

In November 1902, Houdini appeared at the St James Hall in Manchester.

chimneys in industrial suburbs. St James' Hall was built in 1884 and closed in 1907 when it was then converted into a cinema.

While in Manchester, Houdini escaped from a police cell in the city.

His next performance took him back to the Palace Theatre at Blackburn where he played to packed audiences between 24 and 29 November. There was probably reluctance as he recalled his harrowing experience at the theatre just a month earlier.

An advert appeared which read:

Re-engagement at enormous cost and positively the last appearance in Blackburn prior to his departure for the continent, of the world famous Houdini whose miraculous feats have staggered humanity and are beyond description.

Houdini was reported to have beaten the house record that he'd set at Blackburn previously by more than £200.

A poster advertising Houdini's forthcoming appearance at the Palace Theatre in Blackburn which announces a re-appearance in the town and a stupendous increase in his salary. (*Image courtesy of Kevin Connolly http://houdinihimself.com/*)

PALACE
THEATRE, BLACKBURN.

Proprietor ... ... Mr. FRANK MACNAGHTEN
Manager ... ...Mr. CHARLES SCHUBERTH

Owing to the Enormous Sensation
created by

HARRY

HOUDINI

THE

CELEBRATED JAIL-BREAKER

AND

HANDCUFF KING

On the occasion of his recent engagement at the above
Theatre, Mr. Frank Macnaghten has

AT A STUPENDOUS
INCREASE OF SALARY

PREVAILED UPON **HOUDINI** TO
RE-APPEAR FOR

SIX NIGHTS AND MATINEE

COMMENCING

MONDAY, NOV. 24th

Prior to his return to the Continent.

NO INCREASE IN PRICES.

DON'T FORGET the DATE is

MONDAY, NOV. 24th

An early photograph of the Palace Theatre in Blackburn.

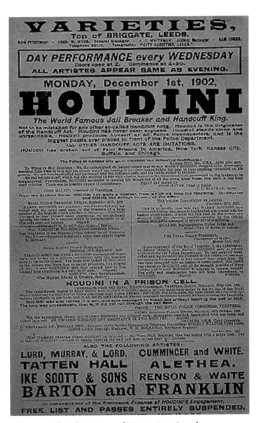

A poster for the City of Varieties, Leeds advertising Houdini's forthcoming appearance on Monday, 1 December 1902.

A photo of a bemused Charlie Peace.

After Blackburn, he next travelled to Leeds and played at the City of Varieties Music Hall from 1 to 6 December. The music hall was built in 1865 and was located in Swan Street. *The Era* described it as *'one of the handsomest and most commodious in the provinces.'*

While there, Houdini made his escape from a cell at Armley Prison (later Leeds Prison) where the notorious cat burglar, Charles Peace, had been held captive before being executed in 1879.

Some theatres refused to pay Houdini's £100 salary so instead he accepted a percentage of the takings. It was a shrewd move. After his well-publicised escape from the prison in Leeds, the demand for tickets was twice that of the amount of seats available. Working on a percentage of ticket sales meant that his earnings easily doubled. Houdini received a percentage of the takings until the end of 1902. At Leeds his share was £200 for the week.

A poster advertising his show read:

VARIETIES.
Top of Briggate, Leeds.
Monday, December 1st, 1902.
HOUDINI
The World Famous Jail Breaker and Handcuff King.
Not to be mistaken for any other so-called Handcuff King. Houdini is
the originator of the Handcuff Act. Houdini has never been exposed.
Houdini stands alone and unreachable. Houdini produces himself at all
Police Headquarters and is the biggest puzzle ever placed before the Police
Department.
All other handcuff acts are imitations.
HOUDINI has broken out of four prisons in America. New York, Kansas
City, Buffalo and Chicago.

Also on the bill with Houdini at Leeds were Lord, Murray and Lord, Tatten Hall, Ike Scott and Sons, Barton and Franklin, Cumminger and White, Alethea and Renson and Waite. Tatten Hall was a very popular comedian at the time who had played many roles in the theatre. He had started his career as a dentist but soon found that 'treading the boards' was far more enjoyable. In later years, he became the touring manager for Gracie Fields.

Houdini's escapades at Leeds were reported in the *Yorkshire Evening Post* of Thursday 4 December:

Locks, bolts and bars have no terror for Mr Harry Houdini, 'the handcuff king and champion jail breaker', who is appearing at the Leeds City Varieties this week.

Today, the Leeds police were afforded an opportunity of testing his skill. First of all, Houdini gave a few exhibitions of freeing himself from handcuffs before the Chief Constable (Major Tarry) in his private room at the Town Hall. Being convinced that the feats were genuine, Major Tarry, in the presence of a number of other prominent officials of the force, had Houdini tested in some of the empty cells. What exactly happened may be gathered from a testimonial given to Houdini after his performance. It reads as follows:

Police Offices, Leeds,
Town Hall, Dec. 4th, 1902.
We, the undersigned, hereby certify that Mr Harry Houdini was stripped and searched in the main Bridewell, in the Town Hall, Leeds, in the presence of a number of prominent police officials of this city. Three pairs of police regulation handcuffs were placed upon him with his hands behind his back and in a perfectly nude condition he was led into a cell, which was doubly locked.

In 2 min. 57 sec. he walked out into the open corridor, having taken off the handcuffs, each pair being open, and opened the door without assistance.

Signed,
A Dalton (Deputy Chief Constable).
Jas. Blakey (Chief Inspector).

The idea of placing Houdini in the cell nude was to make sure that he had no instrument concealed about him. He subsequently opened the door of the cell in which Charles Peace was once confined. Houdini has performed very similar feats at Bradford and in several other large towns. He is an American by birth and before he took to the stage was by trade a locksmith.

A prisoner, who caught sight of Houdini from behind a barred gate this morning, was heard to exclaim, 'I wish you were in here, old man. We'd soon be able to get out and have a pint.' Tomorrow, a prominent local detective is to try some peculiar leg-irons on Houdini. If the latter fails to free himself from them, he has promised a donation of £25 to the Police Orphanage.

Houdini stripped of his clothes and handcuffed and locked in a cell.

While Houdini played his last night at the City Varieties in Leeds on Saturday 6 December, his friend, Chung Ling Soo was playing his last night at the nearby Coliseum. Although hugely popular, Chung Ling Soo stole much of his act from Ching Ling Foo, a Chinese magician who was also a friend of Houdini's. There was great rivalry between the two men.

A drawing of Harry Houdini which appeared in the *Yorkshire Evening Post* of Saturday 6 December 1902.

Ching Ling Foo, Chinese magician and friend of Houdini, whose act was stolen by his rival, Chung Ling Soo.

Houdini next played at the Empire Music Hall in Burnley between 8 and 13 December. Burnley was known for its cotton mills, which used row upon row of power looms, and its coal mining which led to its generation of electricity in the town in the late 1800s. With the Leeds and Liverpool Canal and the arrival of the railway, goods were able to be transported in bulk bringing much prosperity to the town. The Empire opened in 1894 and could accommodate 1,935 people.

The *Burnley Gazette* of Wednesday 10 December carried a story under the headline *REMARKABLE FEATS*. It read:

EMPIRE   THEATRE   OF   VARIETIES,
BURNLEY.
Lessee and Manager......MR. W. C. HORNER.

MR. C. G. COTES' VAUDEVILLE COMPANY.
MONDAY, DEC. 8th.   SIX NIGHTS.
MATINEE, TUESDAY, DEC. 9th, at 2.

HOUDINI.

MISS ESTA STELLA.   W H. LIDDY.
W. H. CLEMART.   ALF. CHESTER.
MISS NELLIE WALLACE.
MR. CHARLES MAY.

3 SISTERS SPRIGHTLY.

TIME AND PRICES AS USUAL.

A newspaper advert showing Houdini and the other vaudeville acts appearing at the Empire Theatre of Varieties in Burnley during December 1902.

Burnley, this week, is giving shelter to a man, a typical citizen of the land of the almighty dollar, of medium height, quiet demeanour and syllable accentuating in his speech, whose performances are enough to give Sherlock Holmes nervous prostration. We refer to Houdini, who is this week at the Empire Music Hall, giving a demonstration of phenomenal abilities in escaping from leg irons, shackles, handcuffs, in short, all the paraphernalia which the ingenuity satellites, of a benevolent judicial system have devised. To escape from the regulation handcuff is to Houdini child's play and he and his performances have naturally been the sensation of every town visited. Houdini does not confine his attentions to handcuffs and leg-irons merely but cheerfully essays breaking out of any gaol those in authority are kind enough to grant his request to be locked up in and generally successful. A good many in Burnley and district will puzzle over how it is done, for Houdini makes a stipulation that in 'indoor' work, so to speak, he is not watched, whilst on the stage he successfully defies locks, bolts and bars within a cabinet.

A representative of this paper saw him, yesterday, in a matinee performance at the Empire. He came upon the stage the personification of decorum, in evening dress, and before commencing his performance announced that that morning he had attended at the Burnley County Police Station and was locked in the end one of the row of cells. Five other cells were locked as well as a gate. He released himself from the cell he was confined in and opened every cell in the corridor and gate, within five minutes. When placed in the first cell, he was handcuffed and got rid of these in addition. He stated, amidst laughter, that he went to the Borough Police Station but they refused to lock him up and he challenged the Watch Committee to have him placed in any cell in the Town Hall, 'under his conditions', and if he failed to break out in less then five minutes, he would forfeit £50 to any hospital they should name.

Houdini then got to work. Two local gentlemen went upon the stage and produced two pairs of

JAIL

BREAKER

IN

BURNLEY.

—•—

HARRY
    HOUDINI

was locked in a cell at the County Police Station in the presence of Supt. Brassington and Sergt. Wynn, December 9th. He released himself by opening the cell door, and proceeded to open every cell in the corridor (6 in number), also opening the large iron gate, all in less than 5 minutes time.

—•—

As Chief Constable Mr. Rawle refused to lock HOUDINI up, HOUDINI WILL FORFEIT £50 TO any charitable purpose named by the Watch Committee if he fail to escape from the Town Hall Cell (under his conditions in less than 5 minutes time.

An article about Harry Houdini's appearance in Burnley in December 1902.

handcuffs and a pair of leg-irons, in which they secured Houdini, who when the operation was completed, was bent half double, in consequence of the 'cuffs' being attached to the leg-irons, and had just enough 'rope' to walk into the cabinet upon the stage. Mrs Houdini drew a veil over her husband's actions and the two local gentlemen, retaining the keys of their hardware, sat down, and with an expectant audience awaited events. A minute went by, two, three, and then excitement rose, as the newer pair of handcuffs, open, were suddenly jerked out of the cabinet and fell with a little clatter upon the stage. A moment later, Houdini drew the curtain aside and disclosed himself free of his cumbersome appendages, which, open, he held in his hands. He was heartily cheered. Then, with his hands tied securely behind him, he walked into his cabinet and almost instantaneously re-appeared with his coat off but with his hands still tied behind him. Then, borrowing a coat, he again vanished into the cabinet, re-appearing a second later with that on and his hands still tied. He was next, with his hands tied behind him, placed in a sack, the mouth of which was sealed, which in turn was placed in a large box, strongly corded. This was carried into the cabinet, Mrs Houdini walking with it. The curtain was drawn and almost simultaneously Houdini emerged from the cabinet free. The box was uncorded and Mrs Houdini was found in the bag, the seal upon the mouth which had not been broken.

Houdini's feats have created quite a sensation in the town and the Empire will assuredly be crowded every night this week. It may be added that Houdini last week, escaped from the cell at Leeds in which Charles Peace was confined.

The *Burnley Gazette* for 13 December read:

Houdini, 'the handcuff king and jail breaker' has had large houses at the Empire this week, to witness his performance. Last night, before a big house, Mr. J.W. Taylor and Colour-Sergt. Whittle of Burnley, secured him in Boer irons and leg irons, which necessitated him assuming a crouching position, and then fastened a second pair of irons on his wrists. These irons were not of the ordinary regulation pattern, but possessed double locks and were, as Houdini admitted, almost twice as secure as the regulation pattern. Nevertheless, he freed himself from them in five and three-quarter minutes and was loudly cheered. Other handcuffs of the regular pattern he made far shorter work of. Tonight's is his last appearance in Burnley, so far as his visit is concerned, and there is sure to be a big house at the Empire to see him.

Houdini broke all box office records at Burnley.

His final date for 1902 was at the City of Varieties in Leeds between 15 and 20 December. His popularity was even greater than that of his recent visit and extra matinees had to be held at a larger theatre, the Coliseum. Houdini once more increased his income.

On Thursday 18 December, ex-Superintendent Lincoln of the city police force produced a straitjacket while Houdini was on stage at the Coliseum. He was locked and handcuffed in the jacket and was then conducted into a cabinet in front of a large and appreciative audience. After six minutes, Houdini re-appeared with the straitjacket over one arm.

The following night, he was nailed into a wooden box on stage by a local carpenter, a Mr Nettleton. Once again he made his escape to much applause.

An advert for the show stated that this was Houdini's last date in the UK before he departed for Russia. However, Houdini's next appearance was at the Rembrandt Theatre in Amsterdam in January 1903.

The tours of the UK in 1902 had brought him much adulation from the British public and his popularity continued to grow.

Freepost Plus RTKE-RGRJ-KTTX
Pen & Sword Books Ltd
47 Church Street
BARNSLEY
S70 2AS

DISCOVER MORE ABOUT MILITARY HISTORY

Pen & Sword Books have over 4000 books currently available, our imprints include; Aviation, Naval, Military, Archaeology, Transport, Frontline, Seaforth and the Battleground series, and we cover all periods of history on land, sea and air.

Keep up to date with our new releases by completing and returning the form below (no stamp required if posting in the UK).

Alternatively, if you have access to the internet, please complete your details online via our website at **www.pen-and-sword.co.uk.**

All those subscribing to our mailing list will receive a free e-book, *Mosquito Missions* by Martin W Bowman. Please enter code number ACC1 when subscribing to receive your free e-book.

Mr/Mrs/Ms ....

Address..

....

Postcode........................... Email address..

Website: www.pen-and-sword.co.uk Email: enquiries@pen-and-sword.co.uk
Telephone: 01226 734555   Fax: 01226 734438
Stay in touch: facebook.com/penandswordbooks or follow us on Twitter @penswordbooks

Chapter Four

1903 – Further Shows

Although Houdini wasn't in the UK during the beginning of 1903, his shows had left a lasting impression and he was still being talked about. The *Leeds Mercury* of Saturday 14 February mentioned Houdini in one of their draughts and chess articles which read:

Patrons of the local entertainment halls have for some time past been mystified by the doings of 'Houdini the handcuff king', who somehow escapes from all manner of apparently hopeless positions in which various members of the audience fix him. I am told that a prominent checkerist, connected with a club not far from York Road, has discovered Houdini's secret and that at our future convivial gatherings after the matches we shall possess the services of a popular and able entertainer.

A studio shot of Houdini in chains.

Houdini with his hands chained behind his back. This was a regular feature of his act.

Houdini preparing to escape from leg-irons, handcuffs and chains.

Houdini's brother Hardeen continued to tour the UK and a notable appearance was recorded in the *Yorkshire Evening Post* of Tuesday 27 January:

Perhaps the most interesting appearance at the Leeds Empire Theatre this week is that of Hardeen, who, like his brother, Houdini, is a handcuff manipulator. He was adorned last night with five sets of handcuffs and two pairs of leg-irons and was to all appearances securely fastened as human ingenuity could devise. In about five minutes he was free, however, and afterwards, extricated himself with equal ease when handcuffed with his hands behind his back. The trunk trick is also very clever.

Houdini's brother, Hardeen, performing a similar act complete with chains and handcuffs.

Six dates have been found for Houdini's tour during 1903. His first appearance was at the Pavilion Theatre in Leicester between 9 and 14 November. There he managed to escape from a cell built by Oliver Cromwell.

His next venue was at the People's Palace, Halifax where he appeared between 16 November and 21 November.

Houdini knew when a fellow escapologist was tying him up. In Halifax, a spectator tied Houdini's hands behind his back but was taking a long time doing so and Houdini got suspicious that the man was more than an ordinary onlooker.

'He must be a so-called imitation handcuff king!' he announced.

A poster advertising a forthcoming Hardeen challenge at the Palace Theatre, Bath during 1903.

The man stopped tying knots for a few seconds and told the audience that he knew nothing about escapology. He continued to tie knots before Houdini entered his cabinet. The escape took longer than it would normally but, even so, he was soon free. However, the challenger was not happy and insisted on tying Houdini up once more. Houdini was not impressed and turned to the audience and asked if anyone knew the man. No one answered from the audience but a man stepped out from the wings and indicated that he knew who he was.

'He is Pollard, the handcuff king from Bradford!' he said. 'He wrote that handcuff exposure in the Strand!'

Houdini turned to the audience and pledged £500 to the poor of Halifax if Pollard would allow himself to be handcuffed by Houdini and managed to escape. Houdini called to the manager of the theatre. 'Mr McNaughton, will you stand good for me?'

McNaughton agreed and the audience cheered. Houdini's assistant, Frank Kukol, brought on stage a pair of manacles which Houdini held aloft for the audience to see. The cuffs were the infamous American Bean Giants. Pollard shook his head in denial and announced that he had only ever escaped from British handcuffs. Kukol produced a pair of British handcuffs and Houdini announced, 'Mr McNaughton, pay this young man £500, when he gets out of these!'

Pollard refused and left as the audience jeered.

Houdini's performance had been due to last just twenty minutes but instead, with the challenge by Pollard, had gone on for over an hour. Both Houdini and the theatre manager knew that newspaper reports, and people telling their friends about the incident, would make sure that later performances were packed out.

A poster advertising Houdini's appearance at the Palace Theatre Halifax in November 1903.

Houdini was later also bound by a local magician who had challenged him to free himself from cord and chains. He managed to escape but later described the way that he had been secured as 'a very dangerous tie'. He continued to play to packed audiences.

Houdini travelled from Halifax to the Empire in Huddersfield where he played between 30 November and 5 December. Huddersfield was a wool and textile town and many people in the audience would have worked in the mechanised

Houdini in dress suit in an early publicity photo complete with handcuffs and chains.

A naked Houdini, stripped so that he can't conceal any hidden keys or lock picks.

mills. By the time Houdini appeared there, the Empire was in decline and was demolished the following year. In Huddersfield, Houdini escaped from a cell completely naked and proceeded to open nine others.

As mentioned, there were many imitators who tried to copy Houdini's act. One annoyed Houdini in Huddersfield when he failed to pay his bills, so much so that Houdini took out an advert in the local paper. It read:

Will the gentleman who calls himself Houdina or Houdiana, and who in a fit of absent-mindedness walked away from Huddersfield forgetting to pay his board bill to Mrs Scott of St Peter's Street, kindly send the lady her money. It is very impolite to disguise yourself under a name which may sound like mine, and then walk away without paying your bills. I will not be responsible for any bills made by this gentleman.

On 1 December, Houdini wrote a column for the *Dramatic Mirror* from Huddersfield concerning his rival, the Great Cirnoc:

Several deaths have occurred lately, among whom may be mentioned Paul H. Conrich, better known as Cirnoc, who has made quite a reputation as a 'Handcuff King'. He had been failing in health, and had just signed a contract with Manager Richards to open in Australia, according to London Era, and died on his way to Sydney, where he is buried. He was about forty-five years of age and had been a performer for many years. He leaves a son and daughter. He was recently married to a lady who used to manage Karo, when Karo toured America.

Houdini tightly secured in handcuffs.

The Great Cirnoc had regularly interrupted both Houdini's and Hardeen's performances in the past and it's curious that Houdini should have paid tribute to him. Some suggested that Cirnoc's interruptions were perhaps planned to gather more interest in Houdini's shows.

Will Goldston in his book *Sensational Tales of Mystery Men* mentioned Houdini's rivalry with the Great Cirnoc:

Houdini brought the escape business to a fine art. He also understood the value of newspaper stories and articles as a form of publicity. He once confessed to me that he spent every cent he could spare in advertising himself. He learnt to swim, and his first sensational trick was an escape from a milk can filled with water. This illusion was invented by one of his assistants.

Sensation! That was Houdini's password. He was not, of course, the first man to escape from handcuffs and boxes, but he certainly was the pioneer in escapes of a sensational nature. He aimed at being different from all other performers, and I have known him to scrap many illusions because he thought he was being imitated.

At the beginning of his performances, Houdini always told the audience that he did not possess supernatural powers. He emphasized the fact that his escapes were tricks – not miracles. In spite of this assurance, many people were firmly convinced that he had the power of dematerialising his body at will. When Houdini's fame had spread through England and the Continent, many imitators sprang up. The American reduced their number in an incredibly short time by means of a scheme which was as simple as it was effective.

He organised a service of professional 'challengers'. These men attended the shows of the various imitators, and challenged the performers to escape from an 'ordinary' pair of handcuffs. These ordinary handcuffs were so constructed that once they were closed they could only be opened with a special key. After a good deal of helpless struggling, the performers invariably admitted defeat.

There was however, one escape act which Houdini could not humble. This was 'The Brother Cirnocs'. The Cirnocs were not imitators in the strict sense of the word, for they were performing in England some time before Houdini came to this country. Their turn was very similar to Houdini's, and, what was more important from the American's point of view, it was equally as clever.

In vain did Harry try to corner the Cirnocs by means of his 'challengers'. At last he gave it up as a bad job. But, realising that he had opponents in England who were just as astute as himself, he decided to delete the handcuff escapes from his programme.

Houdini is recorded as visiting Wakefield many times although the dates are uncertain. There are stories of him visiting Wakefield Bridge because he wanted to catch a glimpse of the ghost of Henry Whalton, a seventeenth century highwayman who was said to haunt the area.

Houdini's next appearance was at the Palace in Blackburn between 14 December and 19 December. Remembering the trouble he'd had there previously with the Hodgson challenge, he wrote in his diary: 'Back to this wretched town. Of all the hoodlum towns I ever worked, the gallery is certainly the worst. Had a tough time with a heel named Wilson.'

A young man had gone on stage to challenge Houdini but appeared more interested in showing him how clever he was. Houdini further wrote: 'He would not let me examine the cuff, so after a lot of speech making, he wanted to walk off the stage. I sneaked behind him and tore the cuffs from his grasp and snapped

A pensive shot of Houdini complete with his book, *The Unmasking of Robert-Houdin*.

Houdini slipping out of chains around his wrists.

Houdini with various means of escape.

them on myself. Well, you ought to have heard the booing that was my share to obtain. I went into my cabinet and found that he had deliberately cut away the whole inside of the lock and it was ten minutes before I had both hands free. Instead of applause, once again I was booed. Then I snapped them on to the rods near the footlights and it took Wilson twenty minutes to take them off himself and he had to use three kinds of instruments to do so. He was applauded and I was booed.'

An advert for Houdini's show at the Palace Theatre, Hull during December 1903.

The incident greatly upset Houdini who wasn't used to such a response from the audience. Because of this, he considered retirement.

A reporter for the *Blackburn Standard and Weekly Express* wrote:

I hear that Houdini having made his 'pile' tends shortly to retire from the stage, for the demand made on him by his performances and the brutality to which he has not infrequently had to submit, are making inroads to his health.

Houdini next appeared at the Palace Theatre, Hull between 21 and 26 December. Whaling had played a major part in the city's fortunes as had the fishing industry. The Palace Theatre had opened in December 1897 and was described as 'a great acquisition to the town'.

The *Hull Daily Mail* of Thursday 24 December reported:

The Palace programme during Christmas will remain as it has been during the week. It is, we are bound to say, a stronger and more generous programme than the management have submitted for a long time. Houdini is the principal attraction but there are a number of others. Especially should be singled out are the turns given by a quintette of Bavarian dancers and Dan Burke, and the two ladies associated with him, as being well worth seeing. There is no Christmas Day concert at the Palace this year.

Houdini's last appearance was between 28 December 1903 and 2 January 1904 at Birmingham. His diary records that the police there refused to lock him up in one of their cells.

Chapter Five

1904 – The *Mirror* Challenge

Twenty-one shows have been discovered for 1904. There are gaps in his timetable and it's quite possible that Houdini played at other venues which have yet to be discovered.

Perhaps the most well-covered of his performances was the one featuring Houdini's appearance at the London Hippodrome where he took part in the *Daily Mirror* Challenge, a story which features later in the chapter.

Back on British soil, Houdini's first recorded appearance was at the Empire Palace in Sheffield between 18 and 23 January. Sheffield was known all over the world for its steel production and many people who came to see Houdini would have been employed at one of the factories in the city. The work was described as having an 'extraordinarily injurious influence upon health.' The Empire opened in 1895 and was very modern at the time with a large stage. It was capable of seating 2,500 people.

The Empire Theatre in Sheffield where Houdini appeared in January 1904.

It's recorded that when Houdini appeared in Sheffield the Chief Constable challenged him to escape from the cell that had once held Charles Peace twenty-five years earlier. This is very similar to the story told when he appeared at Leeds between 1 and 6 December 1902. Peace was held in the Sheffield cell but then hanged at Armley Prison in Leeds leading to the accounts involving two separate cells.

On the morning of Tuesday 19 January, Houdini, accompanied by Mr Alan W. Young, the manager of the Empire, called into the central police station at Water Lane to arrange to give an exhibition of his mysterious powers. He found that the Chief Constable (Commander

Scott) was happy to oblige him but rather than make a later appointment, he locked him up straightaway. In the presence of the Deputy Chief Constable (Mr G.H. Barker) and a sergeant, Houdini was stripped of all his clothing which was locked in a cell. He was then locked in another cell, the one which had once housed Charles Peace. The door was closed and triple-locked. The officers then retired below and locked the iron gate at the foot of the steps. The locks were said to be similar to those at the Bank of England. In five minutes, Houdini ran down the steps fully dressed, opened the corridor gate and presented himself to the startled officers.

A photo of notorious villain, Charles Peace.

Houdini received an impressive letter from Commander Charles Scott which praised his escape. He was issued with the following signed declaration:

Sheffield, Jan. 19, 1904.
This is to certify that Mr. Harry Houdini was this day stripped stark naked and locked in the cell which once contained Charles Peace. The cell was searched and triple-locked, but Mr. Houdini released himself and redressed in five minutes, having also opened the iron gate of the corridor.
  Charles J. Scott, Commander (R.N.)
  Chief Constable, Sheffield. Witness to the foregoing feat,
  George H. Barker, Deputy Chief Constable

During January, Mr George Wale, for twenty years an attendant at the South Yorkshire insane asylum, challenged Houdini to escape from one of the straitjackets used to restrain homicidal maniacs. The challenge was accepted and Mr Wale appeared on the stage of the Empire Music Hall in Sheffield on the afternoon of Saturday 23 January. He bound Houdini up in the jacket, Houdini retired to a small tent on the stage and within eight minutes, re-appeared free of the restraint. On examination, the mechanism of the jacket proved to be wholly uninjured.

An advert for the show which appeared in the *Sheffield Daily Telegraph* of Friday 22 January stated that due to Houdini's popularity, thousands of people were being turned away nightly.

A correspondent of the *North Mail* wrote in the *Dundee Evening Post* of Saturday 30 January:

A publicity shot of Houdini in chains and handcuffs.

I have on various occasions had the honour of securely handcuffing and leg-ironing Houdini and he has always been able to release himself with the utmost celerity and ease. On one occasion I suggested that he should try some experiments on some quite strange, unsuspecting clients and so we took a stroll down the Strand and Houdini led the way into a gunsmith's shop where handcuffs were sold. Approaching the counter, behind which a somewhat austere assistant stood erect, awaiting customers, my companion inquired whether he could purchase a pair of handcuffs, adding that they must be strong.

The assistant smiled with superiority and produced several pairs of the 'latest'. These Houdini toyed with for a few moments, then inquired if it was possible for anyone to escape from them once they were securely fastened and the key removed. The assistant looked flabbergasted at the mere suggestion. Then Houdini asked the assistant to snap a pair upon his wrists which was done.

Then, turning to me, the 'handcuff king' requested me to be so kind as to fasten another pair on, which I did. With the excuse that he wished to try them, he disappeared into a dark corner, and in a few moments returned with the handcuffs hanging loose from his hands and remarking, 'I am afraid these are not strong enough.'

I shall never forget the look on that assistant's face. However, Houdini enlightened him as to his identity and the mystery was cleared up.

Then we went to another shop but here Houdini was known, he having fooled them before and they said they didn't care for any more. From here, we went to Bow Street police station and, making our way to the inner office, where a large assortment of handcuffs are hung upon the wall, Houdini asked the officer in charge to be so kind as to handcuff him as securely as he could. But here again the 'King' was known so the officer looked him up and down with scorn and remarked: 'We've got something better to do with our time.'

At this the dauntless little American triumphantly exclaimed, 'That's just what I wanted you to say.' And then we both left speedily. They were taking charges. New Scotland Yard has also been beaten in a similar manner and none of their irons could hold Houdini.

It appears that as Houdini was becoming more well known, several establishments, including police stations, were becoming less eager to facilitate his escapes from their establishments.

The *Derbyshire Times and Chesterfield Herald* of Saturday 30 January noted:

A drawing of Houdini on stage which appeared in the *Dundee Evening Post* of Saturday, 30 January 1904.

Much interest has been displayed in Derbyshire in the performances of Houdini the 'Handcuff King', who boasts of having escaped from 59 police cells. But he has a rival in Matlock, who set him a hard task on Saturday. The Matlock individual, with several friends, visited the Empire, Sheffield, and, after witnessing Houdini's escape from several pairs of 'bracelets' secured Houdini's hands behind his back with a pair of New York Secret Service Police handcuffs, belonging to a Matlock resident. Houdini, I am informed, tried in the smaller cabinet for nine minutes to free himself and then entered the larger cabinet in order to obtain more freedom of movement. It took him 14 minutes to get loose, and when he did come out, I am told that his wrists were bleeding from the efforts to slip the darbies and he publicly recognised the thorough manner in which he had been secured. The Matlock expert contends that he had escaped from the same bracelets in 1 minute 20 seconds and that he had undone every one of the handcuffs at the Matlock Police Station. If this is so, he has evidently missed his vocation.

Houdini's next booking was at the Empire Theatre in Liverpool between 25 January and 6 February. Liverpool was a major port whose fortunes had grown considerably during the industrial revolution and it had once participated in the

LIVERPOOL

CITY POLICE OFFICE

DALE ST., FEB. 2nd, 1904.

I certify that to-day Mr. HARRY HOUDINI showed his abilities in releasing himself from restraint. He had three pairs of Handcuffs (one a very close fitting pair) round his wrists, and was placed in a Nude State in a Cell which had been previously searched. Within Six Minutes he was free from the Handcuffs, had opened the Cell, and had opened the doors of all the other Cells in the Corridor; had changed a Prisoner from one Cell to another, and had so securely locked him in that he had to be asked to unlock the door.

SIGNED.

LEONARD DUNNING,

HEAD CONSTABLE.

HOUDINI

APPEARS AT THE

EMPIRE THEATRE,

Every Evening this Week.

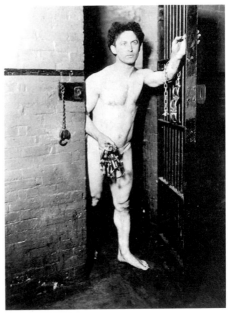

A notice from Leonard Dunning of the Liverpool city police force stating that Houdini had managed to escape from one of their cells.

Houdini, pictured almost naked, releasing himself from a police cell.

Atlantic slave trade. The population rose greatly in the 1800s due to the famine in Ireland and by 1851, approximately a quarter of Liverpool's residents were Irish. The Empire Theatre re-opened in 1896; it had formerly been the Alexandra Theatre.

An article in the *Daily Express* during February read:

Wizard in Gaol.
Open cells and is taken for the Devil.
His 61st escape.

Liverpool
City Police Office
Dale Street, Feb 2nd 1904.
I certify that to-day Mr. Harry Houdini showed his abilities in releasing himself from restraint. He had three pairs of handcuffs, one a very close-fitting pair, placed round his wrists, and he was placed in a nude state in a cell which had been previously searched. Within 6 minutes he was free from the handcuffs, had opened the cell door, and had opened the doors of all the other cells in the

corridor, had changed a prisoner from one cell to another, and had so securely locked him in that he had to be asked to unlock the door.

Signed

Leonard Dunning,

Head Constable, Liverpool. Feb. 2, 1904.

Mr. Dunning has since been knighted and is now head of the Police Constabulary, being located in London, his official title being His Majesty's Inspector of Constabulary, London, England. For him it is literally true that stone walls do not a prison make, nor iron bars a cage. Were he a criminal, his clear, straightforward eyes negative the suggestion, he would be a nightmare to the police of Britain, for he would walk out of gaol as coolly and smilingly as he did twice out of Liverpool Bridewell yesterday. It was an eventful day at the sinister-looking building that stands off busy Dale Street. High police officials, clever detectives, leading city business men, who hold office on the watch committee, all sustained a severe shock by their loss of faith in what they had regarded as an inviolable stronghold. No one has been known previously to escape from the bolts and bars behind which Liverpool quarters its criminals.

In the afternoon Houdini had a pleasant interview with Head Constable Dunning.

'Want to try our locks? Certainly. You're welcome; but, of course, we will take some precautions.'

'I want you to do so,' replied Houdini. 'I will strip naked. You can then handcuff me and put me in your strongest cell, and after you have searched me and the cell you leave me, locking the door. I will join you in a minute or two.'

Houdini was as good as his word. Not only did he escape, but he had torn from his hands and arms three pairs of handcuffs, which had been put on him by officers with absolute belief in their restraining power. Even these feats were not enough for this man, who does things that would have made Jack Sheppard die of envy. He felt sure there was nothing in Bridewell to baffle him. Running along the corridor, he opened the doors of other cells, which he had thought were all empty. When he reached No. 14 and flung open the door, he confronted a prisoner.

'I don't know which of us was the more surprised,' said Houdini to an Express representative. 'Here was I, standing absolutely nude before a terrified, miserable object. Poor fellow! What a shock it was for him. He was an Irishman just recovering from a drunken bout.'

'Arrah!' he said, when he had recovered; 'I thought it was the devil!' The shivering prison-breaker hurried the wretched prisoner out of cell No. 14 into

No. 15 and locked him in. Then he ran along the passage to greet the head constable and the other officials. Only 6 minutes had elapsed since he had been locked in the cell naked and handcuffed. The cell door was inspected and found uninjured. Then one of the gaolers, walking along the corridor, espied door No. 14 open and a prisoner gone.

'That's all right,' said the irrepressible Houdini. 'I've had him out and locked him up in No. 15.'

Hearty laughter followed the narration of this achievement, and the officials went to No. 15. So securely had the Irishman been locked up that it was necessary to call upon Houdini to unfasten the door. The Irishman was found in a somewhat bewildered state, but he probably 'sobered' quicker than he would have done in less eventful circumstances. Houdini left the Bridewell the proud possessor of the certificate which is reproduced at the head of this article.

In the evening Houdini, accompanied by an Express representative, again walked into the Bridewell to settle a point which had been raised since his feat in the afternoon. Was the door which had been fastened against him single, double, or triple locked? The matter could easily be settled. Houdini would just do the trick again. Only this time he would do it with his clothes on, as time was pressing. Liverpool's Bridewell is as an unsightly a place as a Bridewell can be. No one would mistake it for a spa hotel or a convalescent home. Beneath a dark arch you pass, and in the great door which you find opposite is a little window which is unlocked when you knock, and through which you are viewed before you are permitted even to stand upon the threshold. Houdini and his companion were admitted.

'More lock-breaking?'

'Yes; I am ready for more, as many as you like.'

Accompanied by a gaoler, Houdini and the Express representative ascended a flight of stone steps and passed along dimly lighted corridors, whose atmosphere seemed, to reek with crime and mystery. Passing through a gate, a row of cells was reached, upon any one of which Houdini might operate. Here was one marked with a strange device. Houdini would try this one. It was a felon's cell – stronger than some of the others, though it could not have been darker or more forbidding. Houdini entered. He was locked in by the Express representative. He was inside, safe and sound.

There could be no doubt about that. At the first turn of the key the lock went forward twice; at the second, once. Houdini was behind a triple lock in the dark, dreary cell. The Express representative and the gaoler left him there, and retired beyond an iron gate which bars the passage.

'The gate is a greater test than the cell,' said the gaoler. 'It's locked before it's locked, if you understand. Shut it, and it's locked, and then you can lock it again.'

The gaoler's hand only secured it when Houdini presented himself. 'That's as quick as I've ever done it,' said he. And then he tackled the gate. A moment's hesitation. The gaoler shook his head, and a smile was just overspreading his features, when lo! Houdini flung open wide the gate. He agreed that the gate was 'tougher', as he expressed it, than the cell.

Houdini is an American. Only his strong arms and his supple, yet powerful hands give the slightest clue of his prison- breaking capacity. He does not look a gaolbird, but the escape he made for the benefit of Express readers was his 61st. Bright-eyed, smart, active, and a good talker, he has travelled far and wide, and has broken out of the prisons of many countries.

'I have never failed,' said Houdini, 'but I don't say there is no cell I cannot break out of. As to handcuffs, the hardest job I ever had was with a pair made at Krupp's. It took me 40 minutes to get out of them, but I did it.'

Will Goldston recalled his first meeting with Houdini in Liverpool in his book *Sensational Tales of Mystery Men*. He said that the incident had taken place 29 years earlier than the publication of the book, which would have been in 1899. It seems more likely that they actually met in 1904 when Houdini was appearing at the Empire. Goldston wrote:

I knew Harry Houdini before I had ever seen him. His reputation had reached me some years before I first encountered him, and, as is the habit of magicians, we corresponded for a considerable time before he gave his first performance in this country.

Strangely enough, it was quite by accident that I first ran into him. About twenty-nine years ago, I was walking down Lime Street, one of the main thoroughfares of Liverpool. It was winter time and snowing hard. As I hastened along, with my thoughts on nothing in particular, I noticed a short figure, coming towards me, with coat collar turned up and head bent to the ground.

As the man got nearer, I observed that he was carrying a small dog beneath his left arm. His clothes were shabby and unkempt, and it was this fact more than anything else which caused me to stare at him with more than usual interest. To my surprise, his face was familiar.

'Excuse me,' I said, grasping him by the arm. 'Are you Harry Houdini?'

'Yes,' was the reply. 'Who are you?'

'I'm Will Goldston.'

'Goldston, my dear fellow!' cried Houdini, shaking me by the hand as if I had been his lifelong friend, 'this is indeed a pleasant surprise.' His manner suddenly changed. 'Tell me,' he resumed, lowering his voice for no apparent reason, where can I get a pair of patent leather boots?'

'Patent leather boots?'

'Sure. I've tried almost every shop in the town. And then I want to find the American Bar. You must take me there.'

We strolled along to a small footwear shop that was known to me, and Houdini bought the boots he required. When he had expressed full satisfaction at his purchase, I escorted him to the American Bar, wondering why he was so anxious to visit the place. I was not left long in ignorance.

When we arrived, I found that a collection was being made for the widow of a poor and unknown member of the profession. Houdini had been told of this, and had decided to give as much as he could afford. In those days he was not getting the big salary that he earned in later years, but subscribed two pounds to the fund.

I have mentioned this somewhat insignificant incident because it was absolutely characteristic of the man – warm-hearted and generous, always willing to help a brother or sister in distress. And later, when he told me that he himself was badly lacking in funds, I wondered what manner of man this strange Houdini could be.

As we left the American Bar, Houdini told me the story of his life – a story that could fill several volumes. 'Do you know, Goldston,' he said, 'I have not had a decent meal for more than five years!'

'In Heaven's name, why not?' I asked.

'In my early days I couldn't afford it, and now I'm too busy.'

At first I thought Houdini was pulling my leg. As a matter of fact, it was not until some years afterwards that I realised he had told me the truth. Although he was earning a hundred pounds a week, Houdini was a starving man!

After we had walked some little way in silence – I hardly liked to call the man a liar – Houdini resumed the conversation. 'Are you responsible for the display of books in the shop next to the theatre?' he asked.

'Yes,' I replied. 'It struck me that your visit to this country would help the sale of my first book, I hired the shop window, and made a terrific splash of the whole thing.'

Some months previously Houdini had given me his written consent to include the explanations of a number of his escape tricks in a book that I was writing. I had had a big placard painted with the words 'How Houdini does his tricks,' and had it, together with several copies of the book, placed in the shop window.

'It's a good idea, and you certainly deserve to get on,' said my companion. 'But it doesn't do me much good, does it?' And he smiled kindly. 'You must call at my apartments to-morrow. I would like you to meet Mrs. Houdini.'

The next day I called and had tea with the Houdinis. There we talked over different matters connected with our profession, and I remember advising the American to go down to the harbour and see a huge advertisement of his name. It was then that I urged him to have his name printed as 'Houdini', with the Christian name 'Harry' in very small type. Houdini thought this a good business idea, and eventually became known simply by his surname.

Before I left, he promised that he would write to me every week when he returned to America. He kept his promise for twenty-eight years, sometimes sending me as many as three and four letters a week. During the whole of that time I only had one quarrel with him. This was due to a stupid misunderstanding.

It happened in this manner. When Houdini was making a big name for himself in America, the Cirnocs appeared in this country. This last was a double turn – father and son, and were indeed a very formidable combination. At a publicity stunt they declared they could escape from any police cell in which they were locked. This they did to the satisfaction of the public – but not to my own. I discovered they bribed the officials who had locked them in.

Houdini had done the same thing in America, but this had been a genuine escape. In justice to my friend I exposed the Cirnocs in a magical book. Houdini got hold of a copy of the paper and wrongly assumed that it was himself I had exposed.

Impetuosity was probably the strongest trait in Houdini's character. He immediately attacked me in a libellous article which appeared in his own American Magical magazine. I was at a loss to understand his conduct, for not only were his statements untrue, but hitherto we had been the closest of friends.

Explanations and apologies followed. Nobody was better pleased than myself to have the whole matter cleared up, for Houdini's friendship was something for which I would not have exchanged a dozen theatrical contracts.

On Saturday 6 February, Houdini appeared at a charity matinee during the afternoon at the Sheffield Empire Palace in aid of the Lord Mayor's Fund for the Unemployed. He was still playing at Liverpool at the time so must have travelled back and forwards for both shows. The house at the Sheffield Empire was crowded and guests included many of Sheffield's leading citizens including the Lord Mayor and Lady Mayoress (Councillor J.R. and Mrs Wheatley).

From two o'clock until half past five, the entertainment continued. Music hall favourites included Albert Chevalier and others who were not only giving their services, but had travelled a considerable distance to get there. Chevalier did one turn and sang 'Dear Old Dutch'. He was followed by Houdini who received a great reception. He began his act with sleight of hand work, involving playing cards, followed by freeing himself from several handcuffs. He informed the audience about his escape from cells at both Liverpool and Sheffield. A tramway conductor from the audience placed on his wrists a pair of cuffs which were said to have been found in a Boer mine. He very quickly escaped and repeated more escapes with other handcuffs brought by members of the audience.

Also on the bill was Inaudi, the human calculator; Charles De Camo and his famous dog Cora; Bella and Bijou, an amusing act who told of their mis-adventures during their first motor car ride and the Harmony Four who provided excellent harmony music. Many other varied and entertaining acts took part in the show and £175 was raised for the fund.

On Saturday 6 February, the *Yorkshire Post* noted:

So easily does Houdini free himself from the fetters with which a sceptical public load him, that no-one realises the mental as well as the physical strain of his feats. Of late, he has been in a state bordering on nervous prostration and he has been recommended to take a rest. He contemplates taking a holiday for a few months and spending it at his home in America.

The next venue where Houdini performed was at the Empire in South Shields. He appeared there between 8 February and 13 February. South Shields was known for its coal mining, alkaline production and glass making, as well as its shipbuilding industry. The population of the area grew incredibly during the industrial revolution with migrants from Ireland, Scotland and other parts of England.

On Tuesday 9 February, Houdini escaped from a police cell at South Shields Central after giving himself up to Superintendent Cowe.

In the *Sheffield Daily Telegraph* of Thursday 11 February, it was announced:

Councillor Cecil Wilson secured a revelation about the Houdini business at the police cells. The wonderful escape was due to the fact that Houdini could put his arm through the trap door and pick the lock from the outside. No prisoner will be given the same opportunity.

The Saturday matinee on 13 February included Houdini escaping from a packing case after he received a challenge from a member of the public during the week.

From South Shields, Houdini and his entourage travelled to the Empire Theatre at Birmingham where he played between 15 and 27 February.

While in Birmingham, Houdini used a local locksmith to fix a pair of 'Bean Giant' cuffs and it's thought that he could have first met Nathaniel Hart there.

Hart was the maker of the handcuffs used in the *Mirror* Challenge at his next venue at the Hippodrome in London. However, it has been suggested that Hart may have never existed and the *Mirror* Challenge was a promotion dreamt up by Houdini and the *Daily Illustrated Mirror* to promote ticket and newspaper sales.

Houdini appeared at the Hippodrome in London from 29 February until 2 April.

On his first night, he escaped from manacles worn by Count de Lorge for fifteen years while locked in the Bastille; two pairs of handcuffs worn by the famous highwayman, Jack Sheppard; the irons that Charles Peace had been held in when he escaped from a train near Sheffield and several other restraints. The total weight of it all was 131 pounds but he managed to escape in twenty-seven minutes.

A newspaper sketch of Nathaniel Hart, the maker of the infamous Mirror Handcuffs.

Houdini continued to perform to packed audiences in towns and cities around the country but when he returned to London, he found that audience numbers had dropped. For publicity purposes, he staged a special performance in front of reporters at the offices of the *Weekly Dispatch* in London. Using antique manacles borrowed from Tussaud's Chamber of Horrors and leg irons used to detain prisoners at the Bastille. He escaped but it didn't improve his box office takings.

Houdini wrote in his diary: 'House very poorly visited. Hope business will pick up.'

This was followed by: 'Superintendent Moy to hand. Very touching man. Touched me for five quidlest!'

The five 'quidlest' referred to the money Houdini was paying to the police to secure their co-operation.

On 4 March, the police refused to lock up Houdini in their Bow Street police station. A police officer wrote back to Houdini on 9 March after he had requested that he be allowed to escape from their cells: 'I am directed by the Commissioner to acknowledge receipt of your letter of the 7th and to say that he regrets being unable to grant you permission to make the attempt of effecting an escape from any police cell in the city.'

This was a blow to Houdini as publicity for his stage act was always gathered by performing other acts to draw attention.

While performing on stage at the Hippodrome, Houdini was approached by a reporter from the *Daily Illustrated Mirror* who challenged him to escape from a specially-made pair of handcuffs. Houdini examined them and refused the challenge. 'These are not regulation handcuffs.' he said.

The challenger motioned to the orchestra to stop playing, and when they did, he announced: 'On behalf of my newspaper, the *Daily Illustrated Mirror*, I have just challenged Mr Houdini to permit me to fasten these handcuffs on his wrists. Mr Houdini declines. In the course of my journalistic duties this week, I interviewed a blacksmith at Birmingham named Nathaniel Hart who has spent five years of his life perfecting a lock, which he alleges no mortal man can pick. The handcuff I wish to fasten on Mr Houdini contains such a lock. The key alone took a week to make. The handcuffs are made of the finest British steel, by a British workman, and being the property of the *Daily Illustrated Mirror,* has been bought with British gold. Mr Houdini is evidently afraid of British-made handcuffs, for he will not put on this pair.'

Houdini repeated that they were not regulation handcuffs and, turning his back on the journalist, he allowed himself to be handcuffed by three other challengers. He escaped in minutes.

The *Mirror* journalist asked Houdini if he could examine one of the pairs of handcuffs from which he'd just escaped. Houdini handed him a locked pair. The journalist banged the cuffs hard on the steps leading up to the stage. They sprang open much to the audience's amazement and delight.

'So much for regulation handcuffs!' the reporter shouted.

Once more he issued the challenge to Houdini. Houdini addressed the audience and said: 'I cannot possibly accept this gentleman's challenge tonight because I am restricted as to time. His handcuffs, he admits, have taken an artificer five years to make. I know, therefore, I can't get out of them in five minutes. There is not one lock in those handcuffs, but a half a dozen or more. I will make a match if the management here will allow me a matinee some day next week to make a trial. It will take me a long time to get out, even if I can do.'

The manager of the Hippodrome, a Mr Parker, agreed to the event taking place on Thursday 17 March. Houdini wrote in his diary that London was in an uproar and that every paper was carrying the story. This was far better publicity than he could have hoped for and surpassed the interest gained by his usual jail breaks.

With all the publicity, over 4,000 people and 100 journalists turned up to witness the feat. The handcuffs were placed on Houdini and he disappeared behind a small screen to make his escape. Over an hour passed, with Houdini occasionally appearing from behind the screen still cuffed. At one point, he requested that the cuffs be taken off so that he could remove his coat. Frank Parker, the *Mirror*'s representative, refused saying that if the cuffs were to be removed, Houdini would be able to tell how they were undone. On hearing this, Houdini produced a penknife and, holding it with his teeth, proceeded to cut his coat off himself. At one point, after about fifty-six minutes, Houdini's wife came onto the stage to give him a kiss. Many believed later that the key to unlock the cuff was in her mouth. Houdini disappeared behind the screen and after an hour and ten minutes, he freed himself. The gathered crowd cheered and applauded him loudly and he was carried on their shoulders. He later wept saying that it had been the most difficult escape of his career.

It was suggested many years after his death that the whole performance had been staged between the *Daily Mirror* and Houdini and his difficulty escaping was just to add more suspense to the

A postcard of the Angel in Islington which features a horse-drawn tram with a poster announcing Houdini's appearance at the Hippodrome, London in 1904. (*Image courtesy of John Cox http://www. wildabouthoudini.com/*)

A representative from the *Daily Illustrated Mirror* handcuffs Houdini during the *Mirror* Challenge of March 1904.

show. After the show, Houdini was presented with a sterling silver replica of the cuffs in honour of his escape. The miraculous act was reported in all newspapers throughout Britain.

The whole event was covered in the *Daily Illustrated Mirror* of 18 March:

Not a seat was vacant in the mighty Hippodrome, yesterday afternoon, when Harry Houdini, the 'Handcuff King', stepped into the arena, and received an ovation worthy of a monarch. For days past all London has been aware that on Saturday night last, a representative of the Mirror *had stepped into the arena, in response to Houdini's challenge to anybody to come forward and successfully manacle him, and had there and then made a match with America's Mysteriarch for Thursday afternoon.*

In his travels the journalist had encountered a Birmingham blacksmith who had spent five years of his life in devising a lock, which, he alleged, 'no mortal man could pick'. Promptly seeing he was in touch with a good thing, the press man had at once put an option upon the handcuff containing this lock, and brought it back to London with him. It was submitted to London's best locksmiths, who were unanimous in their admiration of it, asserting that in all their experience they had never before seen such a wonderful mechanism. As a result the editors of the Mirror *determined to put the lock to the severest test possible by challenging Mr. Houdini to be manacled with the cuffs. Like a true sportsman, Mr. Houdini accepted our challenge in the spirit in which it was given, although, on his own confession, he did not like the look of the lock.*

Mr. Houdini's call was for three o'clock yesterday, but so intense was the excitement that the 4,000 spectators present could scarcely restrain their impatience whilst the six excellent turns which preceded him, cheered to the echo on other occasions, got through their 'business'. Waiting quietly and unnoticed by the arena steps, the Mirror *representative watched Mr. Houdini's entrance, and joined in giving his opponent-to-be in the lists one of the finest ovations mortal man has ever received. 'I am ready,' said Houdini, concluding his address to the audience, 'to be manacled by the* Mirror *representative if he be present.'*

A hearty burst of applause greeted the journalist as he stepped into the arena and shook hands with the 'Handcuff King'. Then, in the fewest possible words, the press man called for 17 volunteers from the audience to act upon a committee to see fair play, and Mr. Houdini asked his friends also to step into the arena and watch his interests.

This done, the journalist placed the handcuffs on Mr. Houdini's wrists and snapped them. Then, with an effort, he turned the key six times, thus securing the bolt as firmly as possible. The committee being satisfied as to the security of the handcuff, Mr. Houdini said: 'Ladies and Gentlemen: I am now locked up in a hand-cuff that has taken a British mechanic five years to make. I do not know whether I am going to get out of it or not, but I can assure you I am going to do my best.'

Applauded to the echo, the Mysteriarch then retired within the cabinet that contains so many of his secrets. All correct chronometers chronicled 3.15. In a long line in front of the stage stood the committee. Before them, in the centre of the arena, stood the little cabinet Houdini loves to call his 'ghost house'. Restlessly pacing to and fro, the Mirror *representative kept an anxious eye on it.*

A drawing from the *Daily Illustrated Mirror* showing Houdini having the specially made handcuffs put on him during his show at the Hippodrome on 17 March 1904.

Those who have never stood in the position of a challenger can scarcely realise the sense of responsibility felt by one who has openly thrown down the gauntlet to a man who is popular with the public. The Mirror *had placed its reliance on the work of a British mechanic, and if Houdini succeeded in escaping in the first few minutes it was felt that the proceedings would develop into a mere farce. But time went by: 5, 10, 15, 20 minutes sped. Still the band played on. Then, at 22 minutes, Mr. Houdini put his head out of the 'ghost house', and this was the signal for a great outburst of cheering.*

'He is free! He is free!' shouted several; and universal disappointment was felt when it was ascertained that he had only put his head outside the cabinet in order to get a good look at the lock in strong electric light. The band broke into a dreamy waltz as Houdini once more disappeared within the canopy. The disappointed spectators looked at their watches, murmured 'What a shame!' gave Houdini an encouraging clap, and the journalist resumed his stride. At 35 minutes Mr. Houdini again emerged. His collar was broken, water trickled in great channels down his face, and he looked generally warm and uncomfortable.

'My knees hurt,' he explained to the audience. 'I am not done yet.' The 'house' went frantic with delight at their favourite's resolve, and this suggested an idea

to the Mirror representative. He spoke rapidly to Mr. Parker, the Hippodrome manager, who was at the side of the stalls. That gentleman looked thoughtful for a moment, then nodded his head and whispered something to an attendant.

Presently the man appeared bearing a large cushion.

'The Mirror has no desire to submit Mr. Houdini to a torture test,' said the representative; 'and if Mr. Houdini will permit me, I shall have great pleasure in offering him the use of this cushion.'

The 'Handcuff King' was glad evidently of the rest for his knees, for he pulled it through into the 'ghost house'. Ladies trembled with suppressed excitement, and, despite the weary wait, not a yawn was noticed throughout the vast audience. For 20 minutes more the band played on, and then Houdini was seen to emerge once more from the cabinet. Still handcuffed! Almost a moan broke over the vast assemblage as this was noticed. He looked in pitiable plight from his exertions and much exhausted. He looked about for a moment, and then advanced to where his challenger stood.

'Will you remove the handcuffs for a moment,' he said, 'in order that I may take my coat off?'

For a few seconds the journalist considered. Then he replied: 'I am indeed sorry to disoblige you, Mr. Houdini, but I cannot unlock those cuffs unless you admit you are defeated.'

The reason was obvious. Mr. Houdini had seen the cuffs locked, but he had never seen them unlocked. Consequently the press man thought there might be more in the request than appeared on the surface.

Houdini astonished his audience yesterday by hacking to pieces his frock coat in his endeavour to secure greater freedom of movement. Houdini evidently does not stick at trifles. He manoeuvred until he got a penknife from his waistcoat pocket. This he opened with his teeth, and then, turning his coat inside out over his head, calmly proceeded to cut it to pieces. The novelty of the proceeding delighted the audience, who yelled themselves frantic. The Mirror representative had rather a warm five minutes of it at this juncture. Many of the audience did not see the reason of his refusal, and expressed their disapproval of his action loudly. Grimly, however, he looked on

Houdini removes his jacket to aid his escape from the *Mirror* cuffs.

and watched Mr. Houdini once more re-enter the cabinet. Time sped on, and presently somebody recorded the fact that the Mysteriarch had been manacled just one hour. Ten minutes more of anxious waiting, and then a surprise was in store for everybody.

The band was just finishing a stirring march when, with a great shout of victory, Houdini bounded from the cabinet, holding the shining handcuffs in his hand – free! A mighty roar of gladness went up. Men waved their hats, shook hands one with the other. Ladies waved their handkerchiefs, and the committee, rushing forward as one man, shouldered Houdini, and bore him in triumph round the arena. But the strain had been too much for the 'Handcuff King', and he sobbed as though his heart would break. With a mighty effort, however, he regained his composure, and received the congratulations of the Mirror in the true sportsmanlike spirit he has shown throughout the contest.

The journalist intimated to the audience that a beautiful solid silver model of the handcuffs would be made, and asked Mr. Houdini's permission to present this to him at no distant date.

Late last night Mr. Houdini sent us the following telegram:

Editor 'Mirror',
2, Carmelite Street,
London. E. C.
'Allow me to thank you for the open and upright manner in which your representative treated me in today's contest. Must say that it was one of the hardest, but at the same time one of the fairest tests I ever had.'
HARRY HOUDINI.

London Hippodrome, March 20, 1904
To Whom It May Concern!
Since my success in mastering the celebrated Daily Mirror Handcuff it has come to my knowledge that certain disappointed, sceptical [sic] persons have made use of most unjust remarks against the result of last Thursday's contest.

In particular, one person has had the brazen audacity to proclaim himself able to open the Mirror Handcuff in two minutes.

Such being the case, I hereby challenge any mortal being to open the Mirror Handcuff in the same space of time that I did. I will allow him the full use of both hands; also any instrument or instruments, barring the actual key. The cuff must not be broken or spoilt. Should he succeed I will forfeit 100 guineas . . .
HARRY HOUDINI

Houdini's challenge to anyone who could escape from the Mirror handcuffs. A 100 guineas prize was offered.

The drawings that illustrated the article were completed by an artist from the *Mirror* who sat within the audience.

On 18 March, Houdini wrote in his diary: 'All English newspapers have wonderful accounts of me escaping out of the *Mirror* handcuffs, greatest thing that any artist had done in England. Extras were out and it was a case of nothing but 'Houdini at the Hippodrome'.

Three days after the challenge was complete, Houdini offered a challenge to the *Mirror*. He told them, 'You challenged me, now I challenge the world!'

He handed the newspaper a statement which read:

London Hippodrome, March 20, 1904.
To Whom it May Concern!

Since my success in mastering the celebrated Daily Mirror *Handcuff it has come to my knowledge that certain disappointed, sceptical persons have made use of most unjust remarks against the results of last Thursday's contest.*

In particular, one person has had the brazen audacity to proclaim himself able to open the Mirror *handcuff in two minutes.*

Such being the case, I hearby challenge any mortal being to open the Mirror *Handcuff in the same space of time that I did. I will allow him the full use of both hands; also any instrument or instruments, barring the actual key. The cuff must not be broken or spoilt. Should he succeed, I will forfeit 100 guineas.*
Harry Houdini.

Once published, Houdini received challenges from all over the country. Will Goldston wrote about the incident in his book *Sensational Tales of Mystery Men*:

I can recall only one occasion when Houdini was baffled in an escape act. That he did eventually succeed in escaping from a pair of specially constructed cuffs after seventy minutes struggling was in itself a great triumph, but he afterwards told me it was the most nerve racking ordeal in all his long magical experience. There was one thing, however, which he refused to disclose. That was the manner in which he freed himself.

A well known newspaper challenged Houdini to escape from a pair of handcuffs made by a Birmingham blacksmith. This man had taken five years to perfect his invention, and it was said that the manacles could only be opened by a special key. Houdini, fearing nobody, and realising the value of the challenge as a free advertisement, readily accepted.

The test was held at the London Hippodrome, and it was generally expected that Houdini would free himself from the wonder cuffs in his customary time of two or three minutes. The manacles were placed on his wrists, and, following his usual procedure, he entered the small cabinet which exposed only his face to the audience of two thousand people.

Five, ten, twenty minutes passed, and still Houdini had not escaped. The audience grew restless. Had Houdini met his Waterloo? There was a cry of relief as he walked to the footlights at the end of half an hour, but when it was seen that his wrists were still secured, it turned to a sigh of disappointment. Perspiring profusely, he examined the handcuffs in the full glare of the electric light, and returned to his cabinet.

A few minutes later, he requested that a pillow might be placed on his knees in order to make his position more comfortable. But still the time went by, and he seemed no nearer success. The audience was amazed.

A poster announcing Houdini's victory after escaping from the *Daily Mirror* handcuffs at the London Hippodrome on Thursday, 17 March 1904.

Fifteen minutes more elapsed, and Houdini asked that his coat might be removed. This request was refused since it would have necessitated removing the handcuffs. So he procured a penknife from his pocket, and slashed the lining of the coat to ribbons.

At the end of an hour, he asked his wife to bring him a glass of water. This she did, placing it on the edge of the cabinet. Houdini took the glass between his hands and drained it. Ten minutes later, he emerged from the cabinet, and flung the handcuffs on to the stage. He was free, and his appearance was greeted with thunderous applause.

How did Houdini escape? Presumably he manipulated the handcuffs by his ordinary methods, but in this case the locks had proved so stubborn that it had taken him over an hour to persuade them to yield. That, at least, is what the public concluded. Perhaps the public was right, it may have been deceived. I do not know.

I only know that on the following day I was told a very different story. A man whose sources of information were usually correct told me that Houdini never escaped from the handcuffs.

After an hour's struggling, said my informant, the magician realised he would never escape. So he asked his wife for a glass of water, and gave her to understand she would have to procure the key at all costs. Bessie, realising the terrible predicament of her husband, called one of the journalists aside, and frankly told him that her husband was beaten. Since failure would have meant the end of everything for Houdini, whilst to the paper it meant but little, she asked to be given the key to pass on to her husband.

This request was granted. It was rumoured that Bessie placed the key in the glass of water and took it to Houdini on the stage. Shortly afterwards, he walked from the cabinet with the handcuffs free from his wrists.

Personally, I think this story is an exaggeration. I can readily believe that Houdini was capable of such a plan when he found his escape impossible, but whether a newspaper man of standing would have consented to deliver up the key is quite another matter. One must remember it would have been a great triumph from the newspaper's point of view to have brought about the defeat of such a celebrated escapologist as Houdini.

When Houdini came in to see me two days later, I put the question to him point blank, 'Say, Harry,' I said, 'they're telling me you unlocked the handcuffs with the journalist's key. Is that true?'

'Who's been saying that?' he demanded.

'Never mind who. Is it true?'

'Since you know so much, Will, you had better find out the rest,' was all he said.

This refusal of information on Houdini's part should not be construed as an admission of guilt. I expected it, for knowing him as I did, I guessed he would welcome the story as a means of quiet publicity, even if it was untrue. On the other hand, if he did actually fail to escape, one would hardly expect him to admit it.

I am afraid we shall never know what actually happened, but you can take it from me that Houdini had the greatest shock of his life. He afterwards told me that he would sooner face death a dozen times than live through that ordeal again.

On 28 March, Houdini was challenged by Bruce Beaumont, who was described as 'a reed thin, 23 year old'. Houdini had heard that Beaumont's wrists were unusually thin and knew that he would be able to escape easily from handcuffs. Instead, Houdini presented him with a locked pair of handcuffs and asked him to open them. After much fuss, Beaumont threw the cuffs down in a rage. He was eventually booed off the stage.

Houdini's performances at the Hippodrome were extended but by the time they reached their end, he was exhausted after performing night after night. His doctor suggested that he take it easier and ordered him to his bed.

While taking it easy in his hotel room, Houdini sorted through the many programmes and press clippings that he'd collected together during his tours. He had been interviewed by a journalist and had mentioned the collection within his article. Soon after Houdini was approached by a retired magician, Henry Evans, better known as Evanion, who sent a note to his room. He told Houdini that he had a selection of handbills that he thought

A portrait shot of retired magician, Henry Evanion.

he might be interested in. Houdini wrote straight back and invited Evanion to his hotel room the following day at 1pm. Houdini waited for Evanion the next day but heard nothing. Houdini's doctor suggested that he was fit enough to take a brief walk so he got ready and took the lift to the ground floor. As he left the lift, the porter announced that an old man had been waiting for him for three hours in the lobby. Houdini hadn't been told of his arrival because of Evanion's scruffy appearance. Houdini approached the bearded, balding Evanion who stood up and introduced himself.

'I have brought you, sir, only a few of my treasures!' he announced.

Houdini couldn't believe his eyes as Evanion produced rare handbills from performances of Robert-Houdin, Phillipe, Breslaw, Pinetti and Anderson. Such priceless items, in Houdini's eyes, he had never expected to see.

Houdini wrote, 'I remember only raising my hands before my eyes, as if I had been dazzled by a sudden shower of diamonds. I felt as if the King of England stood before me and I must do him homage.'

Evanion told Houdini that he had a huge collection at his home near Kennington Park Road. Houdini was weak with illness but ignored his doctor's advice and the next day, travelled to 12 Methley Street where Evanion and his wife lived in a basement room. Houdini sat amazed as he was told by Evanion about all the magicians that he'd met during his fifty-year career and was shown endless memorabilia relating to the many acts.

An advert for Zam-buk featuring a sketch of Houdini from the *Daily Express*.

An advert for Zam-buk showing Houdini which was featured in the *Yorkshire Evening Post* of Friday, 5 February 1904.

Some of the best items in the collection had been left to him by James Savren who was a collector of items relating to British magicians. Savren had been a barber and during his career had assisted many magicians such as Anderson, Cornillot, Doebler and Herrmann. From what he learnt from other performers, Savren produced his own act.

Evanion was 72 years old when Houdini met him and too old to perform. He made a small living from selling material to the British Museum and to other collectors interested in items related to magic.

Houdini couldn't believe what he was seeing and spent many hours in the company of Evanion. He was still not back at the hotel by 3.30am the next morning. Worried, his doctor and his brother, Theo, went looking for him and found him at Evanion's basement room. They insisted that he returned back to his hotel. Houdini agreed but not before he had purchased a large quantity of items from Evanion.

In the *Sunderland Daily Echo and Shipping Gazette* of Monday 28 March, the newspaper told of an 'accident' to Houdini. Whether the accident was real or just to promote the wonder-cure 'Zam-buck' isn't certain:

The man of the moment is Houdini, the handcuff expert and prison breaker. His mysterious power of escaping from locked cells has baffled the police in all parts of the country. Houdini, however, has his difficulties. While performing at the Palace Theatre, Halifax, the other week, he found the handcuffs to fit so tightly that they cut lumps of flesh out of his wrists. The bleeding was staunched as quickly as possible and Mrs Burns, 5 St James Street, Halifax, his landlady, brought him some Zam-buk as the best thing for healing the wounds. Pain and inflammation were at once ended and all the cuts, scratches and sores so perfectly healed up that Houdini was able to resume his performance at once.

Houdini, in praising Zam-buk now writes:

'Although having had to use some preparation or other for similar accidents for the last 16 years, during my experience as handcuff king, I must candidly say that never has anything given me such remarkable relief. Since the Halifax incident, I have frequently had occasion to use Zam-buk and I heartily recommend it as a wonderful healer, a great receiver of pain and an article I would not care to travel without.'

The article appears to refer to an incident at the Palace Theatre in Blackburn two years previously, although it states, wrongly, *While performing at the Palace Theatre, Halifax, the other week, he found the handcuffs to fit so tightly that they cut lumps of flesh out of his wrists.*

A macabre article appeared in the *Western Times* of Tuesday 29 March. It read:

Houdini, the man who cannot be manacled, and Datas, the man whose memory is almost infallible, must each of them have some faculty abnormally developed. The man who does not forget has already caught the eye of the medical faculty. He has received £2,000 on the understanding that on death his head shall be handed over to a famous London hospital.

A comical tale was told about Houdini and Datas, who was billed as the 'Memory Man'. One night Datas approached Houdini stating that he had digs in the city but couldn't remember where they were. Houdini consoled him and invited him back to his lodgings but found that his landlady was out and he didn't have a key so couldn't get in. The irony was that Datas, the Memory Man, had forgotten where he was staying and Houdini, the king of locks, was unable to break in.

On 15 April, Houdini visited the Vine Street police station in London and once more was locked up in a cell and duly escaped.

On 18 April, Houdini arrived at the Palace, Hull where he performed until 23 April. On the first night, he announced that there was nothing supernatural in what he did and that everything he did was accomplished by natural means.

At his invitation, swarms of people brought their own handcuffs onto the stage and he allowed himself to be manacled by three of them. Two minutes elapsed and he handed them back, open, to their puzzled owners. He also performed the box trick, assisted by his wife, which caused much wonder.

The *Hull Daily Mail* of Wednesday 20 April carried an interview between the newspaper's representative and Houdini. It read:

```
               HULL PALACE.
To-night, Saturday, last night of " SATURDAY
                 TO MONDAY."
Monday, April 18th, and during the week at 7 & 9
               HOUDINI,
    The Handicuff King and Prison Breaker.
ELSIE ROBEY,            FRED COWAN,
Speciality Artiste.           Comedian.
               L I N D.
GLADY MAVINS,          RICH & RICH,
    Coon Artiste.        Eccentric Comedians.
ETHEL RA LESLIE,          SAM MAYO,
    Vocalist.                 Comedian.
LEONARD FLETCHER,     HORACE WHITE,
    Speciality Artiste.      Ventriloquist.
               FRANCO PIPER,
            The Great Banjoist.
POPULAR PRICES.               TEL. 905.
Box office open from 10 to 4.  Saturday, 10 to 2.
```

An advert for Houdini's appearance at the Palace in Hull during April 1904.

Click, click, click! Away went the keys of the typewriter. Houdini was typing as if for dear life. 'Eighty words a minute,' he said.

'Has this anything to do with prison breaking and handcuff defying?' I asked of the only man in the world who makes his living by breaking out of gaols.

Houdini smiled. 'You see I'm a busy man,' he said. 'Don't think all the work I do is done between the hours of seven and eleven in variety theatres.'

'Is typewriting, then, your hobby?' I suggested. 'Or are you writing a book?'

'A book!' he ejaculated, 'two books.'

'You don't say so,' said I.

'You'll have to go a long way to find a man who works harder than I do,' Houdini assured me.

'Then what do you work at off the stage?'

'First of all I am my own agent and manager. You have no idea what a lot of work that means. But I must have been born to work. Look at this.'

Houdini produced a huge book of newspaper cuttings. Long extracts from the American press they were and they all bore Houdini's signature.

'What's all this?' I demanded. 'This looks like industry, certainly.'

'That's a bit of my journalistic work,' he explained. 'I contribute columns regularly to American theatrical papers on European happenings. I call it my "European Letter" and judging from the way it is received, it is in great demand, I should say. That takes up considerable time every week.'

'And about those books? Are you writing your life?'

'No. I am writing two books – one on conjuring and the other on conjurors. The latter is what I consider the work of my life. If God spares me to carry out my idea I mean to make it the greatest and most complete book that has ever been written about conjurors. I am not doing it with a view to making

money. I know from the start it wont pay. But as a rule, a man doesn't expect his hobby to pay and I am doing this for a hobby. To me the lives of conjurors and everything connected with them has an irresistible fascination. Why, there is one conjuror who died many years ago whose grave I have bought so that it may never be disturbed. This book of mine I am going to call 'Biographies of Old Conjurors'.

'And the material for it?'

'The material I am collecting. I hunt up everything I can find about conjurors. I haunt the bookstalls. I make inquiries wherever I go. Once I came across a whole list of records which some other collector had brought together and left to his son. I bought them. They are invaluable to me for my purpose. I have got numbers of pamphlets and programmes connected with conjuring, dating from the year 1700 onwards. One handbill I have has to do with a conjuror named Buchinger, who had neither hands or feet, yet used to do the cup and ball trick and conjuring. There is already a book devoted to the lives of conjurors (Thomas Frost's) but it is not complete by any means and it has many inaccuracies. I mean my book to be as free from error as possible and therefore I spare no pains to make sure of my facts.'

'Why your great interest in conjuring?' I asked Houdini.

'Because I am a conjuror. I rather fancy myself as a conjuror. I began it when I was a lad in Appleton, Wisconsin, where I was born on the 6th April, 1873, of Austrian parents who had emigrated twenty years before.'

'Was your father a conjuror?'

'No,' laughed Houdini. He was a Wisconsin lawyer and a busy one too; too busy, indeed, to take notice of me. That was why I was glad to find surreptitious work in a show at a shilling a day. My mother nearly found me out once. She was passing the 'twopence-halfpenny show' where I was engaged and heard the man in charge cry out, 'Step up and see little Ehrich, the Prince of the Air.' That is one of my first names, Ehrich. She was tempted to go in and see a lad of the same name as myself but she did not enter because she felt afraid of seeing something happen to the boy. She told me that a boy with the same name as myself was performing in a show and I did not explain.

'How long did the show life last?'

'I managed to keep it up for over two years. Then my parents thought it was time I did something to earn my living and they apprenticed me to a locksmith. That was because I had always displayed a talent for dealing with locks. I remember how I used to open my mother's boxes and cupboards and my father's drawers with a button-hook. While I was with the locksmith, I devoted a good deal of time to lock picking. I was very lazy, if I must tell the truth, and I found it was easier very often to pick a lock than to smash it open.'

'Meanwhile, I suppose you still took an interest in shows?'

'I went to all the shows I could, especially where there was conjuring. Whenever I saw a conjuror I knew by instinct, it seemed, how he did his tricks and I used to amuse my friends by doing them. I gradually became drawn into amateur conjuring for charities, that and opening handcuffs. Once, at a church bazaar, I offered five dollars if anyone could fasten me up. A policeman tried and I got free in twenty minutes. It was a very nasty test. I got free from ropes, too. It happened that the manager of a show was at the performance and saw me. He took a great interest in me. He asked me if I wanted to go into the business. I said I did. He made investigations as to what I could do. He locked me up in a prison cell and I broke out. He gave me an engagement and I was with him five years at £1 a week – which I thought good pay.'

'And how did you come to leave him?'

'Martin Beck, the manager of the great Orpheum Circuit (something like a Moss and Thornton tour, a circuit in America is) saw me and was very much impressed. He took me in hand, developed me and made me. I owe all the position I have made to him. Since I joined him I have gone on prospering and have prospered since I left him. I am proud to think that he is coming over from America in a week or two especially to see me and I may tell you that before long I am going to America for a rest. The work has told heavily upon me of late and last week I collapsed under the strain. I have made arrangements to complete this tour shortly and then I take a holiday.'

On Saturday 23 April, Houdini appeared on stage at the Palace, Hull, for his last night.

The *Sheffield Daily Telegraph* of Saturday 23 April reported: 'After a very brief absence, during which his reputation has grown considerably, Houdini makes a return visit to the Empire.'

Houdini played at the Empire Palace, Sheffield from 25 until 30 April. The *Sheffield Daily Telegraph* of Tuesday 26 April reported on his appearance in the city:

Houdini is on his mettle. He was full of challenges at the Empire last night. His remarkable handcuff performances when he was last in Sheffield have stimulated the rivalry of members of the local police force. They feel their reputation is as stake. When a stranger can come in to the city, free himself from their strongest handcuffs and get out of their heaviest-locked cells, they not unnaturally feel that something is wrong; if Houdini's performances are not all tricks. Prominent members of the force are alleged to have claimed that they have done, and can do again, all that Houdini has done. This reached Houdini's ears last evening before his appearance on the Empire stage; and he faced the crowded audience with challenges that should produce the Houdini II, if there is such a one in Sheffield.

With a strongly-marked foreign accent, intensified by a slight nervousness, he introduced himself with a challenge. He would give £1,000 to anyone who could duplicate his handcuff business. Since he had left Sheffield, he had heard that one of the police inspectors had escaped from the locked cell at the police station. Houdini is only a little, slightly-built, highly-strung man but he has a strong belief in himself and his claim to be the handcuff king. So the police inspector, although he might have had a lifelong experience of the cells, could not, in Houdini's opinion, have escaped from the cell by fair means. Boldly he told the audience that if the inspector did escape, it was by means of a duplicate key. Then how did Houdini escape? Upon that point he was silent. But he was ready with another challenge. He will give £100 to the inspector if he can open one of the cell doors, even with instruments.

Houdini had clearly thought out his plan and made his offer as tempting as possible. He will put the £100 in the cell, and lock it up, and if the inspector can get it – it is his. All he asks of the inspector is that he will back his own claim by £5. If the inspector fails to get into the cell, Houdini takes the £5 and will hand it to the police orphanage.

This, however, was only the beginning of the challenges. He had heard that the inspector had cast reflections upon his recent success at the London Hippodrome, when, after a struggle lasting over half an hour, he freed himself from the special handcuffs prepared on behalf of one of the London newspapers. These handcuffs Houdini had with him last night. As soon as he heard of the police inspector's boast, he wired to London for them. They are very heavy instruments with a double-triple lock and Houdini told our representative that they defy the strongest locksmiths in the world. Yet he opened them when locked up in them. If the police inspector could open them, there was another £100 for him. He has a chance of getting rich this week. Houdini does not ask him to put them on his wrists as Houdini had them at the Hippodrome. He will pay the £100 if the inspector can open them in any way he pleases. It is about the most sporting challenge there could be.

'He can bring along his friend the locksmith with him and if they together can open the handcuffs inside five hours, I will pay them £100.'

He added to our representative after the performance that he will also make the inspector a present of the handcuffs.

Later on, he issued another challenge. This time, he was more moderate in his offer of money. There is £25 for anyone who can get out of the German transport chains as Houdini does. All these challenges ought to make things lively at the Empire this week. They seem to be fair offers, for Houdini invites *people to bring their own handcuffs. The only stipulation he makes is that they must not be tampered with.*

As soon as he began his performance, four stalwart men marched to the platform each prepared with a pair of handcuffs. All four pairs were placed on Houdini's arms together. Then he entered what he calls his 'little ghost house', a small tent arrangement remarking that he kept his performances as secret as possible simply for the sake of controversy. 'Some say I do them this way but I assure you I do them that way.'

The four pairs of handcuffs were off his arms, opened, in an incredibly short time. The big trunk show was the greatest mystery. His hands were tied behind his back, he was tied up in a bag and locked in a big trunk. Then the trunk was passed into the tent; Houdini immediately appears out of it and when it is opened, his wife is found locked up inside. At both performances the little man had great receptions.

The *Shields Daily Gazette* of Thursday 28 April carried a story under the headline *HOUDINI'S RIVAL*. It read:

Houdini, the handcuff king, has got a rival. This is James Day, who in the ordinary course of life is a postman at Aston.

At the Gaiety Theatre, Birmingham, yesterday morning, Day gave an exhibition of his powers before a large audience, including agents, managers and artists.

Day escaped from three pairs of police regulation handcuffs in two and a half minutes, retiring to a small tent on the stage, and from an apparently impossible complication of cuffs, leg-irons, unslippable clips and neck irons, fastened by experts at the business, in six minutes.

His record time for one pair of cuffs is five seconds. In a short time, Day is to make a public appearance at the Gaiety.

Two years later, it was reported that James Day had resigned from the post office and was following a career in variety. He amazed audiences with his handcuff escapes and papers contained reports of his 'letter box feat' but didn't state what it involved.

The *Sheffield Daily Telegraph* of Saturday, 30 April carried a story about one of Houdini's challenges under the headline *A PATIENT AUDIENCE*. It read:

The programme at the Sheffield Empire Palace does not usually demand patience on the part of the audience. But last night hundreds of spectators occupied their seats, gazing on a stage, the prominent features on which were a lady standing by a curtained enclosure, which concealed from view the famous 'handcuff king' Houdini who was endeavouring to release himself from two fixed handcuffs which had been brought in response to his challenge.

The audience saw the hands of their watches pass ten and twenty minutes. At three minutes to eleven it was evident that in many cases the mind was sorely troubled between the licensing laws and the famous performer. In numerous instances the palate which suggested visions of an adjoining hostelry evidently had a stronger influence than the thoughts of the 'handcuff king'. The curtain enclosure quivered as if to stimulate the spectators. The conductor of the orchestra wiped his brow, the trombone player got into the 'lower area' for his notes and the instrument seemed sadly to need lubricating. Eleven o'clock passed and an audible sigh went around the house. Having thus relieved their feelings, the impatient members of the audience settled down quietly to await the events. Fifty minutes had elapsed and still Houdini was concealed. The orchestra played a dreamy waltz. The audience began to grow a little restless. The lady by the side of the enclosure held her ear to the curtain. Evidently a few words passed between her and the performer and then, like a flash of lightning, Houdini emerged from his hiding-place, holding high the cuffs that had previously held him fast. He was greeted with cheers. The man who challenged him was cheered an hour before; but, sad to relate, his portion was now groans.

He is accused of having brought a tampered handcuff. Houdini had said before he accepted the challenge that he would give £100 if it could be proved that his statement was not true. The incidents at the commencement and at the close of the performance were certainly entertaining and there is a probability of the interest being continued tonight.

A few words are perhaps necessary to explain how it all came about. When the procession of gentlemen from the audience mounted the platform with cuffs to test the dexterity of Houdini, one of their number was observed to be holding a rod, apparently over a yard in length, on each end of which was fixed a cuff. The house was crowded and there were evidently many present who knew that something unusual was likely to happen. Houdini examined the manacles and then declared before the audience that they were not of the regulation pattern and that they had been tampered with. His challenger approached the footlights and with a dramatic gesture declared himself to be 'Thomas Sharpe, the handcuff king of Sheffield'. He denied that they had been tampered with. But Houdini persisted in his statement and gave the name of a man who had written to him stating that such was the case. He asked if the man who had written to him was present. A pin might have been heard to drop as the query went around the house.

There was great joy; the man was present. He walked on the stage and with the style of an expert he examined the cuffs. He then proceeded to address the audience and claimed to be the 'handcuff king' in Sheffield after Houdini. 'Let 'em all come,' somebody remarked and one wondered if Sheffield would yield any more experts of this description. Eventually Houdini accepted the challenge, under protest. It might have been a strong test for him; it was certainly an ordeal for some of the audience to sit the performance through. But there was great enthusiasm when he succeeded and then he challenged Mr Thomas Sharpe, who had brought the manacles in question, to visit the Empire tonight and be handcuffed by him.

The story of Houdini and Thomas Sharpe continued at the following night's performance and the story was told in the *Sheffield Daily Telegraph* of 2 May:

There was another hour of great excitement during Houdini's turn at the Empire on Saturday night. The house was crowded, mostly with admirers and sympathisers, but there were obviously a few malcontents present. It was generally anticipated that the man Sharpe, whose handcuffs gave Houdini so much trouble on Friday night, would appear to submit in his turn to being handcuffed by Houdini and would attempt the task of releasing himself. But there is a difference between the ability to make locks and the ability to pick them. After Houdini had been on about half an hour, and no Sharpe had come to the front, notwithstanding Houdini's frequent inquiries, Mr Alan W Young, the resident manager of the Empire, came on to the stage and announced that he had received from a man named Brown, of Matlock, a message purporting to come from Sharpe, to the effect that Sharpe would not accept Houdini's condition that he would not be allowed to see the handcuffs before they were put on him. Since receiving that message, however, he had had further information that Sharpe denied its authenticity but also that Sharpe, under any circumstances, was not coming up.

Several other persons appeared in the capacity of challengers, carrying each a pair of handcuffs. Houdini first approached a young man, who handcuffed him with his hands behind his back. It was exactly a quarter-past ten when, his hands handcuffed behind him, Houdini disappeared into his red velvet tent on the stage. Exactly as the third minute of waiting was completed, Houdini bounded out of the tent in triumph and held the handcuffs from which he had completely released himself, up before the house in such a way that all present could see. A storm of cheering broke forth.

Meanwhile, the young man with the handcuffs was trying to open one of the cuffs which was still locked, and, failing to do this, he came forward and said,

'They are out of repair now; they won't open with the key.' Houdini replied:
'Then I will open them without the key,' and he took them back to his tent. The
job took him somewhat longer than getting out of the handcuffs had done but
when he again appeared it was to show both cuffs hanging open. They were
then returned to the discomfited challenger and Houdini then went on with
the rest of his performance, showing the trick of taking off and putting on a
coat with his hands apparently tied behind his back; and afterwards exhibiting
his remarkable box trick.

Houdini wowed Sheffield audiences at the Empire Theatre in Charles Street. The
Sheffield and Rotherham Independent reported that Houdini performed in front
of an 'enthusiastic crowd.'

While performing at the Empire, Houdini first met 9-year-old Randolph
Douglas. Houdini was amazed by the boy's knowledge of locks and stage magic.
The boy was a fan and Houdini kept in touch with him and his family for many
years sending notes, letters and postcards.

When Houdini appeared in Dover ten years later, he made a special trip after
the show to see Douglas and was introduced to a trick that became an iconic part
of his act. The story is told later in the book.

While at Sheffield, Houdini received a challenge from Howill and Son which
said: 'Having witnessed your show, and if you think you can escape from any
trunk, you are mistaken.' Houdini, of course, escaped from the trunk and the
stage was set for him to be offered a whole manner of challenges other than
escaping from handcuffs, locks and manacles.

From Sheffield, Houdini travelled to Leeds to appear at the Empire beginning
on Monday 2 May and ending on Saturday 7 May.

On 4 May, the Sheffield Royal Hospital received a guinea as a result of a bet
that Houdini could not get out of a certain lock within half an hour, whereas
he accomplished the feat in twenty minutes. Their books record the amount
under 'General donations' with the note 'Moss Empire re challenge to H
Houdini 1.00.'

Houdini's next appearance was
at the Hippodrome in Brighton
between 9 and 14 May.

The London and Brighton Railway,
opened in 1841, brought day trippers
from London to the seaside resort.
Many of the major attractions were
built in the Victorian area including
the Grand Hotel (1864), the West

An advert for Houdini's show at the Empire in
Leeds during May 1904.

Pier (1866) and the Palace Pier (1899). The Hippodrome opened in 1901 and had formerly been a skating rink.

While at the Hippodrome in Brighton, Houdini escaped from a box constructed by a local staircase maker. The day after the challenge, the *Mirror* presented Houdini with the solid silver handcuffs that he'd been promised earlier.

Also on the bill were Bert Leslie (refined comedian), Dora Martine (graceful and daring gymnast), The Ilfords (novelty gymnasts), the Carina Sisters (artistic musical melange), The Cabiacs (aerobats), Mdlle Flora Lumiere (the Human Butterfly and Kaleidoscope, Serpentine and Fire dancer), J.W. Bray (comedian), Ergotti and King Luis (troupes of Risley acrobats) and animated pictures of all subjects.

Houdini with the *Mirror* handcuffs.

Houdini played at the Empire and Hippodrome in Bristol for the week commencing Monday 16 May. At the beginning of the twentieth century, Bristol had a population of 330,000. At the end of the nineteenth century, the main industries in the city were tobacco and cigarette manufacture, paper and engineering. There had also been a coal trade which had led to the building of the Somerset Coal Canal.

The Empire and Hippodrome in Old Market Street opened in 1893 and could accommodate 2,530 people. *The Era* described it as 'a handsome building faced with red bricks, with dressings of Bath stone introduced in bands and mouldings, and the frames and sashes of the pointed doors and windows are painted in light and dark tones of peacock blue.' Cary Grant (then Archibald Leach) had his first show business job at the theatre as a lime-lighter.

A poster announcing the presentation of solid silver manacles by the *Daily Mirror* to Houdini. The event took place during the matinee performance on Saturday, 14 May 1904.

A torturous challenge was reported in the *Western Daily Press* of Saturday 21 May:

The Bristol Hippodrome where Houdini appeared during May 1904.

Lovers of the inexplicable and mystifying have had plenty to occupy their minds this week in the accomplishments of Mr H Houdini at the Empire and Hippodrome, Old Market Street, and the announcement that this marvellous prison breaker, who comes smiling out of the most formidable manacles and chains, had been challenged, was the means of drawing a great crowd to last night's second performance. The challenge was from an able seaman named Brown of HMS Renown *who doubted Houdini's ability to free himself when secured by what is known as a 'Tomfool's knot' on the wrists and a 'Bowline Bight' on the elbows, while that gentleman agreed to forfeit £10 if he did not succeed in doing so.*

The feat, being particularly difficult of accomplishment, the contest was awaited with considerable interest and when Houdini and Brown appeared on the stage, there was much cheering. The latter brought with him another sailor and was accompanied by several friends, so that Houdini asked for four gentlemen to form a committee on his behalf. A larger committee than four, however, was quickly made up, including navy men and a press representative, who officiated as timekeeper, whilst in the wings were grouped an interested crowd of individuals, including a police inspector. Brown brought two lengths of thick rope and he and his companion, after Houdini's coat had been removed, commenced tying his wrists with such force that he winced with the pain. The elbows were next pinioned and so severe was the strain that Houdini protested that if there was a doctor in the house he had better be in readiness as he feared his arms would be broken. His collar and tie were taken off and the loose ends of the rope knotted tightly around his throat, after which the second rope was made fast to the neck piece, passed around his chest, and tied again to the elbows.

The operation of tying up occupied exactly 13 minutes and Houdini went into the audience to show that the knots could hardly have been made tighter. His hands, owing to the stoppage of circulation, were cold and numb when he stepped into his cabinet and began his formidable task. The minutes passed quickly, and when a quarter of an hour had elapsed, some doubt was felt as to whether he would succeed. Another ten minutes elapsed and a minute later, or, to be precise, 26 minutes and 10 seconds from the time he entered the cabinet, Houdini emerged and freed himself from the few remaining turns of rope, amidst thunderous applause and prolonged cheering. He appeared quite overcome and after bowing his acknowledgements, went into the wings and nearly collapsed. The ropes were examined by Brown and his companion, who were just enough to admit that the challenge was fairly won. Neither of the ropes were cut or frayed in any way.

In conversation subsequently, Houdini said, 'They hurt me terribly, my hands were quite dead and it was the most exquisite torture conceivable for the first two or three minutes. But I'm glad I did it.' It was also pointed out that the challenge issued by Brown made no mention of the knots around the neck. On examination, Houdini's cabinet proved to be nothing but a wooden framework surrounded by curtains and did not contain either a trap-door or instrument of any kind.

Houdini visited Evanion again and bought more memorabilia from him before setting sail with Bess and Hardeen to New York for a short holiday on 27 May.

Travelling onboard the *Deutschland*, Houdini met with Martin Beck who had been touring England looking for acts for the Orpheum circuit. Beck couldn't understand why, with all of his money, that Houdini was travelling second class. He offered to pay to move him up to first class. Houdini thanked him but refused saying it was just as uncomfortable to be seasick in first class as it was in second class.

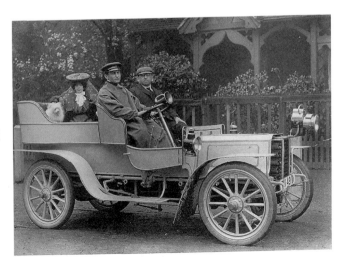

Houdini at the wheel of his brand new 14hp Humber Tourist Car which was manufactured at the Humber factory at Beeston, Nottingham. Shown in the photo are Bess and Harry Houdini together with Martin Beck and the Houdinis' dog, Charlie.

The Empire Theatre, London.

The Empire Theatre in Leicester Square.

Houdini's assistants including James Collins, James Vickery and Louis Goldsmith together with his baggage arriving at the Empire stage door in Leicester Square.

Houdini appeared at the Empire in Leicester Square between 29 August and 3 September 1904.

With the money that Houdini made in Britain, he bought himself a motor car. The story was reported in the *London Daily Mirror* of 4 June. The caption read: *Houdini, the 'Handcuff King', who escaped from the 'Mirror' handcuffs, has bought a Humber motor-car, and taken it to America with him on his holiday.*

Houdini admitted that driving made him nervous.

By August, Houdini was back in Britain and appearing at the Empire Theatre in Leicester Square commencing 29 August until 3 September.

After a successful week, he travelled to Glasgow to appear at the Zoo Hippodrome. The show lasted, unusually, three weeks, starting on Monday 5 September and ending on Saturday 24 September.

Glasgow was famous for its manufacture of chemicals, textiles and engineering and particularly for its shipbuilding industry. The Hippodrome was separate from, but connected to, the zoo. The theatre included variety and circus acts. The zoo was open from 10am to 10pm with animal performances four times daily. The theatre was the idea of Tom Barrasford who joined forces with Edward Henry Bostock (of Bostock and Wombwell Menageries fame). It was a novel idea but seemed to work well.

The *Yorkshire Evening Post* of Tuesday 6 September carried a story under the headline *THE HANDCUFF KING'S SALARY OF £100 A WEEK*, which read:

> *At Glasgow, yesterday, Moss Empires (Ltd) sought to interdict Harry Houdini, the Handcuff King, from appearing last night at the Glasgow Zoo Hippodrome. Defendant's agent said they paid Houdini £100 a week.*
>
> *The Sheriff: I wish I were a Handcuff King. (Laughter.) It seems very remunerative.*

The Moss Empire circuit, who were very powerful at the time, tried to obtain a court order to stop Houdini appearing at the Hippodrome. They claimed that they had an exclusive contract with Houdini that stated that he wouldn't perform in opposition theatres. The court order was refused and for three weeks, Houdini was all that people talked about in Scotland.

The *London Daily News* of Wednesday 21 September carried a story about a dispute at the Glasgow Hippodrome. It read:

> *At Glasgow yesterday, an attendant at the Glasgow Hippodrome was charged with having assaulted one of the audience. The man who said he was assaulted wished to test the genuineness of Houdini, the Handcuff King and placed thumbscrews upon his hands. Houdini freed himself from them and the man then asserted that Houdini had a key secreted upon his person which enabled him to open the screws.*

> *The audience clamoured for an apology and the prosecutor was assaulted but the charge against the attendant was found 'Not proven'.*

The *Glasgow Times* of 23 September, 1904 reported:

> *You might have walked on the heads of the surging, struggling, swaying mass of people almost from George's Cross to the Normal School. A stranger within the city gates might well have wondered what strange happenings were abroad to bring out such a curious congregation. And yet the explanation was simple. Houdini, the Handcuff King and Prison Breaker, was announced to have accepted a most unique challenge which he would try in front of the spectators in the Zoo.*

Thousands turned up at Glasgow Zoo to watch Houdini escape from a specially constructed wooden box. To the pleasure of the audience, he managed to free himself within fifteen minutes.

While appearing at the Hippodrome, Houdini was challenged by Lockie, Graham & Co, who were local saddlers. They had made a straitjacket for a private insane asylum and were convinced that Houdini wouldn't be able to escape from it. The manager had reservations and asked Houdini if he would like to try the challenge in private rather than in public. Houdini accepted the challenge and for 15 minutes was tied up in the contraption. It took him just over 55 minutes to escape.

Houdini also escaped from a packing case constructed by a local company of carpenters, J & G Findlay, who insisted on building the case on stage so that it couldn't be tampered with. News of his planned escape from the case drew huge crowds. The box was lifted on to a platform so that people could see that Houdini had no means of escape from underneath. So many people turned up that thousands couldn't get into the theatre and waited outside until it was announced 15 minutes later that Houdini had freed himself. A huge cheer was let out. The event caused much disruption in the streets and all traffic had to be stopped.

Houdini reappeared minus his shoes which he lost during the escape. The carpenters were baffled and examined the box which was just how they had left it, nailed and tied with ropes. When Houdini left through the stage door, he was lifted onto the shoulders of admirers and carried back to his accommodation at New City Road. They were reluctant to let go of him and carried him upstairs to his room. From his window, he talked to the gathered crowd until they dispersed. Months after Houdini had left Scotland, his escapades were still much talked about.

From Glasgow, Houdini travelled to the Regent Theatre in Salford for a week's shows commencing 26 September. However, he was so popular that his show was extended to two weeks.

The Regent Theatre opened in 1895. *The Era* noted:

Encouraged by their success in this country, and noticing the rapid increase of the population of Salford caused by the completion of the Ship Canal, Mr James M. Hardie and his partners, Miss Von Leer and Mr Frank A. Gordyn, resolved some months ago to build a handsome theatre in a convenient position.

Once again, Houdini escaped from a cell in the town. He presented himself at the Town Hall on Monday 26 September and offered to make his escape from any cell offered. Mr J.W. Hallam, the Chief Constable, decided to put his powers to the test. As in other cities, he was stripped naked, locked in a cell while his clothes were put in another cell. Two minutes after being locked up, he had escaped and re-appeared in the company of the police, in a room nearby, fully clothed.

An advert in the newspaper of Thursday 6 October stated that Houdini had been a great success in Salford and was being retained six nights longer. He played at the theatre until Saturday 8 October.

During an appearance at the Regent Theatre, Houdini had a run in with a fellow escapologist, 'The Great Mysto'. Mysto had boasted that he was much better than Houdini and this annoyed him. Two years previously, Mysto had written to Houdini requesting an audition. Houdini said of Mysto at the time, 'Carl Mysto at this time was working in pubs, doing magic and passing his hat. He was a tramp. I gave him a pair of pants and a few old shirts and half a dollar. He gave a trial show but did not make good. He was a common bum and a dirty one at that!'

The Great Mysto's real name was Jim Pickles and he was originally a plumber. He was born in Bradford and later became a professional escapologist and conjurer. Mysto was also billed as 'The Great Carl Mysto'. In the early 1900s, he was seen as a rival to Houdini. When Mysto heard that Houdini was appearing in Salford, he was eager to see his show and to meet him. However, Houdini was far from happy with other escapology acts which he denounced as fraudsters and charlatans. He knew of Mysto's popularity and following and on Friday 30 September, Houdini decided to reveal all the tricks of Mysto's act. He wheeled onto the stage a coffin which was identical to the one used by Mysto in his act and revealed how Mysto made his escape. He announced that he hoped that the public would 'never again have to see a coffin used as an accessory to public entertainment.'

Hearing of this act of treachery, Mysto later confronted Houdini in his dressing room. A fight broke out and Mysto punched Houdini to the floor. Because of the altercation, Mysto decided to perform his act at a rival theatre during the same week as Houdini.

The *Daily Mirror* of 4 October carried the story and, for a short while, Mysto became quite well known. There was a sudden demand for his act in smaller theatres and Mysto took many bookings. This convinced other acts that there was money to be made exposing the tricks of the trade especially revealing how handcuff escapes were performed. The Great Mysto was still performing in theatres in 1939 by which time, he was claiming to be Chinese.

The *Manchester Courier and Lancashire General Advertiser* of Tuesday 4 October reported:

> *The performances of Harry Houdini, 'the handcuff king', at the Regent Theatre, Cross Lane, Salford, continues to be the item on the programme for another week. There were full houses last evening and Houdini had a very gratifying reception. Again, the delightful easy manner in which he executes the various tasks imposed upon him was remarkable as it was astonishing and amusing, and clearly proved Houdini to be, in his own particular line, an artist of exceptional character. Houdini enlivens the performance with a pleasant vein of humour.*

Houdini's next date was at the Empire Palace of Varieties Theatre in Bristol from 10 to 15 October. Houdini's love of his mother became evident while in Bristol when he told a local reporter, '*I have been all over the world except to Australia, and I'm not going there! It's a bit too far to get back from shouldst anything happen to my mother. She is a dear, my mother is, and I've bought her two homes, one in the town and the other in the country. She'll never want.*'

The *Western Daily Press* of 11 October reported:

Old Market St., Bristol. 1446.

A street scene showing the Empire Theatre in Bristol where Houdini appeared in October 1904.

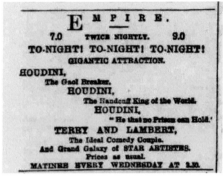

An advert from the *Western Daily Press* of Tuesday, 11 October 1904 announcing Houdini's appearance at the Empire Theatre in Bristol.

A studio portrait of Houdini pointing.

In an excellent all-round programme at the Bristol Empire and Hippodrome this week are a fair sprinkling of American artistes. Heading the bill, of course, comes Houdini, the wonderful jail-breaker and handcuff king. His turn is certainly remarkable and has broken more records in the way of 'draws' than, probably, any other artiste now on the music-hall stage. On Monday night, he was handcuffed by five members from the audience; he was free in a few seconds; he was tied by the wrists and placed in an overcoat; in less time than it takes to write, the coat was being worn by an assistant and Houdini was free; he was tied in a sack, sealed, placed in a well-strapped and locked barrel and covered with a curtain; one, two, three and Houdini was bowing to his audience and someone else was found enclosed in his barrel. It is electrifying. Houdini has a strong company backing him up, a company which contains two or three turns equally capable of 'starring' were Houdini not present.

From Bristol, Houdini travelled to the Hippodrome in Liverpool where he played for two weeks between 17 and 29 October.

Houdini wrote in his *Dramatic Mirror* column on 19 October:

When I landed in England in May 1900, no one knew that a handcuff could be made useful as a stage effect. Now, alas, I see hundreds billed as 'World's Greatest Handcuff Kings,' so I changed my billing to 'Jail Breaker' and they all took that title too. All you have to do in England to become a 'jail breaker' is to buy an English handcuff with two keys and you are made. But there is one thing I will say – no one tries to steal your name or change their name to sound like yours, as is the case in Germany. Here in England, they do not go so far, and make good with their own names, which is something that German artists ought to think over. I believe in the motto: 'Live and let live,' but then I am not an undertaker.

The *Manchester Courier and Lancashire General Advertiser* of Friday 28 October wrote: '*Houdini, who is this week at Liverpool, has accepted a challenge from four seamen of HMS* Eagle *RNR to free himself from recognised ship irons used years ago for mutiny on the high seas.*'

The seamen said that they planned to manacle and truss up Houdini in the old fashioned punishment method and he was to lie on his back, with his hands manacled to his knees and between his arms, holding him in an immovable position while wearing heavy leg-irons locked on his ankles.

On 1 November, Houdini was reported as having been interviewed by the *Halifax Evening Courier*. The reporter stated, '*I noticed on Houdini's arms several scars, as though some tiger had clawed him. He said that he had been in Blackburn and had been put in manacles that would have made an executioner wince. The gentleman who did the trussing business had superabundant strength.*'

Houdini is thought to be referring to his Blackburn performance of 1902 when he was trussed up by William Hope Hodgson and it appears that the scars were still visible two years later.

There is a gap between Houdini finishing his show at Liverpool on 29 October and his next recorded appearance at the Tivoli Theatre in Leeds on 14 November. As the article mentioned appeared in the *Halifax Evening Courier of* Tuesday, 1 November 1904, it's assumed that Houdini was appearing at the Palace Theatre in Halifax between 31 October and 5 November. If it was a two week run, it would fill in the missing dates.

Houdini's name not only became synonymous with escapes. A successful coursing greyhound, called Houdini, owned by a Mr A.J. Humphery, toured the north during 1904 winning many contests. Meanwhile, sporting notes in the *Nottingham Evening Post* mentioned that Sir J.E. Backhouse had called his colt foal Houdini.

The *Nottingham Evening Post* of Saturday 12 November carried a story about Birmingham's own Houdini, whose name was becoming synonymous with any escape. It read:

Houdini's feats have been imitated in very effective fashion by a prisoner in the custody of the Birmingham police.

A deserter from South Wales Borderers, William Elliott, was taken to the lockup in Steelhouse Lane. The doors and windows are all barred night and

day and the only communication with the exterior world is by means of a
small slide little more than a foot square through which inquiries are answered
from the office.

Yet during the momentary confusion incidental to the change of police
duty, Elliott vanished completely. The police have no idea how the escape was
effected.

Houdini next appeared at the Tivoli Theatre in Leeds. He played from Monday 14
November to Saturday 19 November.

A prominent Leeds city councillor heard that Houdini had had hand bills
printed for his show and intended to pass them out in the streets. The councillor
called Houdini to his office. He arrived there with his manager, Harry Day, and
Harry Flounders from the Tivoli. Proceedings were threatened if the handbills
were distributed but Houdini stated that the handbills would be distributed
regardless of what action the councillor took.

When the three men returned to the theatre, they found that the manager,
Edgar Waller, had locked up all the bills and wouldn't hand over the key. Harry
Flounders stated: 'Houdini thereupon changed his business from breaking out
and broke in to secure the bills which were then distributed by Houdini, Mr Harry
Day and myself in the main streets of the city. This took place from four o'clock
until time for the show to start but the bills were distributed and no proceedings
were taken.'

Harry Flounders stated, while telling this story, that Houdini had a special
solid steel bar forged for a challenge although he didn't say what the challenge
involved and the event isn't mentioned in the newspapers of the time. However,
all was revealed, years later, in the *Yorkshire Post* of Sunday, 22 December 1928,
when a reader, who was in the audience, wrote:

It was in either the late Tivoli or early Hippodrome days that Houdini
introduced a new trick. He had an iron bar, about 4ft 6 inches or 5ft long. The
two ends were turned into rings. Pairs of handcuffs were fixed at each end, one
bracelet being locked on the ring at the end of the bar, and the other on one of
his wrists so that when he was fastened up, his hands were the length of the bar
apart as in the drawing. I noticed when I first saw the trick that the bar was not
much thicker than a lead pencil.

However, when fixed as stated, Houdini offered £50 to anyone similarly
fixed who would get free. He then went into his cabinet and in a few minutes
came out with the handcuffs off his wrists and carrying an iron bar in one
hand.

Now, I did not believe it was the same bar. It was easy to have a substitute concealed and it struck me that there was only one way to do this trick. To unlock the handcuffs, you could have a key or keys concealed, but you must get your hands together, so why not bend the bar across the knee until the hands were close enough to get the key?

The illustration featured in the *Yorkshire Post* of Sunday, 22 December 1928 showing Houdini with the bar.

I had an iron bar made but, as I was too modest to go on the stage myself, I arranged (after instructing him how to do the trick) with the late Charlie Parker, who was working the cinema pictures and lighting effects at the City Varieties. At the last minute, Charlie 'duffed' but explained it all to the son of a prominent city councillor.

The most important point, as I had told Parker, was to insist on going into the cabinet to do the trick but Parker forgot to mention this, so my deputy's deputy, in full view of the audience, started and partly bent the bar over his knee. Houdini immediately stopped him and unlocked the cuffs, remarking that any fool could do that. He said the bar was thin for convenience but he would have a thick steel bar forged that could not be bent.

Houdini, next day, had thousands of bills printed, challenging the councillor's son to do the trick on Friday night but before the bills were distributed, the councillor heard of it and tried to have the whole thing stopped.

But the thick forged steel bar that Houdini had made was really a piece of iron tube, about an inch thick, which made it just as easy to do it my way and substitute a straight bar afterwards. However, there was no payment of the £50 that I and my friends were going to divide.

While Houdini entertained at the Tivoli, his rival, Frank Hilbert appeared at the Empire performing very similar stunts including escaping from handcuffs and the box trick. However, his act was different from Houdini's because at the end of the show, he told the audience how it was all done.

The *Leeds Mercury* of Tuesday 15 November noted: '*He seems to have keys for the handcuffs secreted all over his person, and the box trick, when you see it, is simple. A false lid and two bags gives the show away.*'

The *Yorkshire Evening Post* of Tuesday 15 November reviewed Houdini's act at the Tivoli:

Houdini, in addition to his handcuff business, at which he is a past master, showed a packed house at the Tivoli last night a model of a prison cell. Enclosed and locked in a sort of barrel, he was duly placed in the cell, which was triply locked outside. In a minute or so, he was outside the cell and the barrel, when opened, contained an attendant.

Another gap appears between Houdini playing the Tivoli in Leeds and him appearing at the Pavilion in Newcastle between Monday 28 November and Saturday 3 December. At the beginning of the 1900s, Newcastle's main industries were coal mining and shipbuilding. It was one of the first cities to be lit by electric lighting.

The Pavilion Theatre was very new when Houdini appeared there having just opened in December 1903. *The Stage* described it as 'spacious and superbly upholstered.'

While at the Pavilion in Westgate Road, Houdini was challenged by the chief warder of Newcastle prison. The challenge involved Houdini escaping from a straitjacket 'for the murderous insane'. The escape took place during the second house of 2 December.

He next appeared at the Hippodrome in Brighton between 5 and 10 December. There were two performances nightly at 6.50pm and 9pm. Matinees were

To-Night.   To-Night.

CHALLENGE!

Mr. E. F. NEWTON,
Principal Warder of the Wakefield Jail,
for 22 years, and

CHIEF WARDER of the NEWCASTLE PRISON
for 10 years,

HAS CHALLENGED HOUDINI to allow himself to be strapped up in a

STRAIT JACKET

such as is used on the **Murderous Insane.**

HOUDINI

HAS ACCEPTED THE CHALLENGE !
FOR THE

Second House To-Night, Dec. 2nd,

At the **PAVILION**, Westgate Road.

WAR TAX INCLUDED

A handbill announcing a challenge to Houdini by the chief warder of Newcastle prison in December 1904.

performed on Wednesday and Saturday at 2.30pm. The Grand Circle was 6s, stalls were 1s, fauteuils (reserved) 2s, boxes 12/6 or 3s a seat, stage boxes 15s or 4s a seat. Children under 12 years old got in for half price to the stalls and fauteuils.

Houdini's next venue was the Palace Theatre in Manchester where he performed between Monday 12 December and Saturday 17 December. The headline in the *Manchester Chronicle* read, *HOUDINI HOME AGAIN* and applauded him as 'the greatest sensation of modern times.'

An article appeared in the *Dundee Evening Post* of Monday 19 December. However, the dates and venues quoted in the article appear to be wrong. It read:

Mr Harry Houdini has, I hear, just finished a very successful week at Liverpool. The week previously, I am told, he astonished beyond measure the hard-headed men and women of canny Newcastle by extricating himself from a straitjacket. This he did at the Pavilion, to the intense astonishment of the whole town, which stormed the hall on the announcement being made that the great gaol breaker had accepted the challenge of a celebrated warder. The usual committee of townsmen watched the proceedings and in nineteen minutes the trussed Houdini was free and shaking hands with his challenger.

A handbill advertising Houdini's show at the Hippodrome Theatre of Varieties in Brighton during December 1904. (*Image courtesy of Kevin Connolly http://houdinihimself.com/*)

Houdini had many imitators. One, 'Arthur the Handcuff King' appeared for one night only at the Town Hall, Motherwell. An advert in the *Motherwell Times* of Friday 16 December stated that he had astonished the world and pulled in crowded houses everywhere. Probably a slight exaggeration!

In December 1904 Houdini was back in London and watched his friend, Chung Ling Soo, perform at the Empire Theatre. As he watched from a box, the crowd repeatedly shouted, 'Houdini! Houdini!'

Chapter Six

1905 – Hilbert and Evanion

For the first time, the first six months of the year were taken up entirely with tours of Great Britain. Houdini's first date was at Barnard's Theatre, Woolwich between 2 and 7 January. Woolwich was an important military and industrial town. Barnard's Theatre opened in 1899 and was very popular during the music hall years.

On 3 January, while in Woolwich, Houdini received a challenge from Thomas and Edge, who were local builders and contractors. He made sure that the area was covered in 'Houdini Challenged' leaflets and the publicity drew a large crowd. Houdini promised to pay £50 to the funds of the Cottage Hospital if he failed. The show took place at the second house of the Thursday evening performance. Houdini was nailed into a packing case which was then roped. Of course, he soon made his escape.

After Woolwich, Houdini appeared at the Palace Theatre in Glasgow between 16 and 28 January. The news that he planned to escape from a locally made hamper at the Palace Theatre again brought much attention and many more people turned up than could fit into the theatre. There was so much excitement while the act was being performed, that many of the people kept outside broke in to see the result.

The Era reported that this was Houdini's sixth week in Glasgow but must have been referring to weeks in different years and not to a run of six solid weeks. The newspaper reported that on Monday 23 January, thousands rushed the doors and the theatre was crowded. On 27 January, the prices were raised and, once again, the place was packed. The newspaper referred to

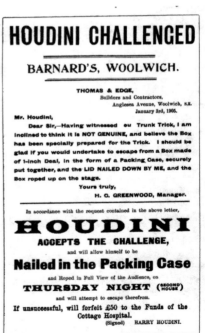

Houdini accepts a challenge to be nailed into a packing case at Barnard's Theatre in Woolwich on Thursday, 5 January 1905.

a three-week run by Houdini at the Zoo Hippodrome in Glasgow which raised receipts of £4,000. This refers to his visit the previous year.

Houdini next appeared at Barnard's Palace of Varieties in Chatham between January 30 and 4 February. Chatham was predominantly known for its naval and army connections and Chatham Dockyard played a vital role providing over 500 ships for the British Navy. Many people at Barnard's Palace of Varieties who had come to see Houdini would have worked in the dockyard or had military connections. He was reported to have been offered a large sum to appear before nobility and officers at Chatham but due to prior engagements, had to turn it down.

New cells had recently been installed in the police station in Chatham when Houdini arrived. To publicise his show, he offered to break out of them. The Kent County Constabulary turned him down because they didn't want it to appear that their new cells weren't completely escape proof. However, Chief Constable Alfred Arnold, head of the Rochester police force, was happy to oblige. Houdini duly escaped and gained the publicity that he wanted.

Houdini's next venue was at St George's Hall in Bradford where he appeared between 13 and 18 February. The show was covered by the local newspaper:

Whilst aware of the fact that imitators have been attempting to give the game away in Bradford, Houdini has never had any qualms about facing the music. According to the little American, there is this distinction between his 'show' and that of those who recently made an 'exposure' at a place of entertainment in the city. Whilst the one reflects the skill of a past-master in the locksmith's business, the other, says Houdini, is nothing more or less than a pure fake. Whatever be the opinion in Bradford on the merits of the rival exponents of the art, there can

An advert promoting Houdini which appeared in *The Era* of Saturday, 11 February 1905.

PLAIN FACTS.

By giving a navvy the part of Hamlet to study, will that make him a

SIR HENRY IRVING?

By allowing an ignorant slavey to sing a song in masculine clothes, will that make her a

VESTA TILLEY?

By giving an undersized, canting hypocrite, with cringing mannerisms, an old dress suit, and a few handcuff keys, will that make him a

HOUDINI?

You may, like a monkey, imitate, like a viper, bite the hand of a benefactor, but you cannot rob a person of his personality.

HOUDINI.

On his Sixth Week in Glasgow at the Palace, Monday, Jan. 23rd, thousands rushed the doors and packed the place, the huge crowd becoming unmanageable. Friday, Jan. 27th, prices were raised, packing the place, never before having held such a large amount of money in one house; and this, after a three weeks' run at the Zoo Hippodrome, during which time

HOUDINI

drew close on to £4,000 in the three weeks.

Week of Jan. 30th, played to the most sensational business of Barnard's Theatre. Receipts so large that Messrs. Barnard can hardly credit amount. This music hall having been established over fifty-five years, has never been known to hold that amount of money, the record having been broken by nearly £100.

A Large Sum was offered to

HOUDINI

for a Special Performance for the Nobility and Officers Stationed at Chatham, but owing to prior Engagement it was impossible to accept.

HOUDINI.

HOUDINI.

HOUDINI.

Under Exclusive Management of **HARRY DAY.**

be no mistaking the tremendous interest taken in Houdini's appearance at St. George's Hall last night.

The attendance was exceptionally large, and judging from the reception accorded the central figure, the only inference to be drawn is that locally, at all events, faith is remarkably strong in Houdini. Bradford has lately developed quite a mania for the handcuff business – the statement has no official significance! – and the crowded state of the galleries and pit, and the excited condition of many of their occupants during the performance, bore ample testimony of this fact.

The usual invitation extended from the platform to the audience for handcuffs, and the presence of a 'Watch' Committee met with a ready response. The first pair of cuffs on which Houdini was asked to try his skill were produced by a man named E. Kendall, of 15, Bronn's Terrace, Back Lane, Bramley. These Houdini used for the purpose of showing how simple it was for a person to extricate himself. This was accomplished by tapping the cuff on a chair.

A more serious test then followed on the initiative of Mr. Jack Spink, of 5, Wellclose Place, Leeds, who describes himself as the 'Handcuff King of the World, under 20 years of age'. Houdini was pinned in a very awkward fashion with his hands behind him. By a dislocation feat he brought his hands in a more workable position, and before one could scarcely realise the fact, he was in and out of the curtained cabinet, free. The excitement was growing, and amid some uproar Spink demanded to be handcuffed. This was done, and on emerging from the cabinet he appeared to have slipped the cuffs, for they were still fastened. A good deal of 'barging' ensued on the stage, which was closely followed by the audience, one of whom reminded Houdini of his £100 challenge, to which he replied that this was still good, providing, of course, he fastened the cuffs on the individual himself.

Eventually another pair of cuffs were produced, and although at first Spink took exception to them on the ground that they were not Bradford police cuffs, he allowed himself to be fastened by a man named Kendall. The sounds proceeding from the cabinet showed the struggle Spink was making to get free, but ultimately he had to come out and admit he was beaten.

A scene of wild excitement followed. Placing Spink's hands through a curtain Houdini speedily released one hand, but the second was too much for him, the master hand explaining it was evident Spink, in trying to release himself, had jammed the levers, and it would be impossible to open the lock. The only alternative was to cut it off. With the cuff hanging to his wrist, the youth proceeded to leave the stage, exclaiming that he would have it filed off in Leeds. But the owner of the cuffs objected to this course, and along the corridor and right away to the railway station the disturbance was continued. Both the *city police and the railway officials declined to interfere, and eventually Spink was allowed to proceed to Leeds on leaving his entire kit of fetters and lock pickers as a deposit with Kendall.*

Spink did not hide the fact that he had come with the express intention of obtaining the £100, but he only succeeded in creating a lot of excitement.

After the excitement had abated and no other handcuffs being forthcoming, Houdini went through a series of very smart illusions, one special feat being the prison cell and barrel mystery. The programme was contributed to by a number of talented variety artistes. The entertainment will be continued during the week.

The Era of Saturday 18 February reported:

Close upon three thousand people are crowding the vast St George's Hall, in Bradford, nightly to witness the handcuff feats by Harry Houdini and the excitement as the tests proceed is intense. All sorts of manacles are brought into use but every effort to secure Houdini fails.

An entry in Houdini's diary for 18 February read: '$2,150 clear salary.' This worked out to about £450, a fortune at the time. This had been his highest salary so far. Houdini's usual salary for a week's entertainment was £150.

After Bradford, he appeared at the Theatre Royal in Stockton between 20 and 25 February before performing at the Alexandra Theatre in Sheffield between 3 April and 8 April. Little is known about these two appearances.

He next appeared at the King's Theatre in Cardiff between 10 and 15 April.

When Frank Hilbert appeared at the Cardiff Empire in a show called 'The Bubble Burst', part of his act revealed how picks and tools could be concealed by a 'Handcuff King',

A poster advertising Frank Hilbert's performance at the Cardiff Empire in 1905.

referring to Houdini, and used to undo locks. Hilbert was a failed escapologist so decided instead to earn his trade exposing the tricks of Houdini. Theatres that couldn't afford Houdini booked Hilbert instead.

While performing his act, a grey haired man with a beard and wearing glasses waved his cane at Hilbert. 'You're a fraud, you're a damn fraud!' shouted the man much to the amazement of the audience. Two women close by him, stood up and one held a pair of handcuffs up in the air.

'This man does not use police regulation handcuffs. He has cuffs of his own but I have some regulation handcuffs here and I challenge him to open them!' she shouted.

The old man was causing a fuss and the theatre manager appeared with two constables. He was waving his cane around in the air and another constable had to subdue him. As they were preparing to eject him from the theatre, his beard fell off. All was revealed. The 'old man' was, in fact, Houdini! Very soon, he was joined by the two women who turned out to be Houdini's wife, Bess, and his sister, Gladys.

Houdini turned to the audience and appealed to them. 'Ladies and Gentlemen, see how they are treating me! It's not right!' he shouted.

Some members of the audience shouted, 'Shame, shame!' A cry of 'Give him fair play!' was heard.

Mr Oswald Stoll, the owner of the theatre, had warned the manager to look out for Houdini because he had suspected that he would try to disrupt Hilbert's act. Houdini had managed to fool the staff at the theatre by being professionally disguised by a local hairdresser. He even wore a fake wax nose.

The manager, a Mr Lea, wasn't happy and when one of the constables asked him what he should do with Houdini, he replied angrily, 'Throw him out!' Lea then grabbed Houdini by the throat, tearing his collar and threw Houdini towards one of the constables. Houdini fell on the floor and one of the constables kneed him in the ribs while covering his mouth with his hand so that he couldn't be heard.

Hardeen was in the audience and ran forward to assist Houdini. His aim was to throttle Lea but he was stopped by a constable.

Houdini in disguise ready to disrupt Frank Hilbert's show.

Houdini was ejected by a side door and thrown four feet into a muddy alleyway. He was in pain and claimed that his leg was broken. Two constables stood him up but as he began to walk away, Lea kicked him in the leg, smiling.

'Don't do that again!' Houdini shouted at the manager. Lea, still smiling, claimed it was an accident.

Houdini and Hardeen later appeared on the stage of the King's Theatre. Still looking dishevelled, Houdini recounted the tale. 'Shame!' shouted members of the audience. As he limped off, he received great applause.

An edited version of the event appeared in a local Cardiff newspaper:

Theodore Hardeen, Houdini's brother, in 1905.

This week Houdini had a rival performing at the Empire, Frank Hilbert, whose act was entitled 'The Bubble Burst: How Handcuff Tricks Are Done.' This led to a good deal of excitement.

On Monday at 6.30pm Houdini called at a hairdresser's shop (J.A. Burridge) in Duke St. where he had his hair tinted grey and changed the shape of his nose with wax. He then made his way to the Empire in the guise of an elderly gentleman wearing spectacles and a moustache and carrying a walking-stick. A companion bought the tickets and they had no difficulty in entering the theatre. Houdini's wife and her blind sister-in-law were also in the audience. During Hilbert's act, Houdini, having a pair of handcuffs with him, challenged the performer to escape from them. However, anticipating such an event the management had 4 male attendants and 3 constables on duty there, and they, attended by the manager, proceeded to eject the challenger, laying him on his back in the wet outside the theatre. The two ladies also challenged Hilbert and were turned out. Later, Hardeen arrived on the scene and threatened to challenge Hilbert every night of the week. He then accompanied his brother, Houdini, in a carriage to the King's Theatre in time for him to give his own performance and to tell his audience of his treatment at the Empire.'

The *Cardiff Western Mail* for Tuesday 11 April also featured the story:

At the Empire, Hilbert's act was normally introduced by his manager, Mr Frederick Leighton. On Tuesday, he accused Houdini of organising attempts to upset the show at various London music halls but assured the audience that Mr Lea, the Theatre manager would not brook any such attempt. During that performance 4 youths were ejected. The same night at the King's Theatre, Houdini claimed to have been offered £125 a week by Mr Stoll but that Mr Beresford had offered him more.

Earlier that day a summons for assault was granted against Mr Lea at Cardiff Police Court. The Chief Constable had now twice refused to challenge Houdini to escape from one of his cells.

The story continued in the *Cardiff Western Mail* for Wednesday 12 April:

In response to Houdini's reference to Oswald Stoll's offer, the latter sent this telegram to Mr Lea:-

'Houdini's services have been offered to me, but I declined to accept them owing to a dislike to his methods. Take no notice of him whatever, except to eject him should he attempt to create disorder in the Empire – Stoll'.

On Wednesday, the two rivals escaped from nailed boxes made by Couzens and Sons, joiners of Bute Road. Between the two houses at the Empire that evening, Mr F. Leighton, Hilbert's manager, was arrested and taken to London by police on account of a debt he had incurred. He was away for 48 hours.

The *Cardiff Western Mail* for Thursday 13 April reported:

Questioned on his reaction to Stoll's telegram, Houdini said he could prove Stoll's original offer, but if that gentleman wanted to take him up, whichever of them might be proved wrong would have to pay £50 to Nazareth House and £50 to Cardiff Infirmary.

On Thursday night Houdini performed a challenge escape from a straitjacket. The *Cardiff Western Mail* of Friday 14 April stated:

On Friday morning, Houdini's case against Mr William Lea, the South Wales manager of Stoll's Empires (that he had taken Houdini by the throat and kicked him, on Monday night) was heard by the magistrates Ald. David Jones and Ald. Edward Thomas. The case was dismissed.

Houdini's next engagement was at the Lyceum Theatre in Newport between 17 and 22 April. Newport had been a port since medieval times and dealt with the coal export from the eastern valleys of South Wales. The Alexandra South Dock opened in 1892 and became a major employer. The Lyceum opened its doors in 1897 and could seat 1,250 people.

When Houdini appeared at Newport, he discovered that his rival, Frank Hilbert, was appearing at another theatre nearby. They both asked Chief Constable Sinclair if they could make a jailbreak from their cells. Sinclair agreed but would only allow both stunts to be performed at the same time on the same day. Houdini, his brother Theo and the manager of the Lyceum turned up at the agreed time of 4pm. A huge crowd turned up to watch the rivals compete with each other. However, Hilbert was nowhere to be seen. The Chief Constable waited for Hilbert to arrive but when he didn't turn up, Houdini was allowed to proceed. He undressed in one cell and left his clothes there. He was then locked in the adjacent cell as officials left the area to allow him to perform his escape. In just five minutes and thirty seconds, Houdini joined the officials, fully dressed. He told the Chief Constable that he had also unlocked the iron gate to the corridor where the cells were housed.

The crowd had grown outside and when Houdini left the police station, they all cheered. He raised his hat in gratitude and then walked quickly towards the theatre with many people following him to the stage door. Many bought tickets and the house was once again packed.

The *Cardiff Western Mail* of Tuesday 18 April reported:

On Tuesday, Hilbert's manager Leighton, appeared at Marylebone Police Court charged with fraudulently obtaining credit of £19 and 18 shillings. In asking for bail, his solicitor claimed the charge had been 'arranged' by Houdini's manager to embarrass Houdini's rival, Frank Hilbert.

Houdini next appeared at the Eastbourne Hippodrome between 24 April and 29 April where he escaped from the police cells in the morning and accepted a packing case challenge on 26 April. With the coming of the railway, Eastbourne became a seaside resort originally constructed by prominent landowner, William Cavendish, as a resort built 'for gentlemen by gentlemen'. It proved hugely popular.

Will Goldston recalled a conversation about the packing case escape in his book *Sensational Tales of Mystery Men*:

On one occasion when Houdini was performing in London, he decided to try out a new packing case escape. The trick was very successful and he was well pleased with the reception he obtained. Halfway through the week he invited me to dine with him, and suggested I should accompany him to the theatre after the meal.

As we were putting on our hats and coats prior to setting off to the show, Houdini turned to me with a startled expression on his face.

'Will!' he cried.

'Yes, Harry?' I replied, not knowing what to expect.

'Do you know how I escape from that packing case?'

'I haven't given it a thought, Harry.'

'You're lying,' Houdini shouted. 'Tell me the truth.'

'I assure you, Harry...'

'Don't lie, Will.' Houdini's manner had become quieter now. 'To be honest, I want to know if magicians are getting wise to my secrets. If you don't know them, I'm not afraid of the others. Please tell me.'

I took a pencil and note-book from my pocket, and sketched an instrument which I thought could be used for the packing case escape. Without speaking, I handed over my diagram to Houdini.

He went deathly pale. My long shot had gone home. 'I'll take this,' he said at last, tearing the sheet from my notebook. 'This has finished me with packing cases. After this performance, I'll have no more.'

From Eastbourne, Houdini travelled to Oldham to appear at the Empire Theatre between 1 and 6 May. During the industrial revolution, Oldham had become one of the most important centres of cotton and textile industries in England.

The *Oldham Chronicle* of 29 April announced :

The principal attraction at the Empire Theatre next week will be the visit of Harry Houdini, the world-famous prison-breaker and handcuff expert. He has escaped out of prisons and cells in this country, the United States, Holland, and Russia, and should prove a big 'draw'. He is supported by a clever variety company, which includes:- Nina Elmo, comedienne; Arthur Aldridge, vocalist; Steel and Laing, vocalists and dancers; Vandinoff, painter in oils; Caban with his performing donkeys, ponies, and dogs; the Sisters Albert, duettists

The Empire Theatre in Oldham where Houdini appeared between 1 May and 6 May 1905.

and dancers; Clive Watts, comedian and dancer; Hanvarr and Anna Lee, in the sketch 'The Golfer and the Maid'; and Miss Ethel Arden and Mr George Abel's company in the sketch 'The Little Stowaway.'

A report of the show appeared in the *Oldham Standard* on Tuesday 2 May. It read:

Last night intense excitement attended the performance at the Empire Theatre of Harry Houdini, extensively known throughout Europe and America as the handcuff king and jail breaker. It was indeed hard to believe that so large a number of persons in Oldham had so much interest in handcuffs as appeared to be the case. Doubtless the instruments of ill repute were, for the most part platonic, but the theatre was crowded. A variety entertainment occupied the earlier part of the evening, and it was not until shortly after nine o'clock that a drop scene was removed and a large cabinet and an assortment of trunks and other articles were revealed. On his appearance, Houdini was unanimously greeted.

A commencement was made by the announcement that he was the originator of the handcuff performance, all other rival shows being imitations. Houdini concluded his remarks by offering to forfeit a sum of £100 to anyone who should free himself from the cuffs used in his feats. He then invited members of the audience to come upon the stage, and to act as a supervision committee. Five persons immediately responded to the invitation, and took their places on either side of the platform. Several handcuffs of various regulation patterns were produced, and Houdini proceeded to demonstrate to the audience how very easy it was to escape. He had only to strike the cuff sharply near the hinge, and the lock would fly open. The action was suited to the word successfully, and some of the house applauded, as if they recognised a useful 'tip'. This, however, was a mere preliminary business, and Houdini proceeded to turn up his sleeves. He proceeded to perform a series of clever and mystifying tricks with great success.

In the variety entertainment which preceded there is plenty to satisfy all tastes. The sketch presented by Miss Ethel Arden and Mr George Abel's company entitled, the 'Little Stowaway' is very dramatic indeed. It is the revival of a piece that in other days won renown, and it lacks nothing either in excellence of acting or scenery. Distinctly clever is Nellie Bowman, and her assumption of the title part is a wonderful and convincing piece of work. She is a pathetic little figure and she sings with commendable taste and expression. The part of the commander is taken by Mr Wm. Clayton in a masterly fashion, and Willie

Amusements.

EMPIRE   THEATRE,   OLDHAM.

MONDAY, May 1st. A Gigantic Attraction,
THE   FAMOUS   HOUDINI,
The Marvel of the Whole Wide World.
Supported by a Vaudeville Company, the equal of which has never before been presented on a stage, and further will never in all probability be excelled.
Grand Day Performance, Monday, May 1st, at 2 o'clock.
Next week : " The World."

Houdini appeared at the Empire Theatre in Oldham during May 1905.

Scott as the comic boatswain is the leader in most of the fun which blends so well with the serious side of the story. Then there is Caban, whose performing ponies, donkeys and dogs have been trained to perfection.

Midget Rose who also takes part in the show is supposed to be the smallest pony in the world, measuring only 23ins. in height, and weighing 58lbs. The revolving table scene is really astonishing, and Caban offers £30 to any person remaining on the table for 30 seconds like the pony. The comedy act 'The Golfer and the Maid', presented by Hanvarr and Lee, is decidedly very clever and meets with the success it deserves. Amongst the other artistes are Nina Elmo, a comedienne with much ability; Arthur Aldridge, a splendid tenor from the Pavilion, London; Steel and Laing, in their comedy acrobatic singing and dancing speciality; Vandinoff, the wonderful painter in oils; Sisters Albert, duettists and dancers; Clive Watts, a clever dancer and Motora, the comic musical motorist.

Houdini next appeared at the Grand Theatre in Wolverhampton between 8 and 13 May. The theatre opened in December 1894 and was richly decorated. During the first night, he was enclosed in a packing case which was then nailed shut by members of the audience. Houdini escaped in ten minutes with his jacket missing and his shirt collar out of place. The local paper announced that Houdini would return the next night and escape from 'a strait waistcoat such as is used for the murderous insane'.

Some reports also state that Houdini appeared at the Empire Palace of Varieties in Wolverhampton on the same dates.

Houdini's next venue was at the Pavilion Theatre in Leicester between 15 and 20 May.

The Era of Saturday 20 May reported:

Harry Houdini, on making his appearance, had a most flattering welcome and after bewildering the audience with the ease with which he escaped from all kinds of handcuffs, introduced for the first time here his latest and greatest prison cell and barrel mystery. It is needless to say that his show, which is undoubtedly the smartest of its kind, is very popular.

He next appeared at the Avenue Theatre in Sunderland between 22 and 27 May. Sunderland had grown as a port, trading coal and salt. Coal mining employed thousands at the four main pits including Wearmouth Colliery which was opened in 1835. Many of Houdini's audience would have had connections with coal miners or the coal industry.

The *Sunderland Echo* of the 23 May reported:

Before bewildering a large audience in the Avenue Theatre last night, Houdini, the gaol breaker and handcuff king paid a visit to the central police station, West Wear Street. Supt Deighton obliged him by locking him in one of the cells, but in three minutes he had liberated himself and was outside greeting the genial superintendent. At the theatre, he told the audience of his latest escape and then completely puzzled them with his exhibition. Among the gentlemen who formed the stage committee was a well known policeman who helped to manacle the artist and always found that his efforts were in vain. From various kinds of handcuffs brought on to the stage by the committee men, Houdini freed himself in a moment. He also put a coat unknown to him on and off while his hands were tied, broke out of a cell with a regulation lock although he was supposed to be also fastened in a barrel, and after being placed in a sealed sack and then in a trunk which was subsequently closed and bound, changed position with a young lady who was outside or appeared to do so, the last two feats being apparently the well known cabinet and trunk trick. They were very smartly executed, indeed the whole of the business was dextrously done by Houdini whose drolleries added not a little to the success of his entertainment. At the conclusion, he announced that a firm had challenged him to liberate himself after being fastened in one of their packing cases and he promised to do this on Wednesday night if the challengers allowed him to use their name.

Two days later, before a crowded house at the Avenue Theatre, Houdini climbed into a large wooden box which had the top nailed on and was then tied up with ropes. This box was then put inside another cabinet. The task had obviously proved more difficult than Houdini had anticipated and it took 28 minutes before he managed to escape, covered in perspiration with his clothes disarranged and his hair messed up. The audience were mystified by his escape.

Houdini next appeared at the Argyle Theatre of Varieties in Birkenhead between 29 May and 3 June. Shipbuilding was prominent in Birkenhead and many naval vessels were built there. The Argyle Theatre of Varieties opened in December 1868 and had seating for 800 people.

A leaflet for the show announced:

TWO PERFORMANCES NIGHTLY
At 6.50 and 9 o'clock.
Monday, May 29th, 1905
AND EVERY EVENING DURING THE WEEK.
THE JAIL BREAKER AND DEXTEROUS HANDCUFF KING,
HOUDINI
WINNER OF THE GREAT HANDCUFF CONTEST!
(Challenged by the 'London Illustrated Mirror,' March 17th, 1904.)
ALL OTHER SHOWS & EXHIBITIONS OF THIS CLASS ARE COPIES OF
HOUDINI
Houdini will introduce his latest and greatest
PRISON CELL AND BARREL MYSTERY.

Also appearing on the bill were Wee Mona, the infant prodigy comedienne and dancer; the Boston Twins, speciality pantomimists, comedians and knockabouts; Rickaby, popular favourite comedian; Ernie Myers, comedian, patterer and dancer; Lily Lonsdale, soprano vocalist; Chas Austin, character comedian and clever mimic and the Brewsters, lady vocalists, aerobatic and speciality dancers.

Houdini's next venue was at Wigan between 5 June and 10 June.

It was while appearing at Wigan that he received a letter from Mrs Evanion saying that her husband was dying of cancer. Houdini returned quickly to London to see him. By the time he got there, Evanion could hardly speak but told Houdini that he was worried about his wife's welfare. Houdini assured him that he would look after her. Reassured, Evanion produced a collection of playbills which he said that he had saved and gave them to Houdini. They included rare handbills featuring Robert-Houdin's performances in London. Houdini later referred to them as 'the central jewel in my collection'.

Evanion died at Lambeth Infirmary on 17 June 1905. Houdini paid all the funeral costs and posted death notices in the newspapers. He was dismayed how few people turned up at the funeral. Shortly afterwards, Mrs Evanion died and, again, Houdini saw to the funeral costs.

From Wigan, he travelled to Blackpool to appear at the Hippodrome between 12 and 17 June. With the rise of the railway, Blackpool had become a popular destination for tourists eager to enjoy the seaside resort.

An advert for the show read:

> *Monster Whitsuntide Attractions.*
> *Glorious Array of Talent.*
> *Commencing Monday June 12th 1905.*
> *The Greatest of all Handcuff Kings.*
> *The Renowned*
> HOUDINI.

Winner of the Great Handcuff Contest, as challenged by the 'London Illustrated Daily Mirror', March 17th, 1904. THE ORIGINAL. NOT A COPY. THE ORIGINAL. Houdini, the Jail Breaker and Handcuff King of the World. Also introducing his latest Greatest Prison Cell and Barrel Mystery. Locked up in Blackpool Police Cell and Escapes in Seven Minutes.

An article in the *Blackpool Gazette and News* from the 13 June read:

The Hippodrome will re-open its doors on Monday next for the season with a very diversified programme which should prove a great attraction. The many friends of Mr. T. P. Duigan, who previously managed the resort, will be glad to hear that he has returned to undertake the reins of management. The interior of the building has been re-decorated and the stage re-constructed, and patrons will find every accommodation in the way of seating arrangements.

Some of the finest turns of the halls have been engaged to appear during the season, and from what we know of next week's programme there is a treat in store for all holiday-makers. The world famous Houdini, of handcuff and prison-breaking fame, is the star turn of the programme.

The prices of admission are of the usual popular and modest figure.

Houdini's show in Blackpool was hugely successful and thousands turned out to see him. The Whitsuntide holiday saw people flocking to the coast for entertainment and Houdini proved a huge draw.

An article in the *Blackpool Gazette and News* from the 16 June read:

Houdini, the entertaining gaol-breaker and handcuff king – appearing this week at the Hippodrome – sets the locksmiths a pretty problem: Can they invent a lock which shall prove an efficient barrier against him? Where he chooses to try, all prisons seem to be imperfect as regards safe custody, for, as if by some mystic spell, the catches of the locks, though they do not fly asunder, slide back mysteriously, and allow him to issue forth – a free man. It is impossible to think that the hard steel mechanism obeys his will, but how does he do it?

That is the secret which many, who are not voluntarily, but forcibly incarcerated, would like to know.

Houdini makes his first appearance in Blackpool this week; and, as in Russia, America, France, and other countries, he has here given proof of his skill. On Monday he was granted permission to try if he could escape from the South King street police cells. He was stripped, and the precaution was taken by the interested officers to search his bushy hair, chance there might be concealed some wire or other instrument helpful in picking a lock. Houdini's clothes were placed in one cell and he was locked in another, the master key of the Chief Constable apparently making him doubly secure. The lock was found more difficult than many which the man of mystery has dealt with, but,

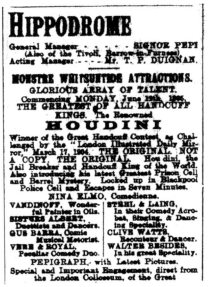

Houdini took part in the '*Monstre Whitsuntide Attractions*' at the Hippodrome in Blackpool in June 1905.

to the surprise of all, he quickly walked out of his prison, got his clothes and, with the eyes of magistrates and officials upon him, he secretly unlocked the iron bar door in the corridor and walked into the police office. And all this was accomplished in seven minutes! Afterwards the following testimony was handed to Houdini:-

Chief Constable's Office
Blackpool, 12th June, 1905.
We, the undersigned, certify that we saw Mr. Harry Houdini stripped naked, searched, locked up in a cell (which was searched) but in seven minutes Houdini had managed to escape from the cell; also opening the iron gate at the end of the cell corridor. There was no chance of any confederacy.
    (Signed) Jno. C. Derham, Chief Constable; Gilbert Blundell, J.P., James Hayes, J.P., John P. Dixon, J.P.
    Houdini had previously given an exhibition on how useless handcuffs are upon his wrists.

Houdini performed a similar act in every town and city that he appeared. However, every audience was new and most, if not all, had never seen his tricks or illusions before making the whole experience something wonderful.

The *Blackpool Gazette and News* from the 16 June reported:

A very strong programme, scintillating with the names of many music-hall stars, characterised the opening week of the Hippodrome. The large theatre was full on Monday evening, and the audience showed its appreciation of the good things prepared for their delectation. First and foremost on the bill is the name of Houdini, the gaol-breaker and handcuff king of the world. He met with a reception worthy of his various feats; and during his 'turn' kept the audience in a state of great excitement.

Sixteen marvellous performing ponies, donkeys, and dogs are presented by the Great Caban; and in the matter of cleverness, it is doubtful whether they can be excelled. Whilst the stage is occupied by Gus Barra, the comical musical motorist, laughter is constantly rippling from the audience. Pretty duettists and dancers are the Sisters Albert; and Steel and Laing provide plenty of fun in their comedy acrobatic singing and dancing speciality. Nina Elmo, a comedienne, has some pretty songs, which she sings to good effect; and Vandinoff, a painter in oils, produces some really fine effects with his brush. The comedy element is contributed to by Vere and Royal, who are described as the 'peculiar' comedy duo; and Clive Watts, beside being a refined raconteur, is a very smart dancer. A very enjoyable evening's entertainment is brought to a close by the Pepigraph, which shows the latest pictures in animation.

An interesting and comical article appeared in the *Hull Daily Mail* of Monday 19 June about a Houdini impersonator. It read:

A man at Blackpool represented himself as Houdini, the handcuff king, getting £165 a week. On the strength of this, he tried to borrow half-crowns. He was put in the lock-up. 'If you are Houdini you can easily get out,' said the police but he stopped in.

The full story was carried in the *Lancashire Evening Post*:

George William Green, a young man, was charged at Blackpool, this morning, with trying to obtain money by false pretences.

Joseph Walter Rome, stopping at the Adelphi Hotel, said that on Friday prisoner went to him in the hotel asking to shake hands. He asked for four shillings and said he would pay back 50s at night. He said that he was Houdini, the 'handcuff king' from the Hippodrome and produced a card bearing that name. Witness did not lend him the money. After seeing Houdini at the Hippodrome, witness obtained a warrant and had the prisoner arrested.

William Corder said that about ten o'clock yesterday morning, prisoner came up to his printing stall in the Winter Gardens and told him he was the 'Handcuff King' and got £165 a week. He ordered some cards bearing Houdini's name and taking away about a dozen with him, said he would see his manager as to whether anything more should be printed on them.

Some time afterwards, witness saw the prisoner distributing the cards in the billiard room, giving one to the secretary.

Harry Houdini said that one of the cards was handed to him on Friday at the Hippodrome. It was not a card he had ordered to be printed. He had had nothing to do with the matter and had never seen the prisoner before in his life. On Thursday, a Fleetwood man came to him and accused him of having borrowed money from him.

The prisoner, who was arrested by Detective Ashcroft, said that he did not recollect anything of it because he had been 'full of drink for days and days.'

The Chief Constable said that Green was a hairdresser and had been in Blackpool three weeks.

Green was committed for 28 days' hard labour.

Houdini next played at the Hippodrome at Hastings between 19 and 24 June. Hastings was another popular seaside resort. The following article appeared in the *Hastings and St Leonard's Advertiser* of 22 June:

The above position would be painful and uncomfortable to anyone but Harry Houdini, the great 'Handcuff King' who is this week delighting and mystifying large audiences at the Hippodrome.

To extricate himself from those manacles is to him mere child's play, for, in company with love, Houdini has always laughed at locksmiths.

Born April 6th, 1873, in Appleton, Wisconsin, U.S.A., and though only 31 years of age, he has been in the show business 21 years, so that it will be seen that his career as a performer began early. In his ninth year he started as a contortionist and trapezist in Jack Hoffler's 'five cent' circus in Appleton.

Houdini padlocked and chained.

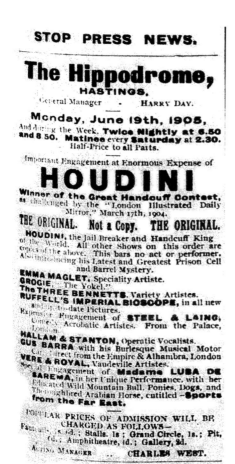

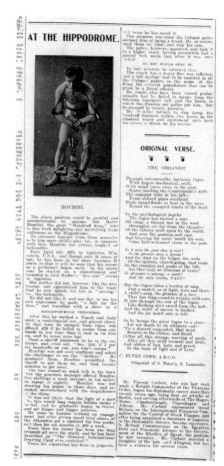

Houdini's appearance at the Hippodrome in Hastings was announced in the *Weekly Hastings Mail and Times* of 17 June 1905.

A cutting about Houdini's act featured in the *Hastings and St Leonard's Advertiser* of 22 June 1905.

His mother did not, however, like the profession, and apprenticed him to the trade that he now spends his life in 'jeering', i.e. the locksmith.

He did not like it, and one day, to use his own expression, he made a 'bolt for the door' and travelled with a show as a slight-of-hand performer. After this he worked a Punch and Judy show, a ventriloquial act, and played clown. At that time he escaped from ropes and offered £10 if he failed to escape from any bonds in less time than it took to tie him up, and he never once lost.

Once a sheriff happened to be in the audience, and cried out, 'Say, kid, if I put my handcuffs on you, you won't escape.'

Houdini was not over confident and asked the challenger to see the 'darbies'. He produced them. Houdini permitted the sheriff to put them on, and took twenty minutes to get away.

The feat caused so much talk in the town that the generous manager offered Houdini five shillings a week increase in his salary to repeat it nightly. Houdini was not drawing big money in those days, and accepted, overwhelmed with the magnificence of the thing.

It was not likely that the light of a man like this would long remain hidden under a bushel, and he gradually began to travel, and get bigger and bigger salaries.

He came to London without an engagement, but after giving small trial shows at the Alhambra got a contract for two weeks, and then for six months at £60 a week.

Since then his career has been one long triumph all over the world, and he has been described as 'The Greatest International Drawing Card ever exploited'.

Twice his reputation has been in jeopardy and twice he has saved it. One occasion was when the Cologne police accused him of being a fraud. He, of course, sued them for libel, and won the case.

The police, however, appealed, and took it to a higher court, having meanwhile had a special lock made that after it was once locked no key would open it. In four minutes he returned free.

The result was a heavy fine was inflicted, and a full apology had to be inserted in all of the Cologne papers in the name of the King, the severest punishment that can be given to a Royal official.

He would also have been ruined professionally had he failed to escape from the Siberian transport cell and the bonds in which the Russian spy police put him. But he escaped in twenty minutes.

Mr. Houdini intends to stop doing the handcuff business within two years, as the constant worry and excitement have been too severe a strain on his nerves.

Houdini's act was incredibly strenuous and he wasn't getting any younger. There was no doubt that it had had an effect on his health and many times, he had told reporters that he was going to give the whole thing up and retire. However, it seems, that he couldn't take it easy and constantly looked for new challenges.

The *Hastings Weekly Mail and Times* of 24 June reported:

STILL AT LARGE!
Houdini accepts Messrs. Bruce's Challenge and escapes.
HIPPODROME 'DRAW'.

Sir,
Hearing that our Chief Constable would not lock you up in the police cells, and after seeing your performance with the mysterious boxes, you need not look

any further for someone to fasten you, for we have in stock a large and strong hamper, and if you will allow us to come on Wednesday we will lock, strap and rope you in this hamper in such a manner, as we are confident will prevent you making your escape, but remember, you are not to demolish or injure the hamper in any way.

Yours faithfully,
FREDK. BRUCE
for Bruce and Co,
2, York-buildings, Hastings.

So ran the challenge sent by Messrs. Bruce to Harry Houdini, the famed gaol-breaker and handcuff expert, who is drawing crowded houses this week to the Hastings Hippodrome. Houdini accepted the challenge, and the town was at once flooded with announcements of the greatest 'draw' of the week. The hoardings were well placarded, and hundreds of handbills distributed, with the immediate result that public interest was aroused, and at the second performance that evening there was a bumper house at the Hippodrome. Every part of the hall was alike – not a vacant seat anywhere, and the standing room was very limited even, so great was the rush for admittance as nine o'clock approached.

Instead of performing his usual feats with the imitation prison cell he carries on his travels he announced that he should at once try his luck with Messrs. Bruce's hamper, but was first persuaded by one of the committee who went from the body of the hall on to the stage, to release himself from a pair of regulation handcuffs, which Houdini did by simply knocking the cuffs on a chain, thereby controlling the spiral spring and releasing the lock, as he explained. He afterwards freed himself from another pair of cuffs, on his wrists behind his back, with equal ease.

The handcuff king explained to the audience that he had made no secret of the refusal of the Chief Constable at Hastings (Mr C F Baker) to lock him up in the police cells. He went to the Central police station, he declared, on Monday morning, as he did at all the places he visited, and asked to be locked up, but 'they would have nothing to do with me; perhaps they thought that I would get out.'

The remark brought a laugh from the audience, and Houdini, smiling in response, said he might have got out or he might have remained in the cell till that evening. He could not say which he would have done, but as he had escaped from prison cells in all the principal cities of the world, he thought he could escape from the Hastings cells were he locked in them.

Before calling upon Mr. Fredk. Bruce to fasten him in the hamper, Houdini craved the indulgence of the house were he too long in making his escape. He would not guarantee to escape, but would try.

The hamper was brought on to the stage by the attendants, and was closely examined by the committee, Houdini offering to forfeit £50 if anyone could prove that it had been prepared in any way for the feat. The stage was covered with a large piece of carpet, to dispel all suspicion of a trap door, and Houdini was then locked and securely roped in the hamper, which was turned over sufficiently to enclose him crouched within before the lid was shut down.

Mr. F. Bruce personally superintended the locking and roping of the hamper. Houdini's voice being heard asking whether he was inside when the process was complete. So far there could be no doubt. The mystery lay ahead. At about 10.5, to avoid reference to seconds, the hamper was shut from view by the placing over of a portable screen, and for the next 35 minutes there was nothing for it but to patiently listen while the orchestra played a quick tune ad-lib, until the very sound grew painful to the ear, so incessant were the repetitions, the conductor at last taking a hint from 'the gods' – of 'new tune.'

Wearily, the minutes dragged, helped on by a few bursts of applause. Ten minutes – quarter of an hour – twenty minutes – twenty-five minutes – thirty – thirty-five. Still no Houdini, and not the slightest movement visible to the audience within the curtain-cabinet. The attendants looked ill at ease on either side, the committee were obviously getting impatient, and the orchestra still fiddled away for dear life.

At 10.40, still allowing a fair margin for odd seconds, the curtain screening the opening of the cabinet was hastily thrust aside, and the 'bottled magician' stepped forth minus his coat and collar – happy and triumphant, but of jaded look.

Houdini, in some 35 minutes, had defeated the attempt of Messrs. Bruce to 'capture' him, and the applause following his re-appearance was naturally deafening. He was applauded to the echo, and well satisfied with himself did he appear, for he had on one more occasion preserved his reputation.

How did he manage it? Ask Houdini! There is a way in which Houdini performs his feats, but the public is never likely to gain the knowledge. The fact that he did not release himself from the hamper in view of the audience, of course, destroyed the major part of the realism of the feat. While such attempts are made in secret there will always be found those who cry 'fake' and 'bunkum', but all the same it is impossible for the onlooker to make such a charge with any degree of fairness. Yet to believe all one sees at such shows – Maskelyne and Cooke's, for instance – would be to invest the performer with powers other than human.

Houdini is certainly one of the greatest attractions ever put on the Hastings variety stage, and his appearance locally says a lot for the enterprise of the new management.

Last evening Houdini was again challenged, this time by Mr Arthur Fisher, late attendant of Colney Hatch, and also by Mr. W.T. Allen, a lunatic attendant, living at 30, North-street. These gentlemen had procured a straitjacket, which had been used especially for the murderous insane by the insane asylum authorities. After wriggling about the stage, Houdini released his arms after six minutes work, and had the jacket off in eight minutes.

Audiences showed incredible patience as some of Houdini's escapes took quite a while. Spectators were left staring at a stage where little was happening with only the orchestra playing to entertain them. The anticipation of the final result kept them hooked and Houdini's reappearance, free of his bonds, always brought huge cheers and applause.

Houdini's act had become pretty standard and one weekly show was much the same as the next, following the same pattern with similar challenges. However, in every town he played, the act was new to the audience and continued to bring the house down.

The *Hastings Observer* reported:

An excellent bill at the Hastings Hippodrome this week is headed by Houdini, the original 'Handcuff King of the World'.

On Monday night, at the second house, there was a very large audience, and when Houdini's turn came, excitement ran high. Some people in the audience who had come prepared with handcuffs were invited to the stage. These included two local Coastguardsmen. In quick succession, Houdini released himself from several pairs of various makes of handcuff. Incidentally he declared that the handcuffs used by the English police were the easiest in the world to get out of. One of the Coastguardsmen brought a big iron arrangement, which, when shut together and locked, secured the wrists, which were separated from each other by a bar of solid metal about two feet long. Houdini said that such things, which were called 'clippers' did not come within his challenge, but he would have a try with them. After being secured, Houdini was free in a couple of seconds.

Following the handcuffing tricks, Houdini proceeded to introduce his gaol-breaking powers, but the officers of the law had declined to lock him up. As he was explaining his model cell, someone in the upper part of the house shouted 'It is faked' more than once. Houdini retorted that he would give £100 to anyone who could expose any 'fake'. The gaol-breaking and box and barrel tricks then performed by Houdini, it is no exaggeration to say, fairly mystified everybody. It did not matter how he was bound and locked, he escaped in a very short space of time.

In addition to Houdini's display, there were several other capital turns. Edna, the charming nightingale (from the Alhambra), delighted everybody. Brogie, as a yokel, went great, Le Celebre Vandinoff did some wonderful lightning oil painting, Hallam and Stanton (operatic vocalists), Arundel and Arundel (speciality artistes), Sisters Albert (singers and dancers), Steel and Laing (acrobatic artistes), and Vere and Royal (Vaudeville artistes) all did well. Madame Luba de Saretta introduced something quite new in her unique performance of an educated wild mountain bull, several beautiful ponies and dogs, and a thoroughbred Arabian horse. Ruffell's Bioscope introduced some up-to-date animated pictures.

A word of praise is due to the orchestra of which Mr. Chas. P. Fox is the able conductor.

Houdini's fame encouraged many other people to take up similar handcuff acts. Some appeared at theatres, some entertained at fetes while others just impressed their friends.

During June, the *Hull Daily Mail* reported the story of a would-be Houdini:

Edward Bell, of Meadow Lane, Birkenhead, has been studying the tricks of Houdini. Arrested on Saturday night for being drunk and disorderly at Tranmere, it took the united force of three constables to overcome him. They twice got the handcuffs on him and he twice slipped them. Finally the police tied his legs together and took him to the lock-up on a hand-cart. He was yesterday fined £2 15s 6d, including costs.

From Hull, Houdini travelled to Scotland to appear at the Gaiety Theatre in Leith between 26 June and 8 July. Leith was known as the port for Edinburgh where modest shipbuilding and repair facilities took place. The Gaiety Theatre in Leith opened in 1899 and saw many big names before becoming a cinema in 1913.

Whilst appearing in Leith, Houdini rented a shop front next to Moss's Empire Theatre in Edinburgh. Frank

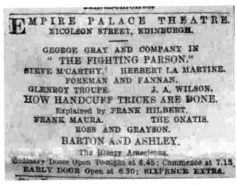

An advert for Frank Hilbert's show at the Empire Palace Theatre in Edinburgh entitled 'How Handcuff Tricks are Done'.

Hilbert was appearing at the theatre busily exposing Houdini's act. Houdini sent Franz Kukol, his assistant, together with a man called George Vickery to the shop front to pose as magicians. Their act, performed every half hour, consisted of them exposing the exposer of Houdini.

A poster for the event read:

Herr Franz Kukol, the celebrated illusionist of Vienna, and Mr George Vickery, the magician of London, beg to inform the general public that they will appear at the large shop at No 23 and 25 Nicolson Street, next door to Moss' Empire Music Hall, where they will give performances every half hour, showing how handcuff tricks are done by all impostors.

These gentlemen confess they do not know how Harry Houdini, who is engaged at the Gaiety Theatre, Leith, this week, performs his tricks. If they did they would not travel as exposers.

Like all other bogus handcuff impostors they do not allow anyone to bring handcuffs. No one is allowed on the stage. No one is allowed to examine the trunk they make use of, as they have a trap in top of the box, similar to other imitators and tear open the bottom of the bag they use!

They cannot open any handcuff unless their own, and they must have a key to fit, just the same as all other exposers.

The whole swindle shown for a penny. Next door to the Empire Theatre, Edinburgh. Open from 11am to 9pm.

Houdini planned to return to America after his last show on 8 July. On his final night, the audience asked him to make a speech. When he finished they all stood and gave him three loud cheers. An awaiting crowd carried him on their shoulders when he appeared at the railway station to travel to Southampton to catch his liner. As they carried him, they sang, 'And when you go, will you no come back?' He was touched by the event and wept at the love he received from his fans.

After sailing on 20 July on the *Kronprinz Wilhelm*, his plan was to tour America for six weeks and then return to Europe for one more tour before retiring for good. However, Houdini was soon back and appearing at venues in Northern Ireland. Little

A handbill advertising a show by Franz Kukol and George Vickery exposing bogus handcuff impostors.

seems to be known of his tour of Northern Ireland or of many of the venues that he played there.

According to an advert in the *Ballymena Observer* of Friday 18 August, Houdini appeared at the Protestant Hall, Ballymena for one night only on Friday 25 August. He was second on the bill after Dr Ormonde who was described as 'King Hypnotist and Monarch of the Marvellous'. The show promised that Houdini would escape from a large iron cage after being securely bound with handcuffs and leg-irons. His show featured an act called the 'Tiger's Den'.

Houdini was still in Northern Ireland in September and *The Era* of Saturday 16 September reported:

> *The new town hall in Newry was packed on Monday to see Dr and Mdlle Ormonde. The Doctor entirely baffled his audience with his numerous tricks and illusions and in his hypnotic exhibition amazed all and proved himself a veritable healer. Mr Fred Ormonde, the lightning cartoonist, did some excellent sketches that of 'Tim' Healy KC MP, being very well received. Houdini, the marvellous handcuff king, went through his remarkable performance with chains, irons and padlocks. Mdlle Ormonde, the 'World's Wonder', entered into a trance, astonishing her hearers by her remarkable and correct revelations. Mdlle Ormonde gave a violin solo, for which she received an ovation, and the entertainment concluded with some excellent animated pictures which were up to date and well received.*

Protestant Hall, Ballymena.

FOR ONE NIGHT ONLY.

FRIDAY, 25th AUGUST, 1905.

The most marvellous Entertainment of the 20th Century is coming, crowded nightly with the elite of each town.

DR. ORMONDE,

King Hypnotist and Monarch of the Marvellous, assisted by the World Famous and Inimitable

"ORMONDE FAMILY SUNFLOWER COTERIE,"

in their Monstre Combination of Varieties including:

HOUDINI

The Greatest Handcuff King and Prince of Jail Breakers. See his extraordinary escape from a large iron cage after being securely bound with handcuffs, leg-irons, &c. Houdini will forfeit £100 to anyone proving he uses trick irons.   Come and see

THE TIGER'S DEN.

The Redoutable Wonder, and Modern Witch of Endor.

Mdlle. ORMONDE,

See the bewildering Indian, Chinese, and Japanese Illusions. Grand Violin Recital by Mdlle. Lorrix Ormonde the sensational and unrivalled modern

PAGANINI.

THE SUNFLOWER COTERIE,

A galaxy of unparalleled talent, every artiste a star of the first magnitude.   See the gorgeous

VIVO-TABLEAUX

Showing the finest display of animated pictures on record.

The Battle of the Sea of Japan, &c., Riots in Russia, Buffalo Bill's "Wild West," Hackenschmidt, General Piet Cronje's Boers and Britishers at St. Louis Exposition, Cicero winning the Derby, Life of a Racehorse, Galton More from a foal to its winning the Derby, Prize Fight, and innumerable interesting events to date.

Come early and secure your seats.

Doors open at 7.15.   Commence at 8.

Prices—3s.; 2s.; 1s.; and 6d.   12.

An advert from the *Ballymena Observer* of Friday, 18 August 1905 announcing, for one night only, Houdini's appearance at the Protestant Hall in an act called the Tiger's Den.

Oddly, it seems, Dr Ormonde and his family were more of a draw in Northern Ireland than Houdini himself. Other dates were undoubtedly played in Northern Ireland but scant information has been found.

The *Aberdeen Journal* of Thursday 14 December reported that Houdini hadn't been paid for his appearance at Leith and the matter was taken to court:

Harry Houdini has had recourse to the Court of Session to obtain from the New Gaiety Theatre, Leith, £100 which he says is due to him in connection with an engagement which he had in the theatre in June last.

The well-known performer stated that he was engaged by Alfred Selwyn on behalf of the defenders to appear in their theatre for a couple of weeks at a remuneration of £150 a week.

The engagement was fulfilled and £150 was paid to him at the end of the first week but only £50 at the end of the second week, leaving the balance now sued for.

The defenders deny that they employed the pursuer and state that he was engaged by Selwyn as agent for a syndicate, the agreement being in his and their interest only. Selwyn had no authority, they say, to enter into any agreement with the pursuer on their behalf. Payment of the balance was

A studio portrait of Harry Houdini.

not made to the pursuer because after taking credit for their own 30 per cent of the drawings, which was the arrangement, the balance remaining was not sufficient to enable them to do so.

Houdini didn't feature much in the British papers for the next year and most of his time was taken up touring America. In 1906, the only mention of him in the British press involved 'Empress', who toured theatres billed as the 'female Houdini,' and Captain E.E. West's racehorse who bore the name Houdini.

Chapter Seven

1907 – University Matinee, Sheffield

Houdini previously wasn't thought to have made any appearances in the UK in 1907. However, the *Sheffield Independent* of Friday 19 April tells otherwise:

A special University matinee is being arranged at the Sheffield Empire for May 4th. A very strong programme will be presented, Miss Hetty King, Miss Nellie Wallace, Mr Ede Forde, Mr John Lawson, Houdini the Handcuff King, Alfred Hurey and Sergeant-Major Enzer being among the artistes who have promised to appear. Of Miss Hetty it is stated that she has just signed a contract to go to America at the nice little salary of £312 a week.

Hardeen was appearing in Sheffield at the Empire Palace at the same time so it's assumed that Houdini was in Britain to visit him.

Houdini spent much of the year touring America and completed his first manacled bridge jump at Rochester Bridge, New York. In his diary he wrote, 'Ma saw me jump!'

Although the jump took place in America, it's worth featuring the newspaper story here as it was Houdini's first manacled leap into a river.

The *Rochester Democrat and Chronicle* of 8 May reported:

Leaps into canal
Crowd of Ten Thousand Sees Houdini Risk His Life.
With a moving picture machine to photograph him as he plunged into the canal and a crowd to cheer or tell of his death, Houdini dived from a truss of the Weighlock bridge at noon yesterday, handcuffed. Two pairs of police bracelets were fastened about his wrists when he made the leap.

Fifteen seconds from the time that the cold water closed over him, Houdini appeared above the surface with one pair of the handcuffs dangling from his right wrist. He sank again, but came to the surface almost immediately afterward with both hands free and waving the handcuffs above his head. His wife and mother were among those who saw him go into the water.

A moderate estimate of the crowd present placed it at ten thousand. The spectators occupied every available bit of space from which a view of the jump could be obtained and had much difficulty in getting to the street afterward.

A publicity photograph of Hardeen in handcuffs and leg irons.

Hardeen posing in front of some of his theatre posters.

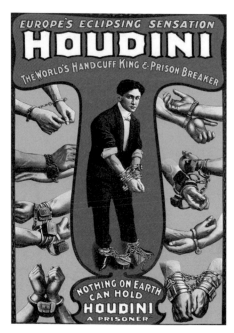

A poster announcing that nothing on earth can hold Houdini a prisoner.

A studio photo of Bess and Harry Houdini taken by Campbell Gray Ltd at Marble Arch, 88 Edgware Road, Hyde Park, during 1907. (*Image courtesy of Kevin Connolly http://houdinihimself.com/*)

Houdini took a preliminary leap into the canal on Monday afternoon. He found the bottom coated with four or five feet of mud. Because of that condition the idea of leaping into the canal with a sack tied about him and with his legs shackled was given up.

Houdini continued to tour America during 1907 and performed further jumps from bridges.

Chapter Eight

1908 – Suffragettes and Safes

The Oxford Music Hall in London where Houdini appeared between 2 November and 28 November 1908.

Houdini returned to Great Britain towards the end of 1908. His first appearance was at the Oxford Music Hall in London between 2 and 28 November.

An advert announced that Houdini appeared in a new sensation, escaping from a locked iron case full of water. Also on the bill were George Robey, Poluskis, Alex Dagmar, Phil Ray, Harry Randall, Will Evans, Carlton the Hanki-Homey Showman, Chas Whittle, Jose Collins, Tate and Tate and the O'Gorman Brothers.

The *London Daily News* of Thursday 5 November reported:

At the Oxford, this week, Houdini, the Handcuff King, enhances an interesting programme by a marvellous display of his art. After adroitly wriggling himself free from a straitjacket, he succeeded in escaping from a large metal pail, filled with water in which he was completely immersed, and padlocked down by a heavy top. The escape takes place behind a tent-like screen and at its end the pail is still found to be water-tight. The time Houdini allows himself is from two to three minutes and if at the expiration of that period he is not free, his attendant has orders to smash the vessel open.

Houdini had planned to jump off Westminster Bridge early in November in a straitjacket and handcuffs but the police refused to give him permission fearing that large crowds would block the traffic. He was threatened with arrest if he went ahead.

While appearing at the Oxford Music Hall in London, he was challenged by five Chinese sailors. They wrote to Houdini but when the letter wasn't answered, they approached the *Star* newspaper. The reason that their letter wasn't answered was because it was in Chinese and three feet long. When translated, the challenge involved Houdini escaping from a 'Sangauw' which was a piece of equipment used to torture criminals in China. The victim would have his feet nailed to two planks of wood, he would be strapped motionless and have a chain around his neck attached to a crossbar above. It all sounded pretty gruesome but amazingly, Houdini accepted the challenge. He insisted that his feet should not be nailed and that two doctors should be on hand in case he got into any difficulty. He also asked to inspect the contraption.

When he went to inspect the device at Limehouse, a reporter from the *Star* accompanied him. After examining it, Houdini was quite happy with the challenge and on the night of Friday 20 November, the five Chinese sailors set up the Sangauw on the theatre stage. The men were said to be dressed in western clothes but had pigtails down their backs.

Once assembled, the device was similar to an upside down triangle. Houdini was strapped to it and chains were wrapped around him, pulled tight and then nailed to far points on the floor. His neck was wrapped several times with rusty chains before the ends were nailed to the crossbar. Houdini then had his hands bound.

The challenge commenced and Houdini struggled for five minutes in which time only one nail had come loose. The nail was hammered back in and the whole thing started again. Slowly, Houdini managed to knock off his shoes and pull his feet up from the straps and free them. By swinging his body, he pulled himself up onto the bar and with his teeth, undid the straps that held his arms. Once his hands were free, he removed the rusty chains from his neck and leapt down onto the stage. The struggle had taken just 16 minutes. The whole experience had been

Suffragettes tying Houdini to a bed during his show at the Oxford Music Hall in London during November 1908.

quite unpleasant and Houdini told the reporter from the *Star* that he would never attempt a similar stunt again using such a torturous piece of equipment.

Next, a challenge was issued by suffragettes. It read:

Dear Sir, We the undersigned, members of the women suffragettes, having heard that it is impossible for you to be secured, and so far, only men have tried to fasten you, we wish you would allow us to secure you to a mattress with sheets and bandages and think that we will be able to fasten you so that you will not be able to effect your escape.

We challenge you to allow us to come on the stage at the Oxford Music Hall, any night during your engagement, and allow us to put our theory into practise.

Signed Peggy Wheatley, 53 Camberwell Road; Mabel Stacey, 16 Old Kent Road, Peckham; Ethel Gibson, 26 Stafford Road, Bow; M Guy-Browne, Clarence Gate; R Cecil, Clapham Park and Maud Ferne, 23 Holmes Roas, Kentish Town.

The challenge took place on Friday 27 November. The suffragettes tied Houdini up and when they were convinced that he couldn't move, one of them lent over and kissed him. Houdini duly escaped.

His next appearance was at the Euston Palace in London between 30 November and 5 December. Houdini, again, broke all box office records while appearing there.

One challenge he received came from William Jordan and Sons which required him to escape from one of their milk churns instead of the usual water cans that were used on stage. He accepted the challenge and escaped during a performance on 2 December. The challenge was a struggle. Houdini was cramped inside the churn and realised that insufficient air holes had been drilled. Shouting out was a waste of time because he couldn't be heard. As he struggled, the churn turned over and as

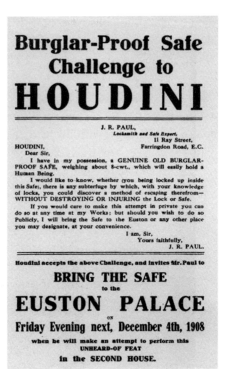

Houdini was challenged to escape from a burglar-proof safe while at the Euston Palace in London on Friday, 4 December 1908.

it hit the stage, one of the clamps became dislodged and Houdini quickly pushed off the lid and the air rushed in.

Another challenge came from a locksmith called J.R. Paul. Paul was a safe expert and defied Houdini to escape from one of his safes which he promised to deliver to the theatre. On the night of the performance, Houdini was locked in the safe on stage. A screen was placed in front of the safe as he made his escape. Houdini later admitted that he'd managed to escape from the safe within 14 minutes but kept the audience waiting in suspense for half an hour before he finally reappeared in front of the screen.

Whilst in London, Houdini was a frequent visitor to the Ivy House antiquarian bookshop at 306 Clapham Road which at the time was owned by John Salkeld. He collected playbills and became friends with Salkeld and his family. Salkeld's wife, Eliza, once gave Houdini shelter from an excited crowd who had watched him escape from police manacles in 1908. Houdini hid in their warehouse until morning and Eliza bandaged his bleeding wrists.

Houdini repaid her kindness by giving her a copy of his book, *The Unmasking of Robert-Houdin* which he signed and dated.

The bookshop was very popular and other well known patrons included Macaulay, Dickens, Thackeray and the Prime Minister, William Gladstone. When Salkeld died in 1908, the *New York Times* featured an article about him which read:

> John Salkeld, who died lately in London at the age of 81, was a second-hand bookseller of the good old type, renowned in fiction, encountered frequently in literary biography, but not often met with nowadays in one's walks abroad. He began to collect old books and sell them in his boyhood. He acquired a large knowledge of books and literature, and was the friend of many eminent bookish men, including Macaulay, Thoms, the elder Dilke, and John Forster. More than thirty years ago he moved down to Clapham Road, where he had a notable bookshop. He had acquired many treasures, and was concerned in many now historic discoveries of rare books and manuscripts. His catalogues of his own collections are treasured in the Bodleian Library.

Houdini's next venue was the Hippodrome in Liverpool where he appeared between 7 and 12 December.

Houdini plunged manacled into the Mersey River from the upper deck of a tugboat on 7 December. The chains and manacles which bound him weighed 22lbs but he managed to escape in just 45 seconds. This was his first handcuffed water jump in England.

The *Dundee Courier* of Tuesday 8 December recorded the incident:

Houdini in chains preparing to leap into the Mersey on 7 December 1908.

Houdini threw himself from the upper deck of the tug Hannah Jolliffe *into the Mersey yesterday afternoon.*

This was intended as a display of Houdini's power in escaping safely under all circumstances from handcuffs and chains, from locks and bars and other impediments. The weather was particularly trying for Houdini on the occasion of his first water jump, handcuffed in England. The air was six degrees above freezing, the thermometer standing at 38 degrees.

Houdini took the leap bravely. In an instant, the plunge was over, the chained athlete disappearing like a shot. In a second or two, Houdini appeared above the surface, carrying the unfastened chains in one hand. They weighed 22lbs, while the locks or handcuffs in which his arms were encased weighed 2lbs to 2½lbs more.

Houdini's head appears above the water of the Mersey. He is holding the cuffs and chains from which he's just escaped.

Houdini is picked up by a small boat after escaping from his shackles in the Mersey.

Houdini said to a press representative:

'The first shock of the cold water nearly knocked me out of my senses but the idea occurred to me, submerged as I was, to save my life and I made a dash for the top.

'The cold,' he added, 'numbed my fingers and made it hard to open the handcuffs.'

'I am glad,' he concluded, 'that all is safely over, for in a water jump like this there is a certain element of risk against me.'

The tide was going out with a very strong current at the time.

Houdini is a teetotaller and non-smoker and expects, he says, to quit these jumps before long.

He added quaintly and curiously: 'I expect the grim fiend is following me up in these tricks and he may catch me some day yet.'

From Liverpool, Houdini travelled to the Hippodrome in Birmingham and performed between 14 and 19 December. A programme from Monday 14 December shows him third on the bill. The entry reads:

Houdini – Presenting his latest and Greatest Creation that of escaping out of an air-tight galvanised iron can, filled with water and secured with six padlocks.

Houdini will forfeit £50 to anyone who can prove it is possible to live or breathe inside the can, after it is filled with water.

On 15 December 1908, Houdini jumped into the reservoir at Edgbaston from a houseboat moored there. The feat took place during a heavy rainstorm. This didn't deter him and he managed to escape in just 42 seconds.

A report of the incident appeared in the local paper under the headline *HOUDINI'S REMARKABLE FEAT*. It read:

Several hundred persons were attracted to the Edgbaston Reservoir yesterday afternoon to witness an extra-special performance by Houdini, the 'Handcuff King,' who is appearing at the Birmingham

A studio portrait of Houdini in chains.

Hippodrome this week. He had undertaken to allow himself to have his arms manacled, then to dive into the water, and appear on the surface after freeing himself of the irons while underneath. Houdini was accompanied by local pressmen to the diving launch, about fifty yards from land and there he undressed. Irons were placed on his elbows and wrists, while a strong iron chain held his arms firmly behind his back. He then dived into nine feet of water and liberated himself under the surface within a minute. He was warmly cheered by the spectators who stood on the banks suffering a drenching from the rain.

His next appearance was at the Grand Theatre in Bolton between 21 December and 26 December. Bolton was a mill town with 216 cotton mills so a fair proportion of the audience would have had connections with the trade.

An advert for the show announced that he would free himself from 'locks, bolts and bars'. Also on the bill were the Regar Trio of lady gymnasts; Ella Lorraine, ballad vocalist; Barney Ives and Company in 'Magic and Illusion'; the Brothers Ford, wooden shoe dancers; the Rizarelis in a sensational

An advert for Houdini's appearance at the Grand Theatre in Bolton between 21 December and 26 December 1908.

revolving trapeze performance; James Brady, eccentric joker; George Bond, comedian; Lyons and Cullum, in a speciality act and Vernon's Imperial Bioscope.

Houdini's last appearance of 1908 was at the Paragon Theatre in London between 28 December and 2 January 1909.

At the end of 1908, Houdini told a London reporter that his leap in chains stunt was about to become more daring. His plan was to pay the owner of a Wright Brothers airplane the amount of $5,000. Whilst in flight, Houdini would leap, manacled, from the plane and land in Piccadilly Circus. The stunt would have not only been very daring but also very dangerous. It would have certainly drawn very large crowds but the event was postponed. Aviation was still in its infancy and a safe way of leaving a plane by parachute had not yet been discovered.

Chapter Nine

1909 – The Water Can Escape

Houdini began the year finishing off his performances at the Paragon Theatre in London. On New Year's Day, he played three performances before returning to his boarding house. He wrote in his diary on that day: 'The poor old deaf landlady had a very bad meal. Went to bed after eating an apple and whatever was fit to eat left from tea.' For all his money and fame, he still continued to stay at downmarket lodgings.

Houdini was obviously still incredibly popular but, oddly, many local newspapers carry no reference to his appearances in their towns or cities. By now, photography was well established but hardly any photos of Houdini in the UK in 1909 appear in the press. The only memorable one is of his leap into Dundee Dock.

One of the first mentions of Houdini in the British press in 1909 comes under the 'Inventions' section of *The Era* of Saturday 2 January. A full page shows a list of recently applied for patents. Towards the bottom of the list is an entry under the headline *COMPLETE SPECIFICATIONS ACCEPTED* which reads: *19,546 – Houdini Illusion apparatus.*

Many of the inventions are featured complete with drawings but no more is mentioned of Houdini's new device.

By now, Houdini was including his escape from a sealed milk can in every show. Together with regular challenges and leaps from bridges, his appearance in a town or city attracted huge audiences.

An advert for Houdini's show inviting people to bring their own padlocks to be used for the water can escape.

His next appearance was at the Palace in East Ham, London between 4 and 9 January. The Palace was relatively new when Houdini played there, having opened just three years previously in 1906.

Houdini accepted a challenge from T. Greenwood of Greenwood and Sons, saddlers and harness makers of 4 High Street, East Ham. The challenge involved him escaping from a bespoke straitjacket. The spectacle took place during the second house on the evening of Friday 8 January and, as usual, Houdini easily made his escape. Ticket prices for the event were 10/6 for a private box; 1/6 for the stalls; 1s for the grand circle; 6d for the pit and 3d for the gallery. Most would have opted for the 3d seats.

From London, Houdini travelled to Liverpool to appear at the Pavilion between 11 and 16 January.

Whilst there, he received a challenge from G.W. Houghton, a champion swimmer, who requested that he escape from an iron chest full of water. Houdini accepted the challenge and the stunt was performed during the second house on the Friday evening of 15 January.

His next venue was at the Regent Theatre in Salford between 18 and 23 January. Houdini was challenged to escape from an extra strong basket purchased from the Henshaw Blind Asylum in Stretford Road. He was chained with locks and the basket was roped. Houdini made his escape during the second house on Friday 22 January.

On Monday 25 January, the *Exeter Gazette* announced that they had engaged Houdini at the Exeter Hippodrome but there's no record of him ever playing in the city.

Houdini next travelled to Northern Ireland to appear in Belfast at the Hippodrome between 25 January and 30 January. While there, he was boarded up using timber which at the same time, was also being used to build the *Titanic*. As usual, he soon made his escape.

After Belfast, Houdini crossed the water to appear at the Palace Theatre, Glasgow between 1 and 13 February before travelling to Manchester to play at the Hulme Hippodrome between 15 and

CHALLENGE!

I, G. W. HOUGHTON, Champion All-round Swimmer of Great Britain, do hereby CHALLENGE " HOUDINI," of the Pavilion Music Hall, Liverpool, to ESCAPE FROM

A LARGE IRON CHEST

constructed on the style of a safe, after it is filled to the top with water. To prove to the Public that I am not asking him to perform an impossible feat, I will undertake **to escape from this Iron Chest after it is filled with water** in less than six (6) minutes, and defy " HOUDINI " to duplicate the performance.

G. W. HOUGHTON,

Champion Scientific Swimmer of the World and Holder of World's Records for several aquatic feats.

9 WALKER ST., WEST DERBY RD.   L'POOL, JAN. 12th, 1909.

The above Challenge is accepted by HOUDINI ; contest to take place 2nd House, Friday night, Jan. 15th, 1909, on stage of Pavilion, Lodge Lane, L'pool.

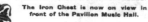

The Iron Chest is now on view in front of the Pavilion Music Hall.

While at the Pavilion Music Hall in Liverpool, Houdini received a challenge to escape from a large iron chest. The challenge took place on Friday, 15 January 1909.

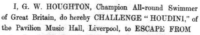

20 February. Harry Foster, a saddler from Hulme, challenged Houdini to escape from a padded cell suit. The escape took place during the second house on Wednesday 17 February.

His next venue was at the Empire at Ashton-under-Lyne between 22 and 27 February. Ashton-under-Lyne was an important mill town which, with its canal and railway links, led to an economic boom in cotton spinning, weaving and coal mining.

Houdini received a challenge from trained nurses and asylum warders who wished to roll him in wet sheets, fasten him down with linen bandages, pour buckets of water over him and tie him to a hospital bed.

He accepted the challenge and performed the feat during the second house on Wednesday 24 February. He had severe difficulties while performing the challenge, however, and injured his wrists badly when he was hung from chains.

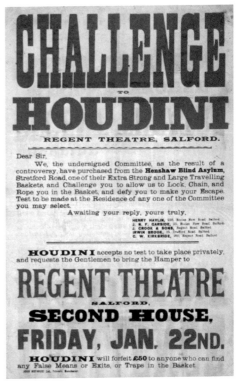

A challenge to Houdini while he was appearing at the Regent Theatre, Salford between 18 January and 23 January 1909. He escaped from a strong basket during the second house of Friday 22 January.

The Hippodrome in Belfast where Houdini appeared between 25 January and 30 January 1909.

An intense portrait of Houdini.

On Wednesday 24 February, Houdini completed a challenge while at the Empire in Ashton-under-Lyne. He successfully escaped from a hospital bed while fastened down.

By March, Houdini was appearing at the Royal Hippodrome in Preston between Monday 1 March and Saturday 6 March. The Hippodrome had recently opened in 1905 and *The Stage* stated *'in the circle, plush velvet tip-up chairs make this part of the house luxurious, whilst other parts of the house are well looked after, and are very comfortable.'*

Houdini was said to have been placed in a cell in Preston and the door shut behind him. No matter how hard he tried to unlock the door, nothing would work and he had to give up his escape. He then leaned against the door and discovered it had been unlocked all the time. This story has been told in several versions, many times, but it's hard to prove if it ever happened.

At Preston, Houdini performed his liberation from a straitjacket act as well as the milk churn escape. A committee of twelve members of the audience strapped him up in the straitjacket. He escaped in a very short time. Then he escaped from the milk churn in a minute and a half and appeared on stage smiling while dripping and panting after the exertion.

Houdini's next appearance was at the Empire Theatre in Bristol between 8 March and 13 March. The *Western Daily Press* of Thursday 11 March stated that he accepted a challenge from Messrs E. Wilkins (foreman), C. Skidmore and T.J. Hacker who worked for a firm of harness-makers in Bristol. Houdini was put in a form of bag, with collar and closed sleeves, made of sailcloth and fitted with extra straps and buckles. The challengers said that such a restraint was used in padded cells. When strapped in the suit, it looked like it was impossible for him to escape from it. It was certainly impossible for him to stand. However, in ten minutes he managed to free himself in front of a large audience and a committee on stage. He received loud cheers for his achievement.

The *Western Daily Press* of Saturday 13 March reported:

An audience in size which probably eclipsed any that had previously attended a single performance at the Empire, witnessed Houdini escape in 17 minutes and 5 seconds from the toils of a crazy crib, used in criminal lunatic wards. The challenge came from three asylum attendants and trained nurses. The crib consisted of a hospital bed furnished with straps to secure every part of the body and including a collar strap which held the head firmly back upon the bed.

Houdini attacked this collar first and before the eyes of a surprised committee succeeded in eventually loosening it and then the other sections of the harness. He was loudly cheered at the conclusion of his performance.

Houdini later stated that he had nearly choked to death due to the pressure of the leather collar around his neck when the bed moved from its original position.

In March, Houdini donated five shillings to the Shilling Collection for the Music Hall Home. Up to that date, 4,568 shillings had been collected for the fund.

During March and April, Houdini returned to Europe and appeared at the Alhambra in Brussels before appearing at the Alhambra in Paris towards the end of March and April. He returned to the UK during May and his first appearance was at the Hippodrome in Blackburn.

John Clempert who billed himself as 'The Man They Cannot Hang'.

While he was away, John Clempert took advantage of Houdini's act but soon found himself in trouble.

The *Manchester Courier and Lancashire General Advertiser* of Wednesday 14 April reported:

> John Clempert, an athlete who is this week appearing at a London music hall and claims to rival Houdini, 'the Handcuff King', was prevented by the police yesterday from diving from Tower Bridge for a wager.

The *Sheffield Independent* of Thursday 15 April reported on Clempert's appearance in court:

> John Clempert, the Russian music hall artiste, who, it had been announced, would dive from Tower Bridge in manacles on Tuesday, but who was arrested by the police before he could do so, was brought before Alderman Howse, at the Mansion House Police Court, yesterday, on a charge of disorderly conduct. Mr A A Strong defended.
>
> Sub-Divisional Inspector Hopkins, of the Tower Bridge police station, said that at ten minutes past one on Tuesday afternoon, the defendant, who was in swimming costume, with handcuffs and chains on him, drove in a cab on to the bridge, and witness suspecting what was about to happen, ran after the cab. The pavement was thronged with people and several men shouted to the defendant to get out and do it from the other side. Witness called to the cabman to stop and he did so. Defendant asked; 'What right have you to stop me?' and witness replied: 'I believe you are going to jump from the bridge and you will not be allowed to.' Defendant became very excited and several times shouted: 'Are you going to pinch me?' A large crowd gathered round and eventually the defendant got out of the cab. He was asked to go away but refused to do so and was arrested for being disorderly by causing a crowd to assemble.
>
> Mr Strong said that the defendant was a Russian and was accustomed to performing similar feats in his own country. He had made a wager to dive from the bridge.
>
> The Alderman said he could not see what possible defence there was to a charge of disorderly conduct. 'You don't mean to suggest,' he asked, 'that a man can be permitted to go to Tower Bridge and amuse himself by jumping in the river with handcuffs?'
>
> Mr Strong: 'He did nothing of the sort. I do not think, at the moment he was stopped, he had any intention of diving from the bridge. He is a foreigner and does not understand what a terrible crime it is in this country to cause a crowd to assemble.
>
> The defendant was bound over in £50 to keep the peace for six months.

METROPOLITAN.

At 6.40 and 9.10.

EXCLUSIVE ENGAGEMENT OF THE GREAT HOUDINI, Zampas, Court Jesters, DIANA HOPE AND CO., FRED ELTON, HORACE LANE AND VIOLET LLOYD, MABEL GREEN, Billie Merson, ETHEL NEWMAN, Ruffell's Bioscope.

Houdini appeared at the Metropolitan in London between 17 May and 22 May 1909.

From 3 to 8 May, Houdini played at the Hippodrome in Blackburn before appearing at the Pavilion in Newcastle Between 10 May and 15 May.

His next venue was the Metropolitan in London where he entertained between 17 May and 22. Also on the bill were Zampas, court jesters, Diana Hope and Co, Fred Elton, Horace Lane and Violet Lloyd, Mabel Green, Billie Merson, Ethel Newman and Ruffell's Bioscope.

From London, he travelled to Portsmouth and appeared at the Hippodrome between 24 and 29 May.

The *Lancashire Evening Post* of Tuesday 25 May carried an advert for Houdini at the Temperance Hall, Preston twice nightly at 7pm and 9pm. It's thought that this must refer to a film he was in because Houdini was appearing at Portsmouth at the time.

Houdini next played at the Palace Theatre, Chelsea between 31 May and 5 June.

The *Era* of Saturday 5 June included a long list of contributors to the Scott Fund. Altogether, £44 9s 3d had been raised and was to be given to the widow of the late George Scott. At the top of the list, and the most generous, was the Great Lafayette who donated £10. Further down the list, it was shown that Harry Houdini had donated 10s 6d.

The *Era* of Saturday 5 June wrote:

A satisfactory appearance of fullness has been presented throughout the week at Mr Henri Gros's cosy hall at Chelsea where Mr J Norman Berlin, the courteous manager, is presenting a programme of much attractiveness. The big name on the bill is that of Houdini, the renowned gaol-breaker, who makes a most interesting escape from a regulation straitjacket. He then proceeds to immerse himself in a galvanised iron can full of water, which is covered in, the lid being secured by half-a-dozen padlocks. The receptacle is wheeled into a recess and the curtains drawn, while an attendant stands with uplifted axe ready to rush in and break open the can in the event of Houdini not making his escape within a given period. Happily, however, no untoward event occurred and the performer made his appearance dripping and triumphant. The feat is preceded by a series of interesting pictures on the bioscope showing the 'Handcuff King', heavily manacled, making a daring leap from the Morgue Bridge into the Seine and freeing himself while in the water.

Houdini wrote a letter concerning 'a little trouble' that he had at Chelsea Music Hall. It read: 'It was of such a nature that the house was sold out at early door money, seats sold on the stage, and thousands turned away. I had three challenges in one night.'

His next appearance was at the Hippodrome in Leeds between 7 and 12 June. His coming was announced in the *Yorkshire Post* which stated that he hadn't appeared in the city for the last four and a half years.

In the *Yorkshire Evening Post* of Saturday 12 June, under the headline *STRAPPED TO A MADMAN'S BED*, an article reported how Houdini was once again strapped to a 'crazy crib' such as those used in asylums. He had performed a similar trick earlier in Bristol. He freed himself in sixteen and a half minutes but was said to be in a crumpled and exhausted condition.

On 12 June, he wrote: 'In Chelsea, Mr. Harry Rickards was in the audience, and I am in possession of a contract which means Australia for 12 weeks, and I am to receive the biggest salary he has ever paid to anyone so far, and I RECEIVE FULL SALARY WHILE ON BOARD THE STEAMER. So I get paid 12 weeks for resting and 12 for working. That is the only condition that I would go all that distance.'

Houdini had always said that he wouldn't travel to Australia, probably because of his sea sickness, but it seems that the offer was just too good to refuse.

The next venue for Houdini was the Empire in Wolverhampton between 14 and 19 June.

A local newspaper carried a report of Houdini's appearance at the theatre. It read:

In acceptance of a local challenge, he suffered himself to be fastened up in a packing case specially made. A large committee were invited upon the stage and when the mysterious Houdini was safely incarcerated in the box all and sundry took turns at knocking nails into it. The case was then crated up and lifted into a cabinet. Houdini had declared his intention of getting out at some time, though he could not guarantee a re-appearance before the final curtain call. After an exciting wait of less than ten minutes however, he appeared before the astonished audience without his coat and with a disarranged collar. The box was in precisely the same condition as when the last nail was knocked in. Tomorrow evening, Houdini will take up another challenge to escape from a straight waistcoat such as is used for the murderous insane.

The Empire Theatre at Wolverhampton. Houdini appeared here between 14 June and 19 June 1909.

Movies of Houdini were now starting to appear regularly at theatres. In June, the Grand Assembly Rooms in New Briggate showed a film showing Houdini's exploits in Paris.

On the evening of Sunday 20 June, Houdini leaped from a bridge, manacled, into Dundee Dock to attract audiences to his show the following week. What was rare was that the news story was accompanied by a photo of him accomplishing the feat.

The *Dundee Courier* of Monday 21 June wrote:

With two heavy leg manacles fastened around his chest and with 'gyves upon his wrists', Harry Houdini dived from the swing-bridge into the deep and dark waters at the entrance to Earl Grey Dock, Dundee, yesterday evening.

Within the brief space of a few seconds Houdini re-appeared above the water free from the iron fetters which had bound him. A huge crowd witnessed the daring act and Houdini's mystifying performance was greeted with loud applause. Seizing a rope which was lowered to him, Houdini quickly pulled himself up to the quay and was driven off in the motor car which conveyed him to the scene.

The preliminary preparations for the dive were made at the King's Theatre, where Houdini is appearing this week. Houdini donned a bathing costume and in the presence of a number of witnesses, the leg manacles were tested and fixed. They were encircled around his neck and passed underneath his arms, being subsequently fastened on his arms immediately below the biceps. The leg manacles were of the regulation police pattern as also were the handcuffs which were attached to his wrists. Houdini donned a dressing gown and in the motor car he was driven to Earl Grey Dock.

Great precautions were to observe secrecy in the matter but when the motor car arrived on the quay shortly after seven o'clock, there was a considerable crowd in attendance and the number increased with that marvellous rapidity peculiar to the gathering of a crowd.

Houdini lost no time. Throwing off the dressing gown, he jumped out of the motor car and rushed to the bridge taking up a position on the rail. The handcuffs were finally adjusted and with his hands locked behind his back, Houdini jumped from the bridge before the amazed spectators.

When he came to the surface a few seconds later, he had freed himself from his fetters. The marvellous man was loudly applauded. One of the assistants had the rope ready to throw to Houdini, who was out of the water and speeding away in the motor car before those who were now hurrying to the scene at the sight of the crowd had time to realise what had happened.

A Courier representative who saw Houdini after the dive was informed that the release affected by him yesterday was the quickest he has yet accomplished.

His performance at the King's Theatre in Dundee commenced on Monday 21 June and ended on Saturday 26 June. While in Dundee during June, Houdini was refused by the police permission to leap in chains from Tay Bridge. A crowd had gathered by the West Protection Wall and the Esplanade to watch the stunt. They weren't to be disappointed. The *Dundee Courier* of Wednesday 23 June announced that Houdini would leap in chains from the bridge of the steamer *Marchioness of Bute* into the Tay and release himself at the bottom

A rare newspaper picture of Houdini leaping into Dundee Dock on Sunday, 20 June 1909.

A bill poster in High Street, Dundee advertising Houdini's show at the King's Theatre and Hippodrome, Dundee between 21 June and 26 June 1909.

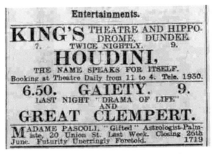

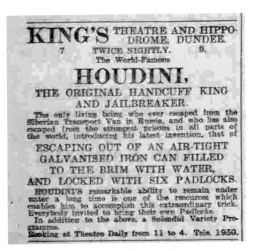

An advert showing that while Houdini was performing at the King's Theatre and Hippodrome in Dundee that the Great Clempert was appearing nearby at the Gaiety.

An advert for Houdini's show at the King's Theatre and Hippodrome in Dundee in 1909.

of the river. The leap took place at 3pm on 23 June. The newspaper offered prizes for the two best snap-shots taken with the first prize being 30 shillings and the second prize 20 shillings. Unfortunately, any photos taken seem to have long since disappeared and none seem to feature in the newspaper. His arrival at Dundee was awaited by huge crowds all eager to get a glimpse of him.

The *Dundee Evening Telegraph* of Tuesday 22 June reported:

> *The name and fame of Houdini, the great handcuff expert, resulted in the attendance of crowded houses at the King's Theatre last night. Houdini performed two very striking acts. In exactly one minute, he released himself from a straitjacket into which he was very securely strapped and his mysterious escape from a galvanised iron tank, full of water and locked with six padlocks, baffled the audience. Houdini had an excellent reception.*

Also on the bill at Dundee were Sevard and Hayes, eccentrics; the Canworths, high-class instrumental and vocal act; Estrella, international barefoot dancer; Sisters Du Cane, vocalists and expert dancers; Stalman and Russell, comedy absurdity; the Kingscope and Syd Walker, comedian.

Houdini's next appearance was at the Palace Theatre in Aberdeen between 28 June and 3 July. The city was known for its shipbuilding and fishing industries. The Palace Theatre opened in 1898 and could seat 1,800 people.

The *Aberdeen Journal* of Monday 28 June reported:

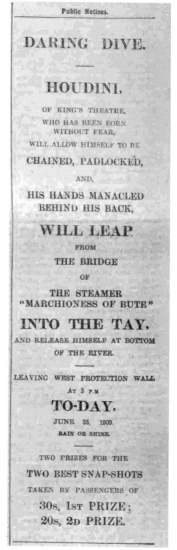

PALACE.

6.45—TWICE NIGHTLY—9.

HOUDINI,

The Original Handcuff-King and Jail-Breaker.

The Only Living Being who ever Escaped from the Siberian Transport Van in Russia, and who has also Escaped from the Strongest Prisons in all parts of the World ; introducing his Latest Invention—that of Escaping out of an Air-Tight Galvanised Iron Can filled to the brim with water and locked with Six Padlocks. Houdini's remarkable ability to remain under water a long time is one of the resources which enables him to accomplish this extraordinary trick. Everybody invited to bring their Own Padlocks.

Supported by a Full Variety Company, including SID WALKER, the latest London Star, presenting the Sketch entitled, "The Debt Collector."

Secure your seats at MACBETH'S, 181 Union Street.

An advert for Houdini's show at the Palace Theatre, Aberdeen, between 28 June and 3 July 1909.

One of the biggest attractions that have been presented to an Aberdeen audience for many years will be Houdini who makes his first appearance in Aberdeen at the Palace Theatre this week. Houdini has performed some almost impossible things in making his escape from the strongest prisons in all parts of the world and on occasion of his present visit, he will introduce his latest novelty – that of escaping out of an airtight, galvanised iron can, filled to the brim with water and locked with six padlocks. There can be little doubt that Houdini will be the sensation locally of the week.

Houdini's show was a great success and played to packed houses daily.

The *Aberdeen Free Press* of 1 July carried the story of Houdini's leap at Aberdeen Channel:

Yesterday afternoon Houdini, who is presently appearing at the Palace theatre, dived, chained and manacled, from aboard a tug into the channel, and after freeing himself from his trammels under water rose to the surface,

Public Notices.

DARING DIVE.

HOUDINI,

OF KING'S THEATRE,

WHO HAS BEEN BORN WITHOUT FEAR,

WILL ALLOW HIMSELF TO BE

CHAINED, PADLOCKED,

AND,

HIS HANDS MANACLED BEHIND HIS BACK,

WILL LEAP

FROM

THE BRIDGE

OF

THE STEAMER "MARCHIONESS OF BUTE"

INTO THE TAY,

AND RELEASE HIMSELF AT BOTTOM OF THE RIVER.

LEAVING WEST PROTECTION WALL

AT 3 P.M

TO-DAY,

JUNE 23, 1909.

RAIN OR SHINE.

TWO PRIZES FOR THE

TWO BEST SNAP-SHOTS

TAKEN BY PASSENGERS OF

30s, 1ST PRIZE ;

20s, 2D PRIZE.

An announcement in the *Dundee Courier* concerning Houdini's leap into the River Tay on 23 June 1909.

and got on board again uninjured. It was announced that the attempt would be made from a point in the bay a little beyond the pier head at 1 o'clock. By that time, hundreds of people had assembled on the pier and on the Torry side of the water to witness what was regarded by all as an exceedingly hazardous feat.

The sea was rough during the forenoon, and about mid-day Houdini was informed by the harbour authorities that it was unsafe to make the attempt, and that no small boat could live in the waves that were coming in. Houdini, however, arrived at the dock gates, from which the start in the boat was to be made, and on being informed of the

PALACE.
6.45—TWICE NIGHTLY—8.

First Appearance in Aberdeen of the World-Famous

HOUDINI,

The Original Handcuff-King and Jail-Breaker. The Only Living Being who ever Escaped from the Siberian Transport Van in Russia, and who has also Escaped from the Strongest Prisons in all parts of the World; introducing his Latest Invention—that of Escaping out of an Air-Tight Galvanised Iron Can filled to the brim with water and locked with Six Padlocks.   Houdini's remarkable ability to remain under water a long time is one of the resources which enables him to accomplish this extraordinary trick. Everybody invited to bring their Own Padlocks.

LOOK OUT FOR HIS SENSATIONAL MANACLED DIVE FROM ONE OF THE ABERDEEN BRIDGES.

Secure your Seats at MACBETH'S, 181 Union Street.

An advert for Houdini's appearance at the Palace Theatre in Aberdeen between 28 June and 3 July 1909.

conditions outside the pier, drove out to see what they were like for himself. Returning he expressed his determination to make the dive, and at once got into negotiations with Captain Forbes of the tug, 'John McConnachie', which was lying at Pocra Jetty. The Captain told him that he had no fear of going out into the bay, but with the sea that was on, it would be impossible to launch a small boat from the tug for the purpose of picking him up after he came to the surface, as they would probably never get it alongside again. It was proposed that the dive might then be made in the channel, but this part of the water being under the jurisdiction of the harbour authorities, they would not allow of that.

By this time thousands of people had arrived on the pier, and they lined the channel all the way from the Pocra Jetty to the pier head, while on the other side of the water there was also a vast crowd. Unwilling to disappoint the spectators who had assembled to see a spectacle, and confident of making the dive even in the stormy weather, Houdini determined to at least go out into the bay and see how the sea actually was from aboard the tug. Accordingly the tug left Pocra Jetty with Houdini and his attendants, Mr Gilbert of the Palace Theatre, and a few other passengers. As the pier head was reached it was seen that it was absolutely impossible to make the attempt there, the waves being so strong. The seas were coming washing over the brow of the tug, drenching those who were even standing on the bridge. The boat was turned about, and for a time it seemed settled that the dive would have to be completely postponed till some other time.

When just about at the head of the channel, however, Houdini expressed his determination to carry out his purpose there, if only the necessary permission could be obtained from the harbour authorities. Captain Crombie was some distance off on another boat, and the situation being explained to him, he offered no objection. Houdini then at once prepared for action. Having divested himself of his clothes he was manacled by one of the attendants. A heavy chain was put around his neck, crossed on his breast and each end fastened to his arms above the elbows. His hands were then carried behind his back and heavy handcuffs placed and locked on his wrists.

A small boat having been set down – the sea here was much calmer than out in the bay – to pick him up when he regained the surface, he dived off the bridge, over the right side of the vessel. A strong wind was blowing and it was cold. The pier was crowded with thousands who were all in tense excitement. Suspense was manifest among all for a time for the odds seemed great against the diver. After about 18 seconds he reappeared, his right hand and arm free, and the fetters in his left hand. A lifebuoy was at once thrown him which he clutched. He was pulled to the side of the tug and hauled on board amid the loud cheers of the spectators on the pier and also from those on board the tug. He went underneath to the engine and got dried and by the time the tug had got alongside the jetty again he was on deck in a long dressing gown apparently none the worse. On landing, he at once drove to his hotel.

On the evening of Friday 2 July, during the second performance, Houdini was challenged by two Aberdeen saddlers, Messrs. William Greig and Charles Sim. An especially large audience had gathered to see the feat. Houdini was dressed in a regulation padded cell suit with extra strong jute straps and buckles. He was then placed in a bag and secured by five straps. After a stiff struggle, the first of the straps was got off in eight minutes. Houdini was still firmly tied but having got his legs loose managed to undo all the straps in 15 minutes. Houdini was cheered again and again for his achievement.

The *Aberdeen Weekly Free Press* of 3 July carried a further story:

Houdini, whose fame as a defier of manacles and even prisons, not excluding condemned cells, is practically world-wide, opened a week's visit at the Palace Theatre, Aberdeen on Monday night. His wonderful achievements have mystified thousands, and at both houses last night the Palace was packed, the audience at the first performance being described as the largest seen within the building since the present arrangement of submitting two programmes on one evening was instituted. The star turn was the sole topic of conversation, and many and varied were the opinions aired as to what would take place. As a prelude to the great act of the evening two cinematograph films, depicting Houdini's notorious manacled dives, one in America and another in Paris, were thrown on the screen. Then the tit-bit of the evening came. The curtain rose revealing a number of zinc tanks and pails, standing within a tarpaulin and guarded by three attendants, and in a brief space Houdini appeared. He had a great welcome. Short of stature but strongly built, even an evening dress suit failing to conceal evidence of broad, powerful shoulders, he addressed the audience in firm, distinct tones, outlining his programme for the evening.

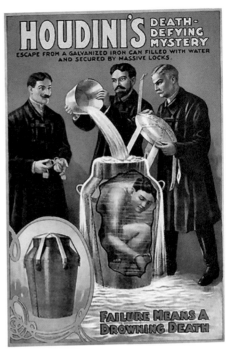

A poster promoting Houdini's water can escape.

The first turn consisted of getting out of a regulation straight-jacket, rather a formidable-looking garment. Two muscular-looking men, who were announced to have lengthy experience of prison work, were commissioned to carry out the fastening-up process. They strapped and restrapped Houdini until he could scarcely breathe, and certainly could not move his arms, which were finally crossed, the ends of the sleeves which overhung his hand being carried around his back and strapped. When the jacket had been ultimately adjusted Houdini commenced to extricate himself from what, to the ordinary individual, would have proved an impossible tangle. Giving himself two or three shakes, he lay down on a mat, wriggled for a brief space, and threw his hand over his head. Continuing to twist and squirm he loosened several of the straps, and finished by throwing the jacket from him. It was a grand feat, and the audience demonstrated in a most hearty manner their appreciation of it.

Better was yet to follow. A large zinc tank resembling in shape a wholesale milk can, was thoroughly examined by a large number of local men, and filled with water. Houdini gave an exhibition of his remarkable powers by remaining in the tin immersed in water for a minute and a half. Then, the dislodged water having been replaced, Houdini again entered the tin. A heavy lid was placed on and fixed down with four locks. A large screen surrounded the whole and after about a minute, Houdini drew aside the curtain having emerged from his prison without disturbing the locks. The audience simply yelled at the performance, which showed that Houdini's fame was worthily merited.

Syd Walker made a successful debut in Aberdeen. His business was thoroughly original, and his punning decidedly clever. A very smart gymnastic turn was given by Hattie Petro and Pete Leon, who are experts at such work. Slatwan and Russell, in a comedy absurdity; Madge Goodall, comedienne and dancer; the Conworths, instrumentalists and vocalists; Estrella, bare-foot dancer, and the Palascope completed an admirable and entertaining programme.

Houdini intimated that he had been refused permission by the authorities to dive manacled from any of the city bridges, but arrangements were being made to charter a ship, from the masts of which he would dive, either today or tomorrow.

While in Aberdeen, Houdini visited the grave of John Anderson who was known as the 'Wizard of the North'. His grave was located within St Nicholas Churchyard. Houdini was born in the same year as Anderson's death and was said to be inspired by him. When Anderson's grave fell into disrepair, Houdini promised to pay for its upkeep.

Will Goldston mentioned Houdini's need to find graves of deceased magicians in his book *Sensational Tales of Mystery Men*:

While in Aberdeen, Houdini visited the grave of John Anderson, the 'Wizard of the North'.

I have already made some reference to Houdini's love of publicity. It was his very life blood. He invented so many schemes for bringing his name before the public that I could fill several volumes on those alone. Some of them failed, most of them succeeded. Had they not done so, he might easily have died a poor and unknown man.

Harry was not blind to the value of sentimental publicity. One of his favourite schemes was to hunt out the graves of any magicians who had

An advert for Houdini's show featured in the *Dundee Courier* of Saturday, 10 July 1909.

lived in the particular town or district in which he was appearing. Then, accompanied by an army of press photographers, he would take a huge wreath to the graveside, standing bareheaded whilst his photograph was taken. On the following day his likeness would appear in the papers with such words as 'Great Magician pays homage to a departed conjurer.' This idea tickled Harry immensely, and incidentally had the desired effect of increasing his popularity.

When he was performing in Paris before the war, he decided to carry out this same programme, and accordingly hunted up the grave and records of Robert Houdin, the eminent French illusionist. He went even further, and inquired for the whereabouts of Houdin's surviving relatives. To his utter astonishment, these good people refused to meet him, and informed him in a manner which left no room for doubt, that they wished to have nothing to do with him.

This public rebuff made Harry very bitter. That anyone should refuse to see him, the great Houdini, was totally beyond his comprehension. I have never learnt the reason for this refusal on the part of Houdin's relatives, more likely than not they desired to be left in quietness. Possibly they hated the thought of publicity. But Houdini could not, or would not, take this point of view.

'Heavens, Will,' he said, 'what's wrong with me? Anyone would think I'm a leper! But they'll be sorry for it before I'm finished.'

'What do you mean?' I asked.

'I'm writing a book on Houdin that'll make those folks of his sit up. He's going to get the worst write up he ever had. He was an imposter.'

'Rubbish, Harry,' I returned, heatedly. 'You know that's not true. Why be so vindictive? Houdin was a great magician, and you know it as well as anyone.'

'He was an imposter, I tell you. I have collected my facts to prove it. And anyway,' he added lamely, 'the public will believe anything I tell them. 'The Unmasking of Robert Houdin' will make everyone take notice.'

'You are making a great mistake, Harry. Nobody will think you a better man for such a beastly action. Houdin is dead and cannot answer back. One of these days somebody will write a book on you, and call it 'The Unmasking of Harry Houdini.''

He looked up sharply at my words. 'If anyone does that it will be you,' he said slowly.

I laughed. 'Maybe you're right.' I replied. 'But if I ever write on Houdini, it will never be out of vindictiveness.'

When the book eventually appeared, it was an utter failure. Although Harry had taken much trouble to delve out his facts, he had also allowed his imagination to run, and the information was not generally accepted as accurate. It was as well. Robert Houdin, 'The French Father of Magic', was a man whom we all loved and respected. His spirit should rest in peace.

Houdini posing beside the container used in his Water Can escape. (*Image courtesy of Library of Congress http://www.loc.gov*)

Houdini jumping from a tall ladder fixed to Brighton Pier during July 1909.

From Aberdeen, Houdini travelled to Brighton where he appeared at the Hippodrome between 5 and 10 July.

By July, Houdini's rival, John Clempert, had tried to replicate Houdini's act as close as he could and in the meantime had revealed the secrets of the Water Can escape.

As mentioned previously, Clempert was born in Russia and had been a professional wrestler and formerly a showman. He was later billed as 'the man they cannot hang'. His act involved him hanging from a trapeze by his legs with a rope around his neck. He would then remove his leg hold and drop 15 feet before hanging in midair by his neck. It seemed inevitable that his act would go wrong and it did one night in Rochester when he injured his spine performing the stunt. While recovering in bed, he decided to perform an act similar to Houdini's which included escaping from prison cells, handcuffs and chains. He replicated Houdini's act as close as he could, including jumping off bridges. Theatre acts could be copyrighted and Houdini took out a suit against Clempert. He promised not to perform Houdini's trademark performances again and the suit was dropped. Little was heard of Clempert again.

Houdini performed at least two recorded outdoor stunts while appearing at the Hippodrome in Brighton. One involved him leaping from a tall ladder beside Brighton Pier and the other diving chained from a steamer.

From Brighton, he travelled to Manchester to appear at the Palace between 19 and 24 July.

The *Manchester Courier and Lancashire General Advertiser* of Tuesday 20 July 1909 noted:

Houdini makes some surprising escapes from apparently sealed tombs, prisons, water tanks and the like. One occasionally found oneself wondering how it was done: but really wonderment was unnecessary. There are no miracles nowadays.

Will Goldston recalled Houdini's visit to Manchester in his book *Sensational Tales of Mystery Men:*

HIPPODROME.   SHEFFIELD.
BARRASFORD'S.

Every Evening, 6.50 and 9.   Matinee, Thursday, 2.30.
THE MOST SELECT ENTERTAINMENT IN SHEFFIELD.
NEXT WEEK! NEXT WEEK!! NEXT WEEK!!!

HOUDINI.	
HOUDINI.	**HOUDINI.**
HOUDINI.	THE ORIGINAL HANDCUFF KING AND
HOUDINI.	JAIL BREAKER.
HOUDINI.	3 CUNARDS 3.
HOUDINI.	ALFRED HOLT.
HOUDINI.	EDIE GRAY and BOYS.
HOUDINI.	PICHEL and SCALE.
HOUDINI.	ERNESTO.
HOUDINI.	FRED HASTINGS.
HOUDINI.	ERNEST MONTEFOIRE and CO.
HOUDINI.	BARRASCOPE.
HOUDINI.	THE WALDRONS,
HOUDINI.	WORLD FAMOUS COMEDY DUO.
HOUDINI.	Box Office Open Daily 10 till 4, 7 till 8.30.

'Phones 4110—4111.

Houdini's appearance at the Hippodrome in Sheffield between 26 July and 31 July 1909.

'*Come immediately, spend two days as my guest. Have arranged rooms for you at my digs -- Houdini.'*

Such was the telegram I received from my American friend when he was performing at Manchester many years ago. It so happened that I had no important engagements at the time, and decided to accept the invitation.

When I arrived at the address Houdini had given me, my astonishment was so great that I could hardly find words to greet my host. The house was an insignificant theatrical residence, with typically cheap furniture and threadbare carpets. At first I was inclined to think I was the victim of a practical joke, for I knew that Houdini was earning well over £300 pounds a week.

'*Tell me. Harry,' I said at length. 'Why in the name of goodness are you staying in a frowsy hole like this?'*

'*Frowsy?' Houdini raised his eyebrows in surprise. 'Frowsy? Is it really now? I hadn't noticed. Anyway, Will, it doesn't matter much. The landlady is a heavenborn cook, she can dish up anything in first rate style.'*

And with that I had to be content. In vain did I try to persuade Houdini to change his lodgings for a good class hotel. 'Appearances count nothing with me,' he said. 'But with some decent food inside me, I feel that all's right with the world.'

The following day was Saturday, and Houdini asked me if I would care to see the show he was presenting at the Manchester Palace. I readily agreed, and was installed in a comfortable seat before the second performance.

Houdini was accorded a tremendous reception when he appeared. Following his usual procedure he performed several minor illusions prior to doing his 'feature' trick, an escape from ropes and chains. When the audience had been worked up to a suitable state of excitement, he told them he was about to present 'the world's greatest act', and asked if half a dozen gentlemen from the stalls would come on to the stage to secure his fastenings.

Several men stepped on to the stage, including myself. The volunteers did their work well, and Houdini was securely bound and chained. But one man with ruddy cheeks and a waxed moustache, was bent on making things uncomfortable for him. 'I don't like the look of this knot,' he said, 'It looks as if it might slip easily.'

Houdini was never happy when people found fault with his performance, and in order to avoid all public embarrassment, he instituted a system which permitted his show to proceed with its accustomed smoothness. While the disgruntled one was airing his protests, Houdini gave a secret sign to a man who was standing in the wings, well out of sight of the audience.

The confederate took the cue and smilingly beckoned to the victim. The man paused, scratched his head wonderingly, and walked off the stage. That was the last the audience saw of him. Incidentally it was the last he saw of the audience.

As soon as the unfortunate interrupter had walked well into the wings, he received a terrific cuff on the ear. In nine cases out of ten, this treatment was sufficient persuasion that silence was by far the best policy at Houdini's performances. In this particular case, however, the victim showed fight. So much the worse for him.

He lashed out wildly with both fists. But from the start he was hopelessly outnumbered. Three or four of Houdini's assistants pounced on him and speedily but effectively silenced him. When the poor man had been knocked almost unconscious, he was placed beneath the stage to recover at his leisure.

As Houdini was returning to the dressing room after the performance, he was approached by the house-manager. 'What in God's name have your men done to that interrupter?' he gasped. 'They've half murdered him!'

'They've done what?' asked Harry, assuming innocence. 'I never told them to touch him. He must have got fresh.'

The battered one was brought forward for inspection. He was indeed a sorry sight. Both eyes were closed, his lips were cut and his nose had assumed elephantine proportions. The assistants had done their work not wisely but too well. However, the magician was not in the least perturbed.

'Really, my man,' he said, producing a five pound note from his pocket, 'you must not upset my staff like this. I'm afraid you made them lose their tempers. However, I will discharge them. Meanwhile, George here will put you in a taxi, and send you safely home. Good night.'

The note changed hands. The victim, torn between a desire to thank Houdini for the fiver and an impulse to dot him in the eye, was led away half protesting by the smiling George.

'Well, well,' said Houdini to me in his dressing room. 'It's all in a lifetime, you know Will, it's all in a lifetime. By the way have you heard that story about the wife who broke her husband's nose with a flatiron...?'

Houdini's next appearance was at Barrasford's Hippodrome in Sheffield between 26 and 31 July.

The *Sheffield Evening Telegraph* of Tuesday 27 July carried a story under the headline *HOUDINI AT BARRASFORD'S HIPPODROME*:

Houdini is an extraordinary individual. He can apparently escape from anything. Handcuffs he defies, prison cells won't hold him, and now a galvanised iron tank filled with water and six times padlocked is insufficient to keep him prisoner. Two packed houses at Barrasford's Hippodrome last night watched him first of all escape from a regulation straitjacket and afterwards execute his latest thrill. Immersed in the water filling a large sized iron jar, the lid of which is secured by six padlocks, Houdini was placed in a cabinet and he emerged dripping within a minute and a half. To remain under water for that length of time is a feat in itself. As to the escape – we give it up!

On the bill with Houdini was an acrobatic novelty act, Pichel and Scale; the Waldrons, featuring an 'excruciating comedy item' in their act; Ernest Montifiore, assisted by a clever child actress in a military sketch; the Cunards, smart simultaneous dancers; Edie Gray and Boys in a dancing scene; Alfred Holt, an American mimic; Ernesto, a juggler and musical equilibirist together with Fred Hastings. Films of Houdini's most daring escapes were also shown.

On Friday 30 July, Houdini was seen, in the Wadsley Cemetery, at the grave of George Wale, a former attendant at the Wadsley Asylum. He laid a wreath of immortelles which read: 'In token of respect of George Wale. Last regards from Harry Houdini.'

Mr Wale was the first person in the British Isles to challenge Houdini to escape from a regulation straitjacket. The performance was given at a special matinee, six years previously, at the Sheffield Empire and Mr Wale himself strapped Houdini in the device. Houdini was successful in his escape but it was a hard struggle, taking a considerable time.

The Sheffield shows were followed by appearances at the Hippodrome in Nottingham between 2 and 7 August. Theatre posters at the Hippodrome billed Houdini as: *'The original handcuff king and jail breaker. The only living being who has ever escaped from the Siberian Transport Van'.*

The theatre had only been open for a year when Houdini appeared and was the pride of the city. It boasted one of the largest auditoriums in the country. There

PALACE, PLYMOUTH.
TWICE NIGHTLY, 7 AND 9.
MONDAY, AUGUST 16TH, 1909, AND DURING THE WEEK.
Performances commence 10 minutes earlier on Saturday only.
HOUDINI,
The Original Handcuff King and Jail Breaker.
BILLY YOUNG   JACKLEY TRIO.
MAY MAIDMENT.   STEWART and MORGAN.
TWO MOB BOYS.   THE PALASCOPE.
BILLY WILLIAMS
The Man in the Velvet Suit

An advert for Houdini's show at Plymouth during August 1909.

was much anticipation at Houdini's appearance and the public flocked in their thousands to see him.

From Nottingham, Houdini travelled down to the West Country to visit Plymouth in Devon.

He appeared at the Palace Theatre in Plymouth between 16 and 23 August. His week at the theatre ran from Monday to Saturday and Houdini made the most of free publicity for the show. As with his other shows, this included a free outdoor publicity stunt.

The Palace Theatre in Union Street, Plymouth, where Houdini appeared between 16 August and 23 August 1909.

The Old 5 horse Car at the Halfpenny Gate, Plymouth.

Halfpenny Gate where Houdini leapt in chains from the bridge while at Plymouth in 1909.

The *Western Morning News* reported that Houdini had made a '*most satisfactory debut*' on his first performance at the Palace on Monday 16 August. It also reported that the show included '*a series of excellent pictures upon the bioscope, showing his famous dives from various bridges around the world, earning much applause.*'

The *Western Morning News* and the *Western Evening Herald* both mentioned that Houdini proposed to leap in chains from a nearby bridge the following evening. Halfpenny Bridge at Stonehouse was just a few minutes walk from the Palace Theatre and the leap took place on Tuesday 17 August at 6pm. The stunt ensured that there was a full house later that evening.

The act included handcuff escapes, an escape from a straitjacket and an escape from a milk can. Houdini invited the audience to hold their breath for as long as they could while he was lowered into the can. Its lid remained unlocked. On stage, there was a large clock which showed the passing of time. After two or three minutes, Houdini surfaced to much cheering and applause.

He submerged once more and the can was topped up with water before the lid was firmly padlocked. Screens were placed around the can as the audience watched in anticipation. His assistants stood nearby with large axes in case of an emergency. Details of a challenge was reported in the local newspaper:

At the Palace Theatre, Plymouth, last night, Houdini read the following letter which had been received during the day:-

August 17, 1909.
Houdini. Palace Theatre.
Dear Sir,– We the undersigned expert joiners and builders, having heard of your abilities of escaping from impossible places, do hereby challenge you to allow us to construct a large and strong packing case from one inch timber and use a two and one half-inch common wire nail into which we will nail and rope you so that it will be an utter impossibility for you to escape.

If you accept our challenge, we demand 12 working hours to build the box and you are not to demolish same in making your attempt to escape.

We will send on the box for examination but insist on the right of renailing each and every board before you enter to prevent preparation on your part.

Awaiting your reply we beg to remain sincerely yours,
GEORGE WEST, 10 Palmerston-street, Stoke.
THOMAS SMITH, 16 Littleton-place, Stoke.
JOSEPH COUCH, 2 Melville-road, Ford.
WM. LANG, 23 Tavistock-road, Stoke.
WM. WOOD, 19 Warleigh-avenue, Ford.
Employees, Keyham Yard, Devonport.

Houdini asked if this was a genuine challenge and was met with a cry of 'Yes.' He inquired if the men were in the house and were told they were. He accepted the challenge and said he would forfeit £25 if he failed. The attempt is to take place at the second house on Friday night.

His proposed daring feat, involving him being securely handcuffed and diving from Halfpenny Bridge at Stonehouse, was reported in the next day's *Western Morning News*:

The name of Houdini has long been foremost in the music hall world and this wonderful manipulator of bolts, locks and chains has won for him the title of 'the world's handcuff king and jail breaker'. For the first time, he is making his appearance at the Palace Theatre and, before a crowded audience last night, he made a most satisfactory debut. By a series of excellent pictures shown upon the bioscope, Houdini's famous dives from various bridges in the world were most effectively seen and these won much applause.

His first real feat last night was an escape from a regulation straitjacket, accomplished in full view of the audience. Houdini invited a local committee upon the stage to prevent any suspicion of confederacy and two Plymouth constables fastened him up in the jacket from which he escaped in about a couple of minutes. This trick aroused considerable enthusiasm and applause. Houdini next presented his latest invention, that of escaping out of an air-tight, galvanized iron can filled to the brim with water and locked with six padlocks. This astounding trick displayed Houdini's remarkable ability to remain submerged in the water for an unusual time, and when he liberated himself and appeared before the curtain, he was cheered heartily by the audience. Those who love mystery should not fail to see Houdini.

Houdini leapt off Stonehouse bridge (Ha'penny bridge or Halfpenny Gate) in chains while appearing in Plymouth during August 1909.

Tonight, at six o'clock, Houdini will make a dive from the Stonehouse Halfpenny Bridge into the river, heavily manacled and handcuffed, and will make his escape from the irons, weighing about 28lb, before coming to the surface again.

Apart from Houdini, the programme is of all round excellence. Making his first appearance locally is Billy Williams, an accomplished Australian comedian, who will, we think, make a name for himself in this country. The Jackley Trio are old visitors to the Palace, but they were never heard or seen to better advantage in their drawing-room entertainment. The solos and duets given by Stewart and Morgan were well received; the two Mor Boys excelled as dancers; May Maidment made a vivacious comedienne and dancer; and Billy Young also contributed liberally by a comedy song and dance. The orchestra, under Mr. John H. Grigg, performed well.

The newspaper continued with a report of the dive from Stonehouse Bridge. It read:

Rain did not deter an immense crowd from assembling at Stonehouse Bridge last evening to witness Houdini, 'the handcuff king', doubly manacled, dive from that structure. Punctually at six o'clock, the intrepid American appeared on the bridge, nude accept for a pair of white knickers. He seemed anxious to make the plunge but for a few seconds, he was prevented by the presence of boats below. Mr. Field, the manager of the Palace and Houdini's men, who were also in boats, shouted to the occupants of the obstructing craft and they tardily cleared the course.

Houdini was speedily shackled by his chief assistant. An arm-iron was placed around the upper part of his arms and fastened at his back, after which his hands were secured with handcuffs. Without betraying the slightest sign of trepidation, fettered and hampered as he was by 18lbs weight of iron and his hands bound behind his back, he stood for a few seconds in an upright posture, drew several deep inhalations until his lungs were visibly distended and then hurled his body forward into space. In falling, he gave a backward kick in order to balance his body. His head cleaved the placid waters and Houdini disappeared from view.

Then followed a period of suspense and to alter slightly Macaulay's 'Horatius':-

'The spectators in dumb surprise,
With parting lips and straining eyes.
Stood gazing where he sank.'

Houdini's head reappeared above the surface in the space of forty-five seconds amid the plaudits of the multitude. He had succeeded in releasing himself from his fetters and at once swam ashore, jumped into the cab in which he had driven out and assumed his clothes on the way back to the New Palace Theatre.

There was much excitement in Plymouth about the jump and the local newspapers carried many reports.

The *Western Morning News* for Wednesday 18 August further noted:

Harry Houdini, the 'Handcuff King', who was performing at the Palace Theatre of Varieties, Plymouth this week gave a remarkable exhibition of his skill yesterday afternoon at Stonehouse. The intrepid performer had previously announced his intention of diving from the Halfpenny Gate Bridge, securely handcuffed, and this caused a huge crowd to assemble on the bridge itself and on the adjoining quays and banks.

Prompt to time Houdini appeared, stripped and poised himself on the parapet of the bridge. He was then handcuffed with his hands behind his back, while elbow locks were also worn, the chain passing around the neck. This accomplished, he immediately dived into the stream and disappeared from sight.

Easily within the minute, the 'Handcuff King' reappeared on the surface, carrying his fetters aloft in his right hand, while the crowd heartily cheered his exploit. Subsequently, Houdini said that he had performed the diving trick over fifty times. He was capable of staying under water well over three minutes, but should he not appear in three minutes there were always ready two or three assistants who would swim to his rescue. The handcuffs and chains weighed 18lb.

Another local paper carried the following report of Houdini's visit:

Harry Houdini, expert prison breaker and handcuff manipulator, who has been mystifying the Plymouth public at the Palace Theatre of Varieties this week, gave a marvellous exhibition of his wonderful powers last evening.

A clearer photo showing Houdini about to do a similar stunt to the one that took place at Dundee Dock. (*Image courtesy of Library of Congress http://www.loc.gov*)

The test arose from a challenge issued by five mechanics and joiners of the Devonport Dockyard that they could make a box from which Houdini could not escape. The 'handcuff king' accepted the challenge, which was decided at the second house at the Palace yesterday.

The challenge excited great interest and every seat was booked and the building packed to overflowing. Many hundreds were unable to gain admission. The mechanics filed onto the stage with the box, which was of inch thick wood, and fastened together with 2½ inch wire nails. As it has been exhibited at the Palace for some days, the challengers, to preclude any suggestion of it having been tampered with, went around every edge and inserted handfuls of fresh nails. Houdini, who was received with tremendous applause, soon stepped into the box, and was,

A challenge from the employees of Keyham Yard, Devonport while Houdini was appearing at the Palace Theatre in Plymouth in August 1909.

after it was seen by the audience that he was really inside, securely nailed in. Previously, ventilation holes were drilled in two of the sides. A strong rope was then passed around the box with half hitches, and was itself then nailed to the wood. The performer was then heard to ask if everything was all right, and, on being assured that that was the case, the curtain was placed around the box. The latter had also been thoroughly examined by the Dockyard men and a committee of the audience, who were on the stage. Houdini was also searched, but no tools were found on him.

During the interval of waiting, the orchestra played several well known songs, which the audience sang to pass away the time. After twelve minutes, the band suddenly stopped and the 'house' was in uproar. Houdini had appeared, perspiring profusely, while during his confinement he had also discarded his dress coat. Cheer upon cheer greeted the performer and everyone, the challengers, committee and audience, admitted themselves to be thoroughly at a loss how to explain the trick. The box was in exactly the same condition as when Houdini was nailed in. There was no sign of an opening anywhere. The *nails, rope and cover were also as securely fastened as they were previously. The box, during the test, was at the request of the challengers, placed on a carpet and not on the stage flooring. The Dockyardmen accepted their defeat and each heartily congratulated Houdini on his success. The box was subsequently inspected by the audience.*

At the first house, a gentleman offered Houdini £10 if he could escape from a straitjacket after being fastened in it by a number of sailors. The challenge was accepted but Houdini got free in a little over seven minutes. The ten pounds will today be handed over to the Mayor with the suggestion that £5 shall be sent to the Variety Artistes' Benevolent Fund and £5 to a local charity.

The records for the Palace Theatre show that Houdini received £150 for the week. The weather was also recorded as 'hot'. Houdini returned to the area in 1913 when he played at the Devonport Hippodrome.

Houdini's next three appearances were at the Empire Theatre, Kilburn between 30 August and 4 September; the Hippodrome in Willesden between 13 and 18 September and at the Palace in South London between 20 and 25 September. Some shows are well recorded in the press whilst others, for some reason, barely get a mention. It's uncertain where Houdini played during the week 27 September to 2 October.

Next, Houdini returned to Glasgow to appear at the Coliseum Theatre between 4 and 9 October.

While appearing at the Coliseum, local engineers challenged Houdini to free himself from a 17th century metal cage which had at one time been used as a punishment for criminals. It wasn't long before Houdini once more made his

Houdini night at the Glasgow Coliseum on 22 October 1909.

Houdini and Company at Charing Cross station, complete with baggage, en route to Liverpool before leaving for Hamburg. The photo was taken on 31 October 1909. (*Image courtesy of Paul Zenon http://www. paulzenon.com/*)

escape. His next two appearances were at the Palace in Oldham between 11 and 16 October and at the Coliseum again between 18 and 23 October.

Towards the end of the year, it's recorded that Houdini had to have a boil lanced from his bottom which was caused by the pressure from the straps of various straitjackets.

Houdini left the UK for Hamburg towards the end of October 1909. He is seen, complete with baggage, at Charing Cross Station, London en route to Liverpool for the journey to Hamburg.

Houdini wrote in *The Magician Annual* of 1909:

In Great Britain I receive my smallest salaries. However, having made so many friends in this country I like to be among them. Of course, I also must have made a few enemies, but that is part of life.

After working contracts which I have signed for Great Britain I expect to accept no more, as two performances a night of the work I do is too trying for my physique.

When I retire, perhaps I shall reside half the year in Great Britain and the other half of the year in America.

Chapter Ten

1910 – Tarpaulins and Cannons

During the first part of 1910, Houdini toured Australia. He became interested in aviation in 1909 and bought his own plane, a French Voisin bi-plane which cost him $5,000. On 18 March 1910, he became the first man to make a powered flight over Australia (Colin Defries had attempted the same previously but crashed on landing). The biplane was shipped to England and Houdini planned to fly himself between venues while touring the country. However, for some unknown reason, he never flew again.

Houdini arrived back in England in August. While he'd been away, his act had been copied by a performer calling herself 'Empress'. She was billed as 'The One and Only Lady Masterpiece'. Her act included escaping from straitjackets, handcuffs, water cans and packing cases. At the same time, companies were selling

A poster advertising Empress who billed herself as the 'Female Houdini.'

tools which they claimed that Houdini used in his act to free himself. Dismayed by this, Houdini offered a £20 reward to anyone who could find such an instrument concealed on his person.

Whilst in England, Houdini gave his address as 84 Bedford Court Mansions, Tottenham Court Road, London and it's believed that he owned a flat there.

His first appearance in England was at the Empire Theatre in Kilburn between 12 and 17 September. This was followed by an appearance at Chatham. It's recorded that Houdini was chained to a cannon in Chatham Town Square in 1910. The exact date isn't known but there seems time between his shows at Kilburn and Poplar for it to have taken place then. The cannon had a 15-minute fuse but Houdini managed to escape in 6 minutes. The cannon turned out not to be loaded.

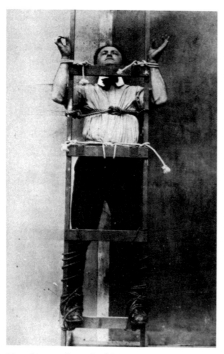

Houdini tied to a ladder with ropes.   A studio portrait of Houdini.

Houdini next appeared at the Hippodrome in Poplar between 3 and 8 October. The posters at Poplar stated, *'The World Famous Houdini'* and showed many of his escapes and stunts from around the world. His show was twice nightly at 6.20pm and 9pm.

His next appearance was at the Hippodrome, Willesden between Monday 10 and Saturday 15 October followed by a visit to Harlesden. Houdini is recorded as being strung by the neck and attached to three ladders in a tripod shape at Harlesden. He was chained and his shoes were stapled to the floor but he managed to escape. There is no precise date given although it's assumed that the event took place in the week after he visited Willesden.

Houdini's entourage at the Hippodrome, Poplar. Several policemen can be seen as well as posters advertising the forthcoming show. A few small children watch.

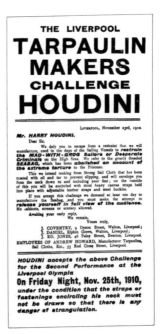

A challenge issued to Houdini at the Islington
Empire during November 1910.

Tarpaulin makers challenge Houdini at
Liverpool during November 1910.

From 31 October until 5 November, Houdini appeared at the Hammersmith
Palace. He was challenged by employees of Moss and Company who insisted that
he wear a special athletic suit and shoes to stop him from concealing hidden
tools. He was nailed into a cabinet but very soon made his escape.

His next venue was the Empire Theatre in Islington between 7 and 12 November.

The challenge at Islington involved Houdini escaping from heavy sacking
which covered his whole body and was then fastened shut with straps. He escaped
and requested that other companies challenged him with similar contraptions.

Houdini's next recorded appearance was at the Grand Theatre in Clapham
between 14 and 19 November followed by a visit to the Olympia Theatre in
Liverpool between 21 and 26 November.

In Liverpool, Houdini was challenged by the workers from a local business,
Andrew Howard, which made tarpaulins and sailcloth for boats. Their challenge,
made on 23 November, was for Houdini to escape from strong sail cloth, treated
with oil and tar to prevent slipping, which would be wrapped around his body
and held in place with straps and buckles. They insisted that Houdini release
himself in full view of the audience and not behind screens or curtains.

Houdini performed the stunt two nights later in front of a packed audience.
He kicked and struggled to free himself and managed to pull the sailcloth down

from around his neck and put his head underneath one of the straps. By taking off his shoes, his feet were soon free from the straps that held his ankles. Soon, his hands were free and he managed to undo the remaining straps and remove the sailcloth before kicking it away. The audience roared with applause.

Another challenge for Houdini was reported in the *Aberdeen Evening Express* of Tuesday 22 November. The article read:

Houdini inside the water can contraption. (*Image courtesy of Library of Congress http:// www.loc.gov*)

Houdini, 'the handcuff king', has received a remarkable challenge from Mr Thomas Nelson, 10-12 Lyndock Street, West Derby Road, who writes: 'I herewith challenge you to escape from the galvanised iron can you make use of if you will allow me to send along sixty gallons of milk and fill the can to the brim before you are locked in. The milk, not being transparent, will not permit the use of your eyes, and I shall bring a large rubber band or some air-tight material to encircle the inside of the cover so as to make the can indisputably air-tight. It is, however, distinctly understood that I have the right to bring along my own committee, also my own locks to lock you in, and that in the case of any accident or failure of your performance, I am no way to be held responsible.'

Houdini has accepted the challenge, the test being fixed to take place at the second house at the Olympia tomorrow night.

Many of Houdini's challengers appear to be cruel and heartless with the express intention of either maiming or suffocating him. However, perhaps that was the intention and it all helped raise the audience's sympathy and attention. Houdini successfully escaped unharmed.

His next venue was the Empire Theatre in Manchester between 28 November and 3 December.

At this time, Houdini took on two more stage assistants. James Vickery and James Collins, who remained as part of the act for the rest of his life. While at the Empire Theatre in Manchester, Collins signed an oath never to reveal any of Houdini's secrets. Together, they worked on a new stage performance, 'The Chinese Water Torture Cell'. Houdini tried to protect the originality of the act by performing it in front of the Lord Chamberlain.

Houdini's next appearance was at the Empire Theatre in Holborn between 5 and 10 December.

The Adventurous Life of a Versatile Artist by Harry Houdini featured a section, taken from a local newspaper, about his appearance at the Empire Theatre, Holborn. It read:

> *The Performer, December 15, 1910.*
> *A Stand For Justice: Houdini's Protest*
>
> *For some mysterious reason, surprisingly little attention has been given in the daily papers to a remarkable 'scene' at the Holborn Empire last Thursday, when Houdini made a plucky and public-spirited protest against prevailing matinee methods. We must, we suppose, attribute to the present obsession of politics the scant attention given to a very unusual incident, of interest alike to the public and the profession.*
>
> *Having received an intimation from the management that, although he was topping the week's bill, his services would not be required at the Thursday matinee, 'owing to the length of the programme', Houdini expressed himself perfectly agreeable to this arrangement, subject to the condition that due intimation should be given to the public that he would not be appearing.*
>
> *This condition not being complied with, he took an opportunity of going on to the stage at the conclusion of one of the matinee turns in order to quietly explain the reason for his non-appearance and to show that it was not his fault that he was breaking faith with the public. He did not urge the audience, as was stated in some reports, to stay until he appeared, but said that he assumed some at least had come to see him perform and that it seemed to him such were certainly to have their money back if they did not see him.*
>
> *The performance went on quietly until 'God Save the King' when the audience took the matter into its own hands, and refused to disperse, calling for Houdini to appear. After a scene of considerable excitement, 150 persons ultimately accepted the management's offer of vouchers for another performance and left the building, but the great bulk of the audience remained until after the conclusion of Houdini's performance at the first evening house, when they trooped out, leaving the place only a quarter full.*
>
> *The queues which formed up for the first house had in the main to be accommodated at the second house, and great difficulty was experienced in controlling the further arrivals for the second performance.*
>
> *The audience's just appreciation of Houdini's protest was voiced in the remarks of a Labour leader who helped to beguile the interval between the afternoon and evening houses by making a speech. He said that he had frequently attended such matinees, and had always attributed the frequent*

failure of some one or more well-known artists to appear to his (or her) personal indifference or indolence, but that now they knew the real reason why the public were disappointed.

In view of a managerial allegation to the afternoon audience that Houdini was not allowed to appear because he had broken his contract, we quote from a further considered protest with which Houdini prefaced his performance at the first house in the evening. He said:

'Before proceeding with my performance this evening, I believe that there is an explanation due to a great many who are assembled here as to the cause of my non-appearance here this afternoon, and if it would interest you to hear, I will explain. I wish to inform you that it is positively no fault of mine, because I was here in the building, ready to work, but the management refused to allow me to go on. I will read a number of letters that I have here, which thoroughly explain the case, and I wish to inform you that I have played a good many weeks on this tour, and never knew exactly where I was going until a few days ahead. I was billed to appear at the Holborn a short time ago, and, without any notification whatever, I was sent to Woolwich, and the public received no explanation why I did not appear here.

Very likely a great many thought that I had broken faith with the public, and last night I received a letter, dated the 6th, after the second performance (about 9 o'clock) which was 33 hours later than dated, notifying me that my services were not required for the matinee performance.'

Having quoted this letter and his reply stating the condition on which he was agreeable to the arrangement, Houdini continued:

'Now, ladies and gentlemen, I wanted to keep faith with the public, and informed the management that I would give the salary that I was earning at the matinee to the V.A.B.F. if they would only allow me to appear, as I knew my reputation was at stake. Being billed, and not appearing, what would the public think? Despite this, I was not allowed to appear, and I trust that those who are assembled here this evening will see my motive in allowing the public to know the real cause of my non-appearance, and that it was positively not my fault'.

The first result of this dignified protest was that Houdini's services were, notwithstanding notice to the contrary, requisitioned for the Saturday matinee.

Houdini, in his speech to the audience that evening, was forcible and to the point, informing them that it was the greatest compliment that had ever been paid him, an audience waiting seven hours in a theatre for him, and that he would never forget it, and he never will.

A newspaper reported at the time:

London, England: Holborn Empire besieged by crowd inside and outside. Unparalleled scenes witnessed in High Holborn. Police reserves called out.

A packed house, to show its disapproval of the management's action, remains at the Holborn Empire, from 2:00 to 9:00 P. M., waiting for Houdini's appearance as advertised. Police forces were called out as the matinee crowd, refusing to leave the theatre, the evening crowd blockaded traffic, being unable to gain admittance. Unparalleled scenes witnessed in High Holborn.

The *Sevenoaks Chronicle and Kentish Advertiser* of Friday 16 December reported:

A strange scene occurred at the Holborn Empire during a matinee performance. Houdini, the Handcuff King, was billed to appear but his turn was not forthcoming. Instead, Houdini came on to stage in his ordinary attire and made a short statement to the effect that he was not allowed to give his entertainment. He also advised the audience to stay in their seats and refuse to leave them until his performance was allowed. They did. When the time came, about five o'clock, for the clearing of the hall in order to let in the crowd for the first evening performance, the afternoon's audience refused to budge. They were still there in large quantities at six o'clock. The police were called in but no attempt was made to clear the house.

The management, to conciliate them, issued tickets enabling them to see another performance. Some were satisfied with these but an orator who spoke from the pit had quite a large audience.

Gradually they dribbled out in twos and threes, though many were still in their seats when the crowd outside was let in. These the management did not attempt to interfere with.

When asked about it, an official casually remarked that they did not take much notice of the trouble. He added that they often have little bothers of that sort. No explanation was given as to why Houdini's performance was not allowed.

Houdini's next venue was again at the Coliseum Theatre, Glasgow between 12 and 17 December followed by a visit to the Empire Palace Theatre in Edinburgh between 19 and 24 December.

When he arrived in Edinburgh, he noticed that many of the children didn't have shoes in the cold weather so he arranged for 300 boots to be handed out at a special performance for the Scottish youngsters. However, word spread like wildfire and many more children turned up to the show than he had expected so

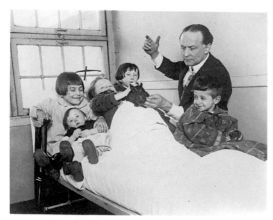

Houdini happily gave shows at hospitals for sick children.

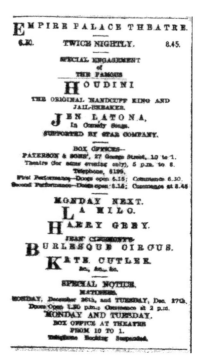

An advert for Houdini's show at the Empire Theatre, Edinburgh which ran between 19 December and 24 December 1910.

he took the rest to the nearest cobbler's shop and he made sure that they all had a pair. Houdini was known for his generosity and was a benefactor to orphans. It was also the ideal time to perform such a deed as it was approaching Christmas and his last show in Edinburgh was on Christmas Eve.

His friend, Arthur Conan Doyle, later wrote of the event, 'He was so shocked at the bare feet of the kiddies that he had them all into the theatre, and fitted them then and there with 500 pairs of boots. He was never too busy to give a special free performance for the youngsters... he was the greatest publicity agent that ever lived.'

The *Scotsman* from 22 December reported:

Extraordinary interest was shown in the challenge to Houdini, the Handcuff King, which was carried out last night on the stage of the Empire Palace Theatre, Edinburgh.

Three expert joiners challenged the performer to escape from a large and strong wooden box or chest which they specially constructed, the condition being that after Houdini had entered it they would nail down the lid, rope the box and nail the ropes to the wood.

The challengers also demanded the right to re-nail each board before Houdini took his place within. The theatre was crowded in every part, and the audience followed the exhibition with the keenest attention. A large committee was appointed, and they took their places on the stage to see that no trickery was practised. The chest was brought on the stage, and the carpenters carried out thoroughly their condition of re-nailing all the boards composing the structure. *Afterwards they drilled air holes in it, and when Houdini entered they fastened down the lid with nails in the most workmanlike fashion. The box was bound with ropes, which were also nailed to the wood.*

When all had been completed, the box, with the performer in the interior, was obscured from the view of the audience with a canvas pavilion, which completely surrounded it. Meantime the band discoursed music, and the audience watched the stage for the first sign of movement. It was almost twelve minutes before the drapery in front of the pavilion was swept aside, and Houdini appeared, showing the box apparently intact, and in the same condition as before he entered it. As he said jocularly, the only difference was that, whereas before he was inside, he was now outside. The audience, after recovering from their surprise, cheered the performer enthusiastically.

The *Edinburgh Evening News* of 24 December reported:

For the second time this week, Houdini picked up the gauntlet thrown down by local challengers and again succeeded in completely bewildering his opponents by his mystifying 'escape'. The challenge was by Messrs. Carson and Leighton in the terms we published the other day. Houdini read this out at the second 'house' of the Empire Palace Theatre last night and expressed himself as being willing to attempt the escape on the condition that the fastenings around the neck did not prevent his breathing. This was agreed to and the 'trussing up' process commenced. When the straitjacket was being adjusted, a 'strong-man' was introduced by the challengers who devoted himself to the business of compressing Houdini to half his natural bulk. When all was fastened, the performer could stand only with difficulty but managed to let himself down full length on the floor. The straps around the ankles and above the knee allowed of a slight bending of the legs, but this was enough for Houdini, and presently the restriction above his knee was seen to give, a smart jerk getting rid of it completely.

The exertions, however, had completely tired the little man out and for a minute or two, he lay prone breathing heavily. Getting to work again, he slipped his feet from their binding and the audience, who by this time were raised to a pitch of the highest enthusiasm, became aware that the shoulder girthing was showing a disinclination to stay on, it too coming away. The rest was easy, a wriggle brought the large strap of the straitjacket out of its 'keeper' and within less than 15 minutes gone, a very much exhausted Houdini crept out of the canvas bag to receive the congratulations of his challengers whose expressions were perfect studies of amazement.

Houdini's last engagement of 1910 was at the Empire Theatre, Newcastle between 26 and 31 December.

Chapter Eleven

1911 – The Brewers' Challenge

Houdini's first shows in 1911 were at the Hippodrome in Bolton between 2 and 7 January.

This was followed by a visit to the Empire Theatre in Nottingham between 9 and 14 January followed by performances at the Empire Theatre in Birmingham between 16 and 21 January.

The first well-recorded appearance came next at the Empire Theatre in Bradford between 23 and 28 January. The event was reported in the local newspaper:

HIPPODROME, BOLTON.
MONDAY NEXT AND DURING THE WEEK.
6-50   TWICE NIGHTLY   9.
MATINEE EVERY MONDAY. 2-30.
HOUDINI
THE ORIGINAL HANDCUFF KING AND JAIL BREAKER.
Tom Bryce & Ella Maynard.   Edith Harmer.
Escourt,   Toltec.   Francis & May
HIPPODROME   PICTURES.
HARRY LEVAINE,
The Great Eccentric Comedian in all his Latest Successes.
FOR PRICES SEE DAY BILLS.

An advert for Houdini's act at the Hippodrome, Bolton between 2 January and 7 January 1911.

Houdini is the 'star turn' at the Empire, and, as demonstrating a sustained interest in him as the original handcuff king and gaol breaker, there were two large houses last evening to witness two astounding feats. One was in full view of the house from first to last. Amid a volunteer committee of ten persons upon the stage he was put into a straitjacket such as is used for refractory patients in asylums, the straps being tightly buckled behind and his arms crossed in the sleeves, and also strapped up as closely as strong men could make it. Houdini then worked his captive form to such purpose that in a minute or so he was a free man, able to hand back the fearful garment to those who thought they had held him securely bound.

The other feat was still more mysterious, although he described it as a trick. He was put into a sort of large milk can, filled with water so that he was entirely submerged, the lid being secured by about half a dozen padlocks. Within very little time, Houdini appeared from the curtain cubicle, and all of the padlocks had been unlocked. The water was still in the tank. Houdini intimated that he was open to accept challenges during the week.

In a good all-round bill the Hadj-Mohammed troupe of acrobats and pyramid builders give a performance which is a masterpiece of its kind. Lee and Kingston, in the sketch 'A Resourceful Lover' are very clever and amusing.

In Jean Clarmont's burlesque circus trained roosters, ponies, a donkey and a dog are utilised with entertaining results. Other turns are by George Rae, Scotch comedian and dancer; Lizzie Glenroy, Scotch comedienne and speciality dancer; the Rawsons (Miss Maggie and Master Jack) in a musical performance; Luigi Salvino, boy instrumentalist; and Fred Shepherd, comedian. There are also new pictures.

Houdini's next appearance was at the Palace Theatre, Hull between 30 January and 4 February followed by a visit to the Empire Theatre, Leeds from 6 until 11 February.

During the appearance in Leeds, Houdini performed the popular milk can escape. However, instead of water, the can was filled with beer as part of a challenge from local brewers, Joshua Tetley and Sons. Houdini was teetotal and it was said that he was overcome by the fumes and passed out while performing the trick and was then saved by Franz Kukol, his chief assistant, who realised that something was amiss and wrenched the can open.

However, an audience member, writing years later to the *Yorkshire Evening Post* of Saturday 22 December 1928, told a different story:

When the curtain went up, the barrel of ale was on a gantry and four brewers' men were on the stage. To a lively tune by the orchestra, they tapped the barrel and filled a jug. They poured out a glass and handed it to Mrs Houdini and she put it to her lips but did not drink any. Then Houdini pretended to take a drink. Then the brewers' men had a glass each. After that, they filled up a tin (which was something like the milk churns you see on the railway) with beer.

Houdini, who was in bathing costume, kissed his wife, and went head first into the tin. Immediately, half-a-dozen men, who were on the

Brewers Challenge Houdini!

Mr. HARRY HOUDINI,
  Empire Theatre, Leeds.

Dear Sir,—
  We herewith **challenge you to allow four of our Employees to fill that tank of yours with beer,** and if you accept our defiance, name your own time. Our men will be at your disposal with the required amount of the beverage.

  Awaiting the favour of an early reply.

  JOSHUA TETLEY & SON, LTD.,
      BREWERS, LEEDS.

CHALLENGE HAS BEEN ACCEPTED

FOR

SECOND PERFORMANCE

TO-NIGHT, THURSDAY, FEB. 9TH

AT

EMPIRE THEATRE.

The above Challenge and Acceptance is unique from the fact that it is positively the first time that such an affair has ever taken place in any part of the world.

The Brewers' challenge at the Empire Theatre, Leeds during February 1911.

A poster advertising the prison cell and barrel mystery.

stage as a committee, fastened the lid on with padlocks all round the lid, the padlocks being locked to staples that were on a collar on which the lid fitted. The can was then lifted into a cabinet and the curtains closed. In a very short period, one of the attendants went into the cabinet and almost immediately opened the curtains and Houdini walked out. The tin was then brought out and the padlocks were still fastened.

I don't think it is any secret now but the upper part of the tin telescoped off the lower part and the lid and padlocks had nothing to do with Houdini's either staying in or getting out. Although I met Houdini many times, I never heard of him being stupefied by the beer as his biographer says. But Houdini was a marvellous showman, a contortionist, and a bit of a strong man. Many of his tricks were not wonderful but he was clever enough to make them appear so. And, by the way, a few nights after the beer episode, he did the trick in the can filled with milk.

A challenge from the naval barracks at Chatham for Friday, 17 February 1911.

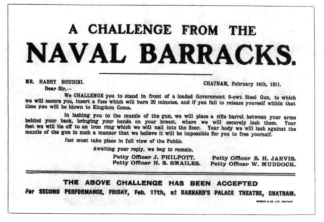

A CHALLENGE FROM THE
NAVAL BARRACKS.

MR. HARRY HOUDINI.   CHATHAM, February 14th, 1911.
    Dear Sir,—
    We CHALLENGE you to stand in front of a loaded Government 8-cwt. Steel Gun, to which we will secure you, insert a fuse which will burn 20 minutes, and if you fail to release yourself within that time you will be blown to Kingdom Come.
    In lashing you to the muzzle of the gun, we will place a rifle barrel between your arms behind your back, bringing your hands on your breast, where we will securely lash them. Your feet we will tie off to an iron ring which we will nail into the floor. Your body we will lash against the muzzle of the gun in such a manner that we believe it will be impossible for you to free yourself.
    Test must take place in full view of the Public.
    Awaiting your reply, we beg to remain.
                    Petty Officer J. PHILPOTT.   Petty Officer B. H. JARVIS.
                    Petty Officer H. S. SMAILES.   Petty Officer W. MUDDOCK.

THE ABOVE CHALLENGE HAS BEEN ACCEPTED
For SECOND PERFORMANCE, FRIDAY, Feb. 17th, at BARNARD'S PALACE THEATRE, CHATHAM.

While Houdini was at Leeds, a crowd of 600 children followed him from the theatre, after the afternoon performance, to his lodgings and then followed him back for the evening performance.

Houdini next appeared at the Barnard's Theatre in Chatham from 13 until 18 February. While in Chatham, he accepted a challenge from four naval officers which read:

> We challenge you to stand in front of a loaded Government 8-cwt, Steel Gun, to which we will secure you, insert a fuse which will burn for 20 minutes, and if you fail to release yourself within that time you'll be blown to Kingdom Come.
>
> In lashing you to the muzzle of the gun, we will place a rifle barrel between your arms behind your back, bringing your hands on your breast, where we will securely lash them. Your feet we will tie off to an iron ring which we will nail into the floor. Your body we will lash against the muzzle of the gun in such a manner that we believe it will be impossible to free yourself.
>
> Test must take place in full view of the Public.

The house was packed on the night of the challenge and Houdini was bound and tied to the muzzle of the gun as stated. He quickly kicked off his shoes and amazingly untied most of the knots with his toes. Although the police chief had not allowed the fuse of the gun to be lit on safety grounds, Houdini still managed to escape with plenty of time to spare.

During February, Houdini met with Alfred Arnold, a police chief, in Castle Gardens, Rochester, to arrange an escape from a police cell. It's assumed that Houdini appeared in Rochester in the week of 20 to 25 February as photos taken at the time are marked February 1911. There's a week missing after this venue.

The next venue was the Empire Palace, Sheffield where Houdini appeared between Monday 6 March and Saturday 11 March. While there, he amazed audiences with the straitjacket and milk can escape.

A challenge was made to him on Wednesday 8 March by Henry Brady, a tarpaulin and sunblind maker of Moorhead, Sheffield. The challenge involved Houdini escaping from a padded cell suit. Houdini accepted the challenge on the condition that there was no danger of strangulation from fastenings around the neck. The challenge took place during the second performance on Friday 10 March.

From Sheffield, Houdini travelled to Cardiff to appear at the Empire Theatre in Cardiff commencing on 13 March and finishing on 18 March.

Houdini, complete with walking stick, in Castle Gardens, Rochester during February 1911. (*Image courtesy of Medway Archives http://www.medway.gov.uk/*)

Houdini pictured with Alfred Arnold, a police chief, in Castle Gardens, Rochester, during February 1911. (*Image courtesy of Medway Archives http://www.medway.gov.uk/*)

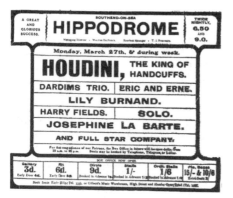

Houdini played at the Hippodrome at
Southend-on-Sea between 27 March and
1 April 1911.

The *Cardiff Western Mail* of Tuesday
14 March read: '*At the Empire Theatre,
Queen Street for the week commencing
Monday 13th March.*

*A brief press report said Houdini
would vary his show during the week.
On Monday he escaped from a large
iron can filled with water. He also*

The Hippodrome at Southend-on-Sea where
Houdini played between 27 March and 1
April 1911.

*showed cinematograph films of himself flying an aeroplane while in Australia, and
of his jumping shackled hand and foot over a bridge in Philadelphia.*

Houdini celebrating
his birthday in
Huddersfield in April
1911. Pictured with him
is his dog, Bobby.

This was followed by performances at the Hippodrome, Southend-on-Sea between 27 March and 1 April.

A challenge by four local joiners, which requested that Houdini escape from a wooden box on 31 March, was published in the local newspaper. At the request of the manager of the Southend Hippodrome, Houdini appeared at a private engagement at a local boat club.

The next venue was at the Palace, Huddersfield where he played between 3 April and 8 April.

A photo shows Houdini celebrating his birthday in Huddersfield. He is pictured in front of his car, surrounded by flowers, with his small dog, Bobby. The photo is marked 6 April although Houdini's birthday was actually 24 March. However, it's recorded that both Houdini and Hardeen claimed his birthday was on 6 April and Houdini wrote much later: 'Re the birthdays, I shall celebrate mine always on April 6th. It hurts me to think I can't talk it over with Darling Mother as SHE always wrote me on April 6th, that will be my adopted birthdate.'

Houdini had several dogs which were much loved. The first, Charlie, accompanied the Houdinis on their first European tours. When Charlie died in 1911, they were heartbroken. In his diary, Houdini wrote: 'Charlie, our dog, dying. Have taken him away from Surgeon Thompson so he can die at home. Bess crying. I don't feel any too good.'

Bobby, a fox terrier, appears in the photo so must have been bought in

Houdini with his dog, Bobby. In the background is a poster advertising an appearance at the Palace Theatre in Halifax. (*Image courtesy of John Cox http://www. wildabouthoudini.com/*)

6.30	**HIPPODROME.** TWICE NIGHTLY	9.0
S	The World Famous	**S**
T	Houdini,	**T**
R	Houdini,	**A**
O	The Original	**R**
N	HANDCUFF KING	
G	And	
	JAIL BREAKER.	
	WILL. DRISCOLL.	
	IRENE MAY.	**A**
	TALLY-HO TRIO	**R**
A	In their Hunting Skit.	
R	F. V. ST. CLAIR,	**T**
R	"The Song Mill."	
A	ALBERT McKELVIN.	**I**
Y	HIPPODROME PICTURES. The Celebrated American Players,	**S**
	MARVIN & RHYDE.	**T**
O	SYD MAY, Renowned Mimic and Popular Star.	**E**
F	NO CHARGE FOR BOOKING IN ADVANCE.	**S**

An advert for Houdini's show at the Hippodrome, Portsmouth where he played between 10 April and 15 April 1911.

SATURDAY, APRIL 15, 1911.

Palace & Hippodrome,

7. BURNLEY. (Tel. 426.) **9.**

TWICE NIGHTLY.

MONDAY, APRIL 17th.

HOUDINI,

THE ORIGINAL HANDCUFF-KING AND GAOL BREAKER.

TOM & NEIL Comedy Boxing and Wrestling Act. "Clothes makes the man."
ENZER TRIO, Jugglers and Ju-jitsu Champion. HAYDEE'S Miniature Vaudeville THEATRE.
DOROTHY WATSON, Entertainer at the Piano. College Chums."
DAVID & MARRIOTT, Operatic Vocalists.

THREE KRAKES, In Comedy Act, "THE ELECTRIC TRAM CONDUCTOR."

MATINEE, Monday at 2-30.

Next week: The World-Renowned DARRACQ, the Sensational Motorist.

A newspaper advert for Houdini's show at the Palace and Hippodrome in Burnley during April 1911.

BARGEMEN CHALLENGE HOUDINI.

HOUDINI, Burnley,
Palace & Hippodrome April 17th, 1911.
Burnley

Dear Sir,
The three undermentioned bargemen HEREBY CHALLENGE YOU to allow them to rope you up, after a sailor's fashion, to a heavy eight feet plank.

They will bind a broomstick behind your knees, then securely cord your wrists under the stick, one on each side of knees.

In this trussed up position they will lay you on your back, YOUR NECK ROPED OFF AT ONE END OF THE PLANK, your feet at the opposite end, and your entire body firmly lashed to this eight feet plank, which is now beneath you.

You must make the attempt to escape in full view of the audience, no cabinets or scenery to be used, otherwise this challenge is null and void.

In behalf of the bargemen,
R. BALDWIN,
R. WATKINSON,
ADAM ASHCROFT

I herewith await your reply.—Yours truly,
GEO. READMAN,
Horse Supt., L. & L. Canal Co.

P.S.—I retain the option of changing the names of one or more of the bargemen mentioned.

The Challenge is accepted by Houdini under the conditions that all fastenings encircling his neck must be tied off with fixture knots, so that during his efforts to release himself THERE WILL BE NO DANGER OF STRANGULATION.

Test takes place at Palace-Hippodrome, 2nd House, THIS (Wednesday) EVENING, April 19th, 1911.

SEATS MAY NOW BE BOOKED. Box Office open continuously from 10 a.m. to 11 p.m.

Palace Theatre & Hippodrome, Burnley.

TUESDAY, APRIL 25, AT 8-0.
DOORS OPEN 7-30. CARRIAGES at 4-45 p.m. TOUR DIRECTION—BARING BROS.

Grand CONCERT RECITAL,

By the ARTHUR NEWSTEAD CONCERT PARTY, including Arthur Newstead, the Famous Pianist; Madame Sobrino, Soprano; Mr. Armstrong Dash, Violinist; Miss Winifred Ponder, Contralto; Mr. Percy Williams, Accompanist. Stalls numbered and reserved, 3/4 unreserved, 2/6. Circle, numbered and reserved 1/6; unreserved 2/-; 1/-, 1/-. Special arrangements for Schools. Box Office now open, 11 to 3 and 5-30 to 10-0. Telephone 426.

Bargemen challenge Houdini at Burnley on 17 April 1911.

the same year. Bess later said that she'd originally seen Bobby in a butcher's shop in Harlem and tried to give him a bone. The butcher wouldn't let the dog have the bone so Bess bought him so that she could feed him. Houdini taught the dog how to escape from miniature handcuffs as well as a specially made straightjacket. He named him 'Bobby the Handcuff King'. He also said that he was the 'greatest somersault dog who ever lived.' In 1918, Bobby's escape act headlined at the dinner of the 14th Annual Society of American Magicians. Bobby died on 15 December 1918, after the Houdinis had had him for eight years.

Houdini's next two appearances were at the Hippodrome in Portsmouth between Monday 10 April and Saturday 15 April and at the Palace in Burnley between 17 and 22 April.

The *Burnley Express* from April 1911 carried the story of Houdini's visit:

During the week, Houdini received another challenge, this time from a number of joiners. It was contained in the following letter:-

'We, the undersigned experienced carpenters and joiners, hereby challenge you to call at our workshop, where we will construct a large and strong box or chest from heavy timber; if you enter this we will nail you in, rope it up and finish by nailing the ropes to the box. We defy you to make your escape without demolishing the same! In fact, you may call any day during our dinner hour, and we will give you the finest, fixing up you have ever had.

(Signed) W.H. Barnes, Wm Cook, Walter Rushworth, employees of Clegg Bros., Blakey Street Sawmills, Burnley.'

Houdini accepted the gage of battle, and the contest took place at the second house last night.

There was a huge crowd, every inch of the theatre being occupied and Houdini had a great reception. The box, a sturdy affair, of strong boards, was brought on, and the men who made it declared it to be genuine, whilst Houdini offered to forfeit £25 if it could be proved he had tampered with it in any way.

To make doubly sure, the joiners put a few more scores of nails in it, and after examining Houdini, fastened him in. The box was then roped, and the ropes nailed to the wood, and when the case was put under the cabinet, it seemed impossible for anything but a needle to get out.

The waiting was not a very entertaining event, and five and ten minutes passed with the audience still staring at a curtain, behind which all was noiseless. At the end of 14½ minutes, however, Houdini appeared, perspiring but triumphant, and was well received with a yell of delight. To all appearances, the box was as it was when he was nailed in – except Houdini was on the outside! The carpenters went to examine it, and the box was also taken outside for public inspection.

The escape, or the means of it, is a mystery. It appeared quite beyond trickery, and yet the feat was accomplished, and Houdini added one more success to his list.

A Burnley youth giving the name of Jessop W. Herbert has written to Houdini offering to be placed in his water cabinet, 'taking all the chances of failure,' and as the gentleman, who considers he is able to extricate himself from the contrivance, has been most persistent, he will be given an opportunity of trying tonight.

HOUDINI'S VISIT TO BURNLEY.

After an absence of nine years, we are next week to have a visit from Houdini, who, by his marvellous escapades from manacles, gaols, and other buildings, in which he has been tethered by police officials as an experiment, has been described as the world's handcuff king. Great interest has been aroused in Houdini's forthcoming performances—there will be a matinee on Monday—at the Palace and Hippodrome, especially seeing that when he was here previously he gained an easy exit from the old Keighley Green Police Station.

A newspaper article concerning Houdini's visit to Burnley.

A further newspaper report from April 1911 read:

A thoughtful Houdini taken in a photographic studio.

Houdini, the handcuff king, made a most remarkable escape from the 'woven' bonds of local bargemen on Wednesday evening. Mr George Readman, horse superintendent of the Leeds and Liverpool Canal Co., on behalf of Messrs, R. Baldwin, R. Watkinson and Adam Ashcroft, on Tuesday issued a challenge to Houdini which the lock-breaker promptly accepted.

The Palace Theatre and Hippodrome, at the second house on Wednesday evening, was crowded to see Houdini escape from the ropes of the bargemen and many hundreds of people were unable to gain admission. The bargemen bound Houdini by the seafaring method of 'splicing' the ropes, or 'weaving' the strands, instead of making knots. The binding was remarkably well done and occupied 25 minutes. Before he began to break his bonds, Houdini explained that this kind of binding was not what he had expected and made his attempt to free himself much more difficult. He then began the struggle, an intensely excited crowd watching his every movement. A full quarter of an hour elapsed before he seemed to have made any impression at all, but it could then be seen that he was freeing his legs. Once he had accomplished that, the rest seemed fairly easy and ten minutes later, he was absolutely free. At the conclusion, he was almost exhausted but was gratified with the tremendous cheering which greeted his successful effort.

Houdini next played at the Hippodrome in Southampton between 24 and 29 April. An advert for his appearance at the Hippodrome read:

HIPPODROME
SOUTHAMPTON
6.55 TWICE NIGHTLY 9.0
MONDAY APRIL 24TH, 1911
And During the Week.
The World Famous
Houdini

The Original Handcuff King and Jail Breaker.
ARCHIE PITT,
Comedian and Raconteur.
ETHEL NEWMAN,
In Comedy Monologue, 'Her Wedding Day'.
BILLY HOBBS,
Coon Comedian and Dancer.
SUSIE AND PROTTI,
Continental Acrobatic Dancers.
HIPPODROME PICTURES,
Return visit of the Mimetic Comedienne
CISSIE CURLETTE,
After her Remarkable Successful American
tour in new songs and old favourites.
THE NORMAN AND LEONARD TRIO
Present a New Musical Incident –
'Ye Squire's Dance'
PRICES AS USUAL
First Performance - Doors open at 6.40; commence at 6.55
Second Performance - Doors open at 8.50; commence at 9.0
NO EARLY DOORS
Box Office 10 till 4. Telephone No. 478.

Carried in *What's on in Southampton* for the week ending April 29, was an article about Houdini's forthcoming appearance:

Houdini, the handcuff king and jail breaker visits Southampton this week. In his present act, he remains under water a longer time than anyone has ever yet succeeded in doing. Houdini in addition to his wonderful skill in prison breaking is a remarkably plucky man. Some years ago, he was by arrangement, escaping from a certain famous prison. It so happened, however, that one of the sentries had not been warned. Catching sight of the supposed prisoner about to clamber up a lofty wall, he put his musket up and threatened to shoot him if he did not at once come back. Houdini took no notice of the warning and the man fired, the bullet whistling by Houdini's head. Thoroughly annoyed at the sentry's action, Houdini, instead of pursuing his flight, turned back and rushed furiously at the sentry. Twice the warder fired at him, missing him each time. Nothing daunted, Houdini grappled with the man, snatched his rifle from him, and then boxed the man's ears well, saying as he did so, 'Don't you shoot at Houdini again.'

Another interesting turn will be Miss Cissie Curlette, the quaint comedienne, who always wins loud applause.

On 29 April, Houdini gave his first performance in England of the Water Torture Cell. A special matinee was performed at Southampton at the end of his appearances at the Hippodrome. The matinee was unadvertised and the cost to enter was one guinea, a high price in those days. It is said that the audience consisted of just one person and he was treated to a performance of a playlet with one act and two scenes called 'Challenged' or 'Houdini Upside Down'. To stop the trick being used by other acts, he copyrighted it as a play rather than patenting it as a magic effect.

Houdini's next appearance was at the Swansea Empire between 1 and 6 May. He was challenged to escape from a box made by three local carpenters. The challenge was completed during the second performance on Friday 5 May.

The front cover, featuring Houdini, of *The Magician Monthly* magazine of May 1911. (*Image courtesy of Marco Pusterla https:// smallmagicollector.wordpress.com/*)

Houdini travelled from Swansea to his next appearance at the Hackney Empire which ran from 8 to 13 May.

While appearing at the Hackney Empire, he was challenged by Messrs. Waters Brothers, of 10 Brett Road, to escape from an air-tight galvanised can, filled with milk to the brim. The escape took place during the second performance on Wednesday 10 May.

During May, the Great Lafayette, a friend of Houdini's, was killed in a tragic fire at the Empire Music Hall. Lafayette arrived in Edinburgh on 30 April 1911 with his dog, Beauty, which had been given to him by Houdini. Beauty, a pit bull, was much loved by his owner and travelled everywhere with him. A day after arriving at the Caledonian Hotel, Beauty died of a stroke. Lafayette was inconsolable. Lafayette announced that his own death wouldn't be far off. He insisted that the dog have a human burial but was told that the only way that that would happen was if it was buried in the grave of its owner. He bought a plot for himself at Piersfield Cemetery and arranged for Beauty to be buried there on 10 May.

On the evening of 9 May, at 11pm, the Great Lafayette was on stage, performing before an audience of 3,000. He was performing an illusion called the Lion's Bride which involved a real lion on stage. As the lion roared, a lantern caught fire on the elaborate set. An asbestos fire blanket was brought down. Panic was averted by the conductor who instructed his orchestra to play the National Anthem. This meant that everyone stood up and were quickly ushered to safety.

Behind the curtain, there was panic as the policy of the theatre was that all exits should be locked. There was nowhere to go and several artistes on stage lost their lives. It was reported, at the time, that Lafayette had made it out onto the street but had gone back in to save the lives of both the lion and a black stallion still on stage. He wasn't seen alive again.

The Great Lafayette with his beloved dog, Beauty, which was given to him by Houdini.

At 5am the next morning, a charred body wearing Lafayette's pasha costume was found beside the dead lion and horse. Two other bodies were recovered which, at the time, were believed to be children but were actually those of two midgets taking part in the show.

The following day, Lafayette's solicitor arrived in Edinburgh and voiced concern that the body found wasn't wearing Lafayette's ostentatious rings. However, the body was taken to Glasgow in preparation for the funeral. Three days later, a workman sifting through the rubble found a severed papiermâché hand which pointed to the spot where an overlooked body lay. The body, adorned with rings, was later identified as Lafayette.

The funeral of the Great Lafayette took place on Sunday 14 May. Houdini sent a wreath in the shape of the head of his dog, Beauty. The event was covered in the *Fife Free Press and Kirkcaldy Guardian* of Saturday, 20 May 1911:

The funeral of the chief victim of the Edinburgh Empire Theatre disaster, Sigmund Neuburger, known throughout the music-hall world as 'The Great Lafayette' took place on Sunday afternoon to Piershill Cemetery, Edinburgh, in the eastern side of the city. The terrible nature of the disaster with its toll of human life, the mysterious personality of the dead illusionist with that compound of Oriental fatalism which showed itself in his actings prior to the occurrence, and the extraordinary turn of events whereby even in death and cremation illusion should linger, all went to provide elements that invested the funeral rites with peculiar interest. Huge crowds lined the route from Morrison Street to the cemetery, a distance of over two miles and the ordinary car and vehicular traffic was suspended.

The urn containing the remains of the 'Man of Mystery' was a massive oak, with a raised three-tier canopy lid. It bore the following inscription on a silver plate: 'The Great Lafayette, who perished in the Empire Palace fire, May 9, 1911.' The urn was lined with lead inside, hermetically sealed. After being deposited in the funeral car, a purple velvet pall on which was worked a white silk cross, hid it from view. It was in keeping with the express desire of the illusionist that the casket containing his ashes should be laid in the vault beside that of his favourite dog 'Beauty,' and great care was taken in the selection of the urn that it should conform to a size that would best meet his expressed wish, and by its position indicate the sense of comradeship that had existed between the dog and his master during life.

The grave of the Great Lafayette complete with a floral tribute from Houdini in the shape of a dog.

The four-horsed car containing the casket with Lafayette's ashes was preceded by the members of Lafayette's company walking bareheaded as it approached the pathway leading to the summit of the mound.

Only about thirty people were present to witness the actual interment of the ashes in the casket containing the embalmed body of 'Beauty.' these included Mr Neuburger (the brother of Lafayette), Mr Sam Lloyd, Mr Nesbit Bailie Smith Elliot, Councillor Boyd, the representatives of the Jewish community and the deceased's more intimate friends. The casket containing the ashes of the 'man of mystery' was enclosed in that containing the embalmed body of Lafayette's favourite dog 'Beauty', and was placed, as was directed by Lafayette himself, between the fore and the hind paws of the dog, the body of which lies *on its side, with open eyes. To be so interred was the master magician's last wish. As the ashes were so laid, the band played the hymn, 'Days and moments quickly flying'.*

The Reverend D Finlay Clark officiated at the graveside and he read a short allocution bearing upon the sad occasion and containing references to the final resurrection of the dead. He also offered up appropriate prayer and this being ended, the casket containing the ashes of Lafayette and the embalmed body of 'Beauty' were slowly lowered into the vault.

Altogether the wreaths numbered over 50. Two or three were very elaborately designed. Mdlle Lalla Selbini, who took the principal lady's part in Lafayette's sketches, and took part in the act 'The Lion's Bride', sent a beautiful floral representation of the proscenium orchestra and drop-screen of a theatre, the whole standing 6ft high by 4ft broad. Picked out in forget-me-nots on the background which formed the drop curtain were the words, 'The Last Act'.

One of the most remarkable was that sent by Houdini, the 'Handcuff King'. It represented the dog, 'Beauty', to which Lafayette was so devotedly attached, a framework of wire and moss being filled in with forget-me-nots. Thousands of flowers had been used in its composition. The inscription read – 'To the memory of my friend, from the friend who gave him his best friend, 'Beauty'.' Mr Martin Harvey's tribute was a plain laurel wreath and there were wreaths also from Mrs and Miss Martin Harvey. Many other wonderful and ornate wreaths were laid.

Meanwhile, ten thousand people witnessed the funeral at Sheffield of the two midgets who lost their lives with Lafayette in the Edinburgh Empire fire. Mounted policemen had to keep the way clear for the procession. A woman was knocked down by a car and seriously injured. The estate of the Great Lafayette was estimated to amount to over £100,000.

Not everyone was so fond of the Great Lafayette. Will Goldin wrote about him years later in his book *Sensational Tales of Mystery Men*:

Callers at my office often become interested in a life size portrait in oils which hangs opposite my desk. Age has darkened it somewhat now, but it is still a picture that commands attention. It shows a slim, middle aged man with pince-nez, his chin resting on his left hand, his eyes gazing thoughtfully into space. There is something queer about the face; it wears an expression difficult to describe. You become uneasy under the steadfast stare from those searching eyes, you feel they are piercing you through and through, and probing into your innermost secrets. Many of my visitors resent this silent examination.

'Who is that man?' they ask.

'*Lafayette,*' *I reply.*

And then perhaps their eyes will wander to a long sword in a glass case hanging on the wall above my head. It is curious how the subconscious mind seems to connect the sword with Lafayette's portrait. They hang at extreme ends of the room, but time and again, I have noticed people glance unconsciously from one to the other.

'*That is Lafayette's sword,*' *I tell them.* '*It was found on his charred body on the stage of the Empire Theatre, Edinburgh. It was given to Harry Houdini, and he passed it on to me.*'

'*Tell us the story,*' *they say.*

So I tell them.

Lafayette was the most hated magician that ever lived. This is strange when one recalls that it was he who established the first class illusionist as an artist worthy of a high salary. He proved to the management of the Holborn Empire that he was worth every penny of the £500 a week he demanded, by taking over the theatre himself for a fortnight, and running it at a huge profit.

He was unsociable to a point of rudeness, and it was for this reason that he was universally disliked. His constant refusals to meet his brother conjurers, both here and in America, made him so intensely unpopular that he was greeted everywhere with the most utter and open contempt.

I have always been convinced that Lafayette was too scared to meet his fellow illusionists. His knowledge of true conjuring was negligible, and, rather than demonstrate his appalling ignorance of the profession of which he was so eminent a member, he preferred to keep his company to himself.

As an illusionist he was wonderful, and as a showman I rank him in the same class as Houdini and John Nevil Maskelyne. Only those who saw the latter two in their heyday can realise how great a compliment this is. But the ability to stage a sensational illusion does not necessitate a knowledge of real magic. It was this knowledge which Lafayette lacked.

He was a mechanical illusionist, pure and simple. He was clever enough to build an entirely different programme from any other magician of his time, and it was in this manner he made his reputation. 'It must be spectacular' was his motto, and well he lived up to it. His act was typified by gorgeous scenery, showy curtains, and loud and soul-stirring music.

Lafayette came from German stock, and started life originally as a scenic artist. It was due to this fact, no doubt, that he picked his illusions with such discriminating taste. I have never learned how he came to adopt magic as a profession, but it was doubtless his position as a scenic painter which first gave him the idea.

He has been called eccentric. That is putting it mildly. I considered him quite mad. He drilled his assistants like soldiers and demanded they should salute him in the street. He bought a diamond collar for his dog. He paid all his accounts by cheque, no matter if the debt was only a penny. A man who does all these things, I repeat, must be mad.

His dog 'Beauty' was his greatest weakness. It was this animal whose portrait was on all the magician's cheques and theatrical contracts. A special bathroom was built for the dog at Lafayette's house in Torrington Square, and at night-time the animal was served with a regular table d'hote meal, complete from soup to sweets. Beauty's portrait hung outside the house with the following quaint inscription beneath: 'The more I see of men, the more I love my dog.'

Lafayette was a great boaster, and resorted to the most irritating form of publicity that has ever been brought to my notice. He had his name and photo printed on a number of small sticky labels, and caused them to be stuck on the exterior and interior of the public lavatories of the town in which he was appearing. This foolish proceeding did him far more harm than good.

He was something of a pugilist too, as a certain Mr. Inglish of Chicago found out to his cost. When Lafayette was performing in that town, he became very friendly with a young and pretty lady whose husband knew nothing of the affair. We can well imagine the gentleman's surprise, therefore, when he entered a restaurant and saw his wife, whom he imagined was appearing as a mannequin in a fashionable dress parade, sitting at a table with the great magician.

'So this is what she does, is it?' thought Mr. Inglish. 'I'll see about it.' He approached Lafayette, and tapped him on the shoulder.

'Do you know this lady is my wife?' he demanded.

'Is that so?' returned Lafayette, not in the least disturbed.

'What do you mean by taking her out to dine without my permission?'

Lafayette made no reply, but hit the unfortunate man a terrific blow on the point of the jaw. It was the easiest way of settling the dispute. Inglish collapsed, and on recovering was asked what he meant by assaulting so eminent a client as Lafayette. Such are the trials of a wronged husband!

How many people know the truth of Lafayette's death? Not many, I can wager. He was burned to death in the disastrous fire at the Empire Theatre, Edinburgh, on May 9th, 1911. It is popularly supposed that he made good his escape, and then returned to save his horse, which was still inside the building. There is little truth in this story.

What actually happened was this. Lafayette always insisted that the 'pass door' – the small iron door which leads from the stalls into the wings – should be kept locked during his performance. This he did in order that no intruders should discover the secrets of his illusions. It was a foolish stipulation, and cost him his life.

When the fire broke out on the stage, he rushed to the pass door to make good his escape. For the moment, he had forgotten it was locked by his own orders. Before he could make his way to the other exit, the stage was a raging mass of flames and smoke, and, overcome by the fumes, he fell unconscious to the boards. When his body was recovered, it was charred beyond recognition.

Houdini played at the Empire in Finsbury Park between 15 and 20 May where he performed a double escape. He was nailed and roped in a box, as he had been done many times before, but the box was then placed in a larger box which was also nailed and roped. Nothing could hold Houdini and he escaped within twelve minutes.

The challenge came from W. Burtle and Sons of 52 Blackstock Road, Finsbury Park. The escape took place during the second performance on Friday 19 May.

Houdini, the elected president, at the Inaugural Meeting of the Magicians' Club in 1911. (*Image courtesy of Marco Pusterla https://smallmagicollector.wordpress.com/*)

Members of the audience at the Inaugural Meeting of the Magicians' Club. (*Image courtesy of Marco Pusterla https://smallmagicollector.wordpress.com/*)

An artist's rendition of the meeting of the Magicians' Club in 1911. (*Image courtesy of Marco Pusterla https://smallmagicollector.wordpress.com/*)

His next appearance was at the New Cross Empire, London between 22 and 27 May.

At 3pm on 27 May, Houdini was elected president of the Magicians' Club which met at the Crown Room of the Holborn Restaurant, London. He promised to pay

An invitation to the inaugural meeting held on 27 May 1911 at the Crown Room, Holborn Restaurant, London. (*Image courtesy of Marco Pusterla https://smallmagiccollector.wordpress.com/*)

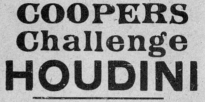

The Coopers challenge to Houdini at Shepherd's Bush Empire on Wednesday, 7 June 1911.

the rent on the club's quarters for the first six months. At the meeting, Houdini was the chairman, Stanley Collins was the secretary and Will Goldston, the organiser.

From London, Houdini travelled to the Palace Theatre, Halifax where he appeared between 29 May and 3 June. While there, he made an escape from underwater at the Whitegate canal lock at Siddal. At 6pm in the evening, a large crowd gathered on the nearby hillside to watch his escape. Employees at the nearby Shaw Lodge Mills watched from their windows in awe.

His last recorded venue of 1911 was the Empire in Shepherd's Bush between 5 and 10 June. Whilst appearing there, Houdini was nailed into a rum punch barrel and managed to escape in 40 seconds. The accompanying poster shows the challenge took place on the evening of Thursday, 7 June, 1911 and that it came from Robert Bedford, Cooper of the Albion Brewery, Shepherd's Bush. Houdini accepted the challenge and stated that 'he would attempt to perform this unheard of feat in the second house.'

In the autumn of 1911 Houdini returned to America and his first show was in Boston where he played to packed audiences.

Chapter Twelve

1913 – The Water Torture Cell

Houdini didn't play any dates in the UK during 1912 but newspapers in Britain still followed his progress reporting that *'he is the lion of the hour in vaudeville in New York just now.'*

His first appearance in the UK in 1913 was at the Empire Theatre in Cardiff between 6 and 11 January.

Houdini was paid £150 for the week to appear at the Empire. A Moss Bros receipt book records this and is signed 'Harry Houdini'. It was reported in the *Cardiff Western Mail* that for the first time, the British public was able to witness Houdini escape from the Chinese Water Torture Cell. He was quoted as saying that the act was first performed on 21 September 1912 at the Circus Busch in Berlin and that the idea had first come to him when he previously appeared in Cardiff. He produced a copy of an older *Western Mail*, from his earlier Cardiff tour, showing illustrations of Chinese tortures. However, copies of the newspaper from that time show no such illustrations.

The poster advertised Houdini as *'The World-Famous Self Liberator'* and showed the Water Torture Cell. He offered £200 to anyone who could prove that it was possible for him to obtain air while in the upside down position.

Cardiff Barracks invited Houdini to escape from a 'padded cell suit'. He accepted the challenge which he completed during the second house of the Friday evening performance.

A poster advertising Houdini's show at the Empire, Cardiff during January 1913.

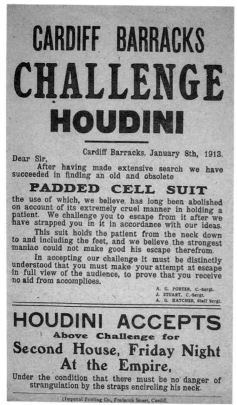

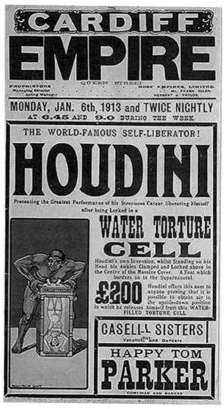

A challenge from Cardiff Barracks to Houdini to escape from a padded cell suit on Friday, 10 January 1913.

A second poster advertising Houdini's show at the Empire, Cardiff during January 1913.

Also on the bill were the Caselli Sisters (vocalists and dancers) and Happy Tom Parker (comedian and dancer).

The following week, Houdini appeared at the Empire in Swansea and his show ran from 13 until 18 January. Also appearing on the bill were Doris Duquesne, Cooper and Lait, Tom Parker, the Great Weiland, the Caselli Sisters, Arthur Young and the Bioscope.

After Swansea, Houdini travelled to the Empire, Bradford where his show commenced on Monday 20 January and ended on Saturday 25 January. Also on the bill were Alec Kendall, Frank Elliston, James Stewart, Alf Chester, the Durant Brothers, Aldon and Loupe, the Real McKays and the Bioscope.

The Era of Saturday 25 January reported:

We are glad to learn from Harry Houdini that his wife has now left the nursing home in London where she was most successfully operated upon by Dr J Forbes

Houdini rehearsing for the Water Torture Cell.

A poster advertising Houdini's show at the Palace, Hull between 27 January and 1 February 1913. Also on the bill were the Durant Brothers.

A photo signed by Houdini on 29 January 1913 while he was at Hull. (*Image courtesy of Kevin Connolly http://houdinihimself.com/*)

Ross. The 'Handcuff King' has received such a number of kind letters of inquiry concerning the health of Mrs Houdini, who, by the way, has now joined him at Bradford, that he is desirous of relieving the minds of his friends and the ever-generous public by announcing, through our columns, the good news of Mrs Houdini's recovery.

It's uncertain what illness Bess was suffering from or what the operation involved. However, by November of 1913, Dr J Forbes Ross died at the early age of 46. His obituary described him as 'a prominent West End surgeon' and stated that he had published a book the previous December entitled, *'Cancer: The Problem of its Genesis and Treatment'*.

Houdini next played at the Palace Theatre in Hull from 27 January until 1 February. An advert for his appearance at the theatre in Anlaby Road on Monday 27 January, shows that tickets were priced at 3d for the gallery, 4d for the Amphitheatre, 6d for the pit, 1s for the orchestra stalls, 1/6 for the grand circle and 5s for the private boxes.

Houdini was advertised as the 'world-famous self-liberator!' and the poster promoted his water torture cell trick. It stated:

Houdini's own invention, whilst standing on his head, his ankles clamped and locked above in the centre of the Massive Cover.
   A feat which borders on the supernatural.
£200 – Houdini offers this sum to anyone proving that it is possible to obtain air in the upside down position in which he releases himself from this water filled torture cell.

Also on the bill were Alf Chester, a comedian; the Durant Brothers (in a funny entertainment, everything in three scenes); James Stewart, the original tramp at the piano; Frank Elliston & Co in a comedy sketch, 'Three and a Fool'; Alec Kendall described at the 'Cheeky Comedian, simply natural, no other excuse'; 'The Real McKays' (Scotland's Representative Juvenile Artists) and Vera Wootton described as 'London's newest star comedienne.'

Also on the bill was the American Bioscope which offered 'New series, up to date.'

A challenge was issued from George Scorrer Ltd while Houdini was at the Palace in Hull. It read:

'Dear Sir,
During your last visit to Hull, you escaped from a Packing Case, but in its construction we were restricted regarding the nails and the manner of driving

them home. WE ARE FAR FROM BEING SATISFIED with the result of that test, and to settle all arguments We defy you to allow us to build A STRONG PACKING CASE, of extra heavy lumber, making use of any size common flat-headed wire nails and no restrictions placed as to the amount or manner.'

The *Era* of Saturday 1 February carried a story under the headline *AN AMERICAN ARTISTE ON ENGLISH CONDITIONS:*

With reference to the cutting from the New York 'Player,' published in our last issue under the above title, we have received from Mr Harry Houdini a copy of a letter which he is writing to the editor of the 'Player,' traversing the wild statements made by the White Rat in his diatribe.

Mr Houdini desires us to publish his letter. He considers that, as the article in question gives so false an idea of English music hall conditions it ought to be severely criticised.

The reply by Mr Houdini is as follows:

To the Editor of the 'Player.'
Dear Sir,
After reading the article of the artiste who so wrongfully attacks English conditions, I feel in duty bound to reply, so as to enlighten many of my brother and sister professionals who may read the article and really believe it.

I do not know who wrote the article but I feel by instinct that it was not an American and if you will look into the artiste whose pen inspired the article, you will find he is not a native-born American. I am simply judging from the tone of the letter in general.

In the first place, I believe it is an artiste who can only have been in England a few weeks, or at the most a month or so, and is judging things with prejudiced eyes.

As I have been in Great Britain on and off more than twelve years, working almost all the time, I am positive the writer of the article is entirely ignorant of manners and affairs in England (speaking theatrically).

In my travels around the world, and I have worked for nearly every manager of any note who plays vaudeville artistes, I can safely say that for fair treatment, for long contracts, and cheap living, England is, without a question of doubt, the best country in the world.

Personally, I think you did very wrong in publishing your letter without investigation, for some of the remarks are entirely unworthy of being published, especially that agents despise American acts, which is not true, as the agents only despise the fresh 'hick' who comes over here, with his 'dis' and 'dat' and 'beau, we tarred 'em over,' and 'cull, we sewed them up' and 'boy, we taught 'em a lesson with the Jasbow.'

Your writer says, 'they have been here a few weeks and looked into conditions carefully.' All he has succeeded in doing is antagonising the entire press against us American performers. I well remember several American performers, failures in London, who returned to America and decried England.

They do not please and then vent their spleen on the inoffensive, unoffending Briton, who has never even heard of them.

English turns also come to America and some make good, others do not do so well, but I very seldom see the English pro running into print and decrying American contracts.

Your informant says that clauses are inserted after you sign them. The entire sentence is a deliberate misstatement, for in all contracts, any and all changes must be initialled by those interested and in any court of law any clauses not initialled are null and void.

I know that there are tricky agents in England but I would like to know a country where there are no tricky agents. If he will look on the Continent he will find that, as a rule, agents in England and America are unborn babes in contract craft compared to a real, good Continental agent.

Some of the material 'pulled' on the continent is worthy of the finest diplomat, as well as the greatest politicians we have, but nothing is illegal in their moves; they simply resort to peculiar methods to gain their object.

Trusting that you will publish this letter in your columns, I beg to remain, sincerely yours,

Harry Houdini.
Member of the IAL since 1901.
Bradford Jan 24, 1913.

Houdini next appeared at the Leeds Empire from 3 until 8 February. Here he was challenged by a local author called S.R. Campion on 3 February. He wrote to say that he thought that Houdini's performance involving the Water Torture

---

HOUDINI

This Week   -   -   -   -   -   EMPIRE, LEEDS.

Business Manager: HARRY DAY, Day's Agency.

An advert announcing Houdini's visit to the Empire, Leeds between 3 February and 8 February 1913.

Cell was excellent. He, however, challenged him to perform the stunt again but with the following conditions – the locks were to be provided by Campion and not examined before the performance, the iron cage had to be discarded, the cell could be put on any part of the stage that Campion desired, the water had to be clean, Campion had to supervise the stunt, Houdini had to escape in four minutes and the locks had to remain the same as Campion had left them.

Houdini accepted the challenge and escaped in the allotted time. Also on the bill was James Stewart, the Three Cape Girls, Aldon and Loupe, Sam Stern, the Durant Brothers, Frank Elliston, Bi Ber Ti and the Bioscope.

The *Yorkshire Evening Post* of Wednesday 5 February carried the story of Houdini's leap into a lake, manacled:

Faithful to his promise, Houdini, who is appearing at the Leeds Empire this week, plunged into the big lake at Roundhay Park this afternoon, before 8,000 people, handcuffed and heavily manacled.

A large platform, standing 14 feet high had been specially erected and a few minutes before 2 o'clock, Houdini mounted it, dressed in the regulation athletic costume, and a police officer handcuffed his hands behind his back, with the regulation handcuffs. The officer also adjusted a pair or irons, which encircled the neck, with a chain running from the hands up to the neck, and a padlock to fasten the chain.

Amidst intense silence, Houdini jumped into the water, which was only five degrees above freezing point. Every minute the crowd grew impatient but when Houdini reappeared with the handcuffs in his hands, and released from the irons, he received a great ovation.

A couple of boats, for life-saving purposes, were close at hand and after Houdini had been safely rowed to the banks, he had to undergo a handshaking ordeal.

It may be interesting to know that Houdini is an expert airman. He was the first successful aviator in Australia. Piloting his Voisin bi-plane, he won the Australian Aero League's trophy at Melbourne on March 15th 1910.

The *Yorkshire Evening Post* of Saturday 8 February wrote about Houdini's appearance at the Leeds Empire:

Houdini issued successfully from the test which he underwent at the Leeds Empire last night when he escaped from a padded cell suit invented by three former members of the Leeds police force. His challengers strapped him into the suit, a sort of combined sack and straitjacket and then, trussed like a chicken, the breaker of bonds began his struggle.

A newspaper advert introducing the Water Torture Cell in 1913.

An advert for Zam-buk in the *Yorkshire Evening Post* of Tuesday, 11 February 1913.

His contortions, as he wiggled serpent-like about the stage, almost made one's bones ache in sympathy and one might have heard a whisper in the house as he strained and shuffled in his strong bonds. A cheer went up from the crowded house when, after seven minutes, the clumsy suit fell to the stage and Houdini stepped forth free.

Houdini next appeared at the Empire in Bristol from Monday 10 February until Saturday 15 February. While at Bristol, he offered £100 for any suggestions of possibilities of a new kind of cell or cage from which he could devise a means of escape.

The *Western Daily Press* of Tuesday 11 February noted:

Houdini, the man of mystery, and also known as the Handcuff King, is the chief turn at the Empire and Hippodrome, Old Market Street, where he presents his latest mystery and last evening, there were crowded houses to welcome him. Houdini is an interesting figure as he claims to be the first human being to fly a mile and in 1910 won the Australian Aero League trophy. He naively added to a Daily Press *representative yesterday that he deserted aviation as it had become commonplace and for two years had devoted his attention to inventing a new and fiendish torture contrivance such as would horrify the most hardened criminal but which he wriggles out of in the most expeditious manner. Houdini was in Bristol four years ago and then mystified the audiences by escaping from all kinds of manacles. On his present appearance, he is endeavouring to arrange with the authorities to allow him to be manacled and thrown from Bristol Bridge. He suggests that a 56lb ball should be attached to his manacled feet, that his hands should be tied behind him, his elbows and knees ironed and generally trussed to the satisfaction of all concerned. He will, after these attentions, escape within a stipulated time. Houdini, however, is still on the alert for new ideas and offers £100 for a suggestion with possibilities of a new kind of torture by which he can devise means of escape.*

Last night at the Empire and Hippodrome, he introduced his water torture cell. This is a chamber filled with water and Houdini's ankles are clamped and locked in the centre of the massive cover. Houdini is then dropped head foremost into the cell, the whole is securely padlocked and iron-bound and there is a £200 guarantee that it is impossible for him to obtain air. Added to this, he is confined within the cell by an iron grill which is only just broad enough to contain him. A committee of inspection last night testified to the proper securing of all locks and then Houdini was suspended head downwards over the tank. After taking a few deep breaths, he was plunged into the water. He was securely locked in and the cell surrounded by curtains. A few minutes elapsed and he appeared amidst thunderous applause, having carried out his undertaking in a most astonishing fashion.

Prior to this performance, he escaped, after many contortions, an orthodox straitjacket properly secured, and a number of able seamen of Bristol issued a challenge. They undertook to truss him to a seven-foot plank in such a way that they thought it impossible Houdini would escape. Houdini, however, accepted the challenge for Wednesday night (second house), providing no slip-knots were used as, he explained, pressure on slip-knots might mean strangulation.

Houdini next travelled to the King's Theatre in Southsea where he appeared between Monday 17 February and Saturday 22 February.

A notice appeared in the *Portsmouth Evening News* of Thursday 20 February which read:

We, a committee of four employees, HM Dockyard, in the ship building department, rated as experts in rigging, slinging and rope tying, herewith deny you to effect your escape from a trussing up we will give you after the obsolete sailor fashion of fastening the raving maniacs or mutineers in the days of the sailing vessels.

If you accept our challenge we stand ready to wager that you will not release yourself.

We intend to lash your body down to a 7ft plank, a broomstick behind your knees, your wrists tied, one on each side, your feet roped off at one end of the plank and your neck fastened to the opposite end.

We will rope and lash you in such a fashion that any movement on your part will be entirely out of the question. Our only condition is that you must make the attempt to escape in full view of the audience. No curtains or screens allowed.

Awaiting your reply, we beg to remain yours truly,

Albert Augustus Blake, 270 Arundel Street, Landport, John Robert Storr, 38 Manchester Road, Fratton, Friend Cronk, 2 King Street, Portsea, A Evans, 40 Herbert Street, Mile End.

Houdini accepted the challenge on the condition that there was no danger of strangulation. The escape took place during the second house on the evening of Friday 21 February. He escaped within half an hour.

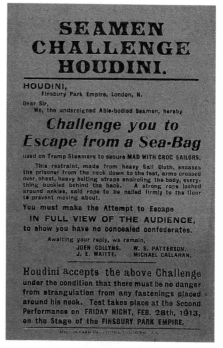

Seamen challenge Houdini at Finsbury Park Empire on Friday, 28 February 1913. (*Image courtesy of Kevin Connolly http:// houdinihimself.com/*)

Robert Falcon Scott's ill-fated team included Lawrence Oates (standing), Henry Bowers (sitting), Scott (standing in front of Union Jack flag pole), Edward Wilson (sitting) and Edgar Evans (standing). Bowers took the photo using a piece of string to operate the camera.

The crowd gathered to see Houdini's leap from Newport Bridge on 5 March 1913. (*Image courtesy of Kevin Connolly http:// houdinihimself.com/*)

Houdini performed the Water Torture Cell escape to packed houses. He promised to perform a diving feat from the South Parade Pier any morning during the week providing that any takings collected were donated to the Scott Antarctic Fund. The fund supported the relatives of the doomed *Terra Nova* Expedition to the South Pole. Most members of Scott's team died while returning home during March 1912 (Edgar Evans had died in February 1912).

His next venue was at the Empire in Finsbury Park between 24 February and 1 March. Houdini accepted a challenge to escape from a sea-bag. On 2 March, he stopped the show to call Franz Kukol onto the stage. He told the audience that Kukol was the best assistant that he'd ever had and that they'd worked together for ten years travelling from Russia to Australia. He then presented Kukol with an inscribed gold pocket watch and chain.

Houdini's setting up of the Magicians' Club in London two years previously seemed to have come to nothing. Lack of funds and a letter from Houdini saying that the rent for the clubroom was too high had meant that the club had progressed

Spectators wait to see Houdini's leap from Newport Bridge on 5 March 1913. (*Image courtesy of Kevin Connolly http:// houdinihimself.com/*)

no further. Houdini decided to correct this and rented quarters at 2 Gray's Inn. The club offered facilities for performing new tricks and illusions, featured books, a writing room, a silence room, a workshop and a museum.

On Monday 3 March, he commenced his show at the Empire in Newport finishing on Saturday 8 March. Houdini jumped from Newport Bridge on 5 March attracting a very large crowd.

The *Nottingham Evening Post* of Wednesday 12 March reported on a court summons for Houdini:

> *At Newport today, Harry Houdini was summoned for obstructing Newport Bridge by giving a public entertainment by leaping manacled from the bridge into the River Usk.*
>
> *The police stated that Houdini, after being warned not to perform the feat, deliberately did so. Thousands of people assembled on the bridge, causing serious obstruction. Houdini, after being turned back by the police, got on to the bridge from the other side by driving up in a taxi-cab.*
>
> *The Chief Constable said he told Houdini he could not give permission for the feat and could not promise that no proceedings would be taken. Houdini's solicitor said his client thought the Chief Constable said he offered no objection. The case was dismissed.*

The incident caused quite a stir and many people took a great interest in Houdini's court appearance. The full story appeared in *The Era* of Saturday 15 March:

> *The remarkable story of how Harry Houdini, the Handcuff King and famous self-liberator, out manoeuvred the Newport police, of how thousands collected to witness his daring leap from Newport Bridge, and of how the traffic was blocked for over an hour was told to the Newport Borough Magistrates on Wednesday, when Houdini was summoned for unlawfully, to the obstruction of passengers, exhibiting a public entertainment on Newport Bridge on March 5 and also for obstructing the highway.*
>
> *The court was crowded. Mr Treharne Morgan, deputy town clerk, prosecuted on behalf of the police and Houdini, who answered the charges in person, was represented by Mr L H Hornby, solicitor, Newport. The case of obstruction was first taken and defendant pleaded not guilty.*
>
> *Mr Morgan explained that Houdini was performing at the Newport Empire last week. Mr J H Milburn, the manager, and Houdini visited the Chief Constable's office and asked if he would give permission for Houdini to jump off Newport Bridge into the River Usk. The Chief Constable replied that he could not give such permission and that he would not give any undertaking, if*

the attempt were made, that a summons would not be issued against Houdini. On the following day, an advertisement appeared in the press intimating that Houdini intended to jump from Newport Bridge into the water at a certain time. In the meantime, the chief constable went into the matter carefully and subsequently came to the conclusion that it would be inadvisable to allow defendant to perform the feat. Consequently, he informed Mr Milburn and Houdini that he could not permit the performance to take place and Mr Milburn and Houdini said that they did not like to break faith with the public after the advertisements had been issued. It was then agreed, proceeded Mr Morgan, that Mr Milburn and Houdini should go to the bridge and be sent back by the police, and Houdini gave his word of honour that he would not attempt to jump from the bridge. On the next day, March 5, about 5.15pm, a motor wagonette drove up to the bridge and in it was a man dressed like Houdini and behind the wagonette was a taxi in which rode Houdini. The wagonette and the taxi were sent back by the police. From four o'clock onwards, large crowds of people had assembled on the bridge, the tram service was stopped, and the roadway completely blocked. At 5.40pm, a taxi drove towards the bridge from the opposite direction and came to a stop in the centre of the bridge. Defendant alighted from it, walked up to and climbed over the parapet, let himself down on to a buttress and plunged into the river – in short, performed the feat that he was advertised to perform.

Mr Hornby: The mere fact of an advertisement in the newspapers is not obstruction and cannot be used in connection with the case. Suppose I inserted an advert to the effect that I was coming from Paris and intended going up in a balloon from Newport, a large crowd would be very likely to collect.

The Chairman (Mr A J Stevens): I am sure they would. (Laughter.)

Mr Hornby: And all the time, I may have no intention of going up in a balloon.

Mr Morgan: The principal ground is that Houdini attended at the bridge and caused a large crowd to assemble.

Mr Hornby: According to your own opening the crowd assembled long before Houdini arrived.

Mr Morgan: I quite agree.

Inspector Cox, of the Newport Borough Police Force, deposed that he was on the bridge at 4.30pm on the day in question and saw a large number of people assembled. An open car and a taxi came up and after a conversation between the Chief Constable and the occupants, they turned back. There were thousands of people on the bridge. About 5.40pm, a taxi came from the opposite direction and drove to the centre of the bridge. Houdini jumped out, mounted the palisade, lowered himself to the buttress of an arch, and jumped *into the water. All the people rushed to one side of the bridge and witness was afraid that the palisading would give way. The passage of the bridge was blocked from 4.30 until six o'clock.*

Cross-examined by Mr Hornby: The taxi was turned back at 5.15pm and returned at 5.40pm from the opposite direction. There were not so many people on the bridge at 5.40 as at 5.15pm and the traffic had been resumed. He did not know that Houdini had had any discussion with the Chief Constable as to which was the safest side of the bridge to jump from.

Mr Hornby: After the taxi was sent back at 5.15, I suppose you thought that Houdini would again appear and go over the bridge? – No, I thought he had gone away.

Mr Hornby: You thought you'd got the better of him? I believe Houdini simply jumped from the taxi, clasped on the manacles, climbed the parapet and plunged into the water? – Yes and he was very smart.

Were other constables nearer to him than you? – Yes.

Did you hear any of the constables say to the taxi driver, 'He will not try it, it is a farce?' – No.

Did they try to stop him? – No, he was too fast.

Mr C E Gower, chief constable of Newport, spoke to Mr Milburn and Houdini visiting his office. The opening statement of Mr Morgan was substantially correct.

Mr Hornby: Houdini asked you for permission to jump from the bridge? – Yes, and I said that I would not give permission or any other undertaking if he attempted the feat, not to prosecute him.

Did you say that you would not give him permission but that you would not put hindrances in his way? – I did not say that.

Do you think that he might have had that impression? – He might have had but I told him I could not give permission.

Did he say on leaving your office, 'Thank you, that is all I want?' – Yes, I think he did say that.

Then he might have been under the impression that you would not put any hindrances in his way? – He might have been.

Did you receive a letter from someone respecting the safety of the bridge as a structure? – Yes.

And was it in consequence of that that you changed your mind in regard to Houdini? – No, it was not.

Did you suggest that he should do his jump at the Docks? – I suggested that he might get permission of the Dock company.

Did Houdini say, 'It is advertised that I am to jump from the bridge and the people will think that I am not keeping faith with them? – Yes.

Did you discuss with him as to the best side to jump from the bridge? – No.

Was there any discussion about a letter? – Yes, I said I would give him a letter that the police were stopping the performance.

Did he say, 'Suppose I get past your men,' and did you say, 'Well, if you do it will be all right?' – No, there was nothing of that kind. I told him if he came up to the bridge he would be stopped and sent back.

Long before Houdini arrived, a large crowd had collected? – Yes.

Then it was not actually Houdini's presence that had attracted them? – It was the anticipation of his presence.

Re-examined by Mr Morgan: Houdini might have had the impression at the first interview that he would not be stopped from jumping from the bridge but he could not have had that impression at the second interview, because he gave a distinct understanding that he would not jump from the bridge.

Mr Morgan: You did not give any undertaking that he would not be summoned? – Certainly not.

Mr Hornby said that Houdini was a showman who went all over the country and the world and he kept in touch with the police. At the first interview with the Chief Constable, he was certainly under the impression that the police would offer no objection to his going over the bridge. The undertaking said to be given by Houdini that he would not jump from the bridge was absolutely disputed. Houdini denied, and denied very strongly, that he gave any such undertaking.

The magistrates were consulting when Houdini interrupted, 'I want my oath against that of the Chief Constable,' he said. 'I did not give an undertaking.'

The Chairman: The case is dismissed.

The second case, that of exhibiting a public entertainment, was then mentioned.

Mr Hornby: One solitary act of athleticism cannot be styled a show, an entertainment or, in the words of the section, 'an exhibition in a caravan'.

Mr Morgan: A taxi-cab and a caravan is a vehicle. The defendant came to the bridge in swimming costume and ready to give an entertainment.

This case was also dismissed without any evidence being given. There was applause in court which was quickly supressed.

Mr Morgan: I intend to appeal in the first case.

The manager of the Empire at Newport, Mr J.H. Milburn, stated that record business had been done, with packed audiences at both houses.

On Monday 17 March, Houdini was at the Olympia, Liverpool where his shows continued to Saturday 22 March.

The Era of Wednesday 19 March reported on the opening of the Magicians' Club:

There was a large and festive gathering at 2 Gray's Inn Road, on Sunday evening, when the Magicians' Club was formerly opened by its president, Mr Harry Houdini. As we stated in our last issue, the new club will provide a long-felt want, as up to the present there has been no special rendezvous for magicians and it should become the headquarters of magic, not only as regards England, but for the whole world.

Conveniently situated just off Holborn, the club premises comprise, on the first floor, a reception and club room, a silence room for correspondence etc.; whilst on the ground floor are a workshop, cloakroom, secretarial offices etc. Luxuriously and tastefully furnished and decorated, the club is replete with every comfort and contains a unique library of technical books and a museum.

Governed by a strong committee of well-known magicians, with Mr Will Goldston at the helm, and with a very moderate yearly subscription, the club should bring together a large following of the art – both professional and amateur. Anyone interested in magic and the kindred arts may join, and Mr Goldston, who has been the prime mover in its foundation, valuably assisted by Mr Houdini and others, is to be cordially congratulated on the result of his hard work and enthusiasm.

Many photos, ornaments and useful articles have been given by well-known masters of magic and just at present the walls of the reception room are adorned with two particular handsome floral offerings: a horseshoe from Mr Houdini and a wand, with the inscription, 'Good luck, M C,' from Mr Goldston. There is a magic clock, which is guaranteed to wake the heaviest slumberer, and remind him of an appointment; an old playbill of Anderson, the Wizard of the North, presented by David Devant; and many other ornamental and serviceable gifts.

Mr Harry Houdini, who was given a very cordial greeting, in formally declaring the club open, paid a warm tribute to its founder, Mr Will Goldston. He extended a hearty welcome to all the members and friends present. It was the only club of its kind in existence, he believed; the subscription fee was very moderate and he sincerely hoped it would be strongly supported. Mr Houdini then read telegrams wishing success to the undertaking from, among others, Mr Chris Van Bern, Mr George Wetton and Mrs Houdini, 'the only handcuff he couldn't escape from', jestingly remarked the president.

The evening was then given over to music, song, magic and merriment. Mr Finlay Dunn gave a humorous sketch at the piano; and others who appeared were Mr Harry Speller (comedian), Mr Cecil Lyle (conjurer), Professor Earle (in card tricks), Harry Houdini (in a clever and neat exhibition of his skill), Mr J Hayman (in parody) and Horace Goldin. The packed gathering, which numbered 130, included many people well-known in the world of magic and variety, in addition to the president and founder being Mr Horace Goldin,

Will Goldston was not only a performer but was employed by Gamages in London where he managed the magic department. He was a lifelong friend of Houdini and was the editor of the Magicians' Annual between 1907 and 1912.

The Hippodrome at Devonport where Houdini appeared between 24 March and 29 March 1913.

Houdini performing the East Indian needle mystery.

Mr David Devant, Dr Wilmar, Mr Oswald Williams, Mr F Cull-Pit, Mr G W Hunter, Mr Harry Day, Mr J Hayman and Mr Finlay Dunn. Mr Stanley Collins is the genial and alert honorary secretary for the first and only club of magic in the world, which already has a membership of 200. It is open daily from 10am till 11pm (Sundays included) and it should be mentioned that the subscription is only a guinea a year and that there is no entrance fee.

Houdini's next appearance was at the Hippodrome in Devonport between Monday 24 March and Saturday 29 March. He had previously played in Plymouth in August 1909. In the early 1900s, Devonport's industry mainly revolved around the navy and the busy dockyard and many in Houdini's audience would have been employed there.

The Era of Saturday 29 March carried a story entitled *HARRY HOUDINI AT THE DEVONPORT HIPPODROME*: It read:

Mr G E Prance, the popular manager of the Hippodrome, Devonport, has as his star turn this week the famous manacled king and self liberator, Harry Houdini, and, thanks to managerial courtesy, our local representative was able on Monday to have a few words with this remarkable man. Mr Houdini, an American by birth, is now thirty-nine years of age. His earliest trick consisted of swallowing needles and thread separately and subsequently expectorating the former duly threaded. This trick he is gratuitously performing at Devonport this week. He then devoted his attention to handcuffs and has submitted himself to all sorts and conditions of manacles but none have yet been discovered to baffle him.

It is his constant effort to introduce some new form of entertainment and after much care and thought, he eventually brought before the public, his water torture cell, a description of which appeared in our issue of a week or two ago. Mr Houdini states that his entertainment entails a terrible physical strain and such being the case, it is his intention to retire after a couple of years' more work. He has never had an accident in performing his tricks but has been very roughly handled by strangers manacling him and who appeared to consider he was made of steel and not of flesh and blood. Mr Houdini is a non-smoker and teetotaller; he further states the show is such a 'nerve-racker' that he invariably sleeps blindfolded, the slightest ray of light always preventing sleep.

The Monday matinee was witnessed by 2,500 bluejackets, whose applause at the termination of the different items was one of the most terrific and gratifying receptions Houdini has ever had.

Houdini's next venue was the Empire Theatre in Newcastle where he played between 31 March and 5 April. To publicise his show, he jumped, manacled, from the Swing Bridge and released himself from his chains underwater to the delight of the gathered crowd.

The Era of Saturday 5 April 1913 carried the story of the jump:

Just on the point of 12 noon on April 1, when the traffic on the Swing Bridge, Newcastle, was at its busiest, a singular and exciting incident occurred. A taxi-cab swung round from Sandhill and was passing over the bridge, when one of the occupants knocked frantically with his knuckles upon the window behind the driver, who at once pulled up. Something was happening inside the car and no sooner had the attention of passers-by been called to the fact, than the door of the taxi flew open and a determined looking man sprang out. Throwing off his coat, he leapt over the barrier on the kerb, rushed across the footpath and scrambled over the side of the bridge, dropping down on the stone buttress.

Three excited men jumped out of the car and followed in wild pursuit. Two of them climbed swiftly over the side of the bridge and down to the platform where the fugitive was now standing, apparently in a state of indecision as to whether to leap into the river or be 'taken'. Before he had taken any action, his two pursuers were upon him and, one of them, drawing chains, handcuffs and other manacles from a large bag he carried, seemingly by a miracle of good fortune, they quickly had the shackles upon their captive, whose hands were handcuffed behind his back, with manacles above the elbow joined by a chain encircling his neck and doubling over his chest, where they were fastened with a heavy padlock.

Then the onlookers, who by now numbered hundreds, gave a gasp, for when the captors stepped back and took a breath after their exertions, the man in the fetters took the desperate step, leapt from the narrow platform into the water, fifteen feet or more below. A row-boat that happened to be in the offing at the time was brought to the spot where the man had disappeared, now indicated by only a few bubbles. Within ten seconds the diver rose to the surface holding aloft in his left hand the chains, handcuffs and padlock with which, a quarter of a minute before, he had been tightly bound.

Immediately, there went up a great shout of applause, such as that to which men with sporting instincts are wont to give vent when a fugitive baffles the police by superior wit or sheer ingenuity. In the present case, however, the police knew nothing about it. It was Houdini, the famous self-liberator and gaol breaker, who had given a demonstration of his remarkable power and it was with motives reconcilable with those of the boy who visits the pantry first and then asks permission to taste the jam that the thing was carried out so hurriedly.

Also on the bill at Newcastle were the Daunton Shaw Troupe, Jack Marks, Bert Errol, Syd Walker, Russell and Held, Yorke and Adams, Dorma Morgan, Recco and Heinz and the Bioscope.

While in Newcastle, Houdini met up with his friend, Chung Ling Soo, and they attended a séance which Houdini debunked. Eventually, Soo fell out with Houdini over a trick called 'The Expanding Die'. Houdini said that he had the sole rights to the trick, which he'd purchased from Will Goldston. However, Soo was performing the trick in Wales. For ten years, Soo had been dismayed by Houdini's attacks on fellow performers and escapologists. He wrote to Houdini, *I am not jealous of you, neither do I fear you!'*

The following year, Houdini performed the act for the first time in England.

Houdini next appeared at the Empire Theatre in Edinburgh between 7 and 12 April.

The ex-police Constable's Challenge required Houdini to escape from an 'insane restraint bag' which was made by the firm of John Macrae who were saddlers and harness makers of Lothian Road. Houdini accepted the challenge and performed it during the second performance on the evening of Friday, 11 April 1913.

The Scotsman newspaper carried the following story from 8 April:

It was as a breaker of 'prison bars' and shackles that Houdini laid the foundations of a popular career on the music hall stage, but on the occasion of this, his second visit to Edinburgh, he discards his accustomed stock-in-trade, and introduces an act of the sensational type – namely, freeing himself from a 'water torture cell'. After the usual imposing preliminaries, Houdini's feet are securely clamped to a board, which in turn serves as cover for a patent cage-like tank, full to the brim with water, in which he is suspended head downwards in the full gaze of the audience. Multifarious bolts and bars are then affixed, and the curtains drawn – even the voluntary 'committee' being now excluded from the proceedings – and in a minute or two Houdini reappears, smilingly triumphant and dripping wet, all the trappings in connection with the tank in the meantime remaining apparently undisturbed. It is extremely clever, and gets the audience wondering how the trick is done.

Houdini performing the Water Torture Cell stunt.

In addition, Houdini makes a selection from his original repertoire, apparently swallowing independently of each other a packet of needles and a skein of thread, and then reproducing the needles, one and all, nicely threaded. Altogether, it was a capital turn, and was warmly received by the large audiences at both 'houses' last night.

As regards the remainder of the programme, principal place is taken by a melodramatic sketch by Horace Hunter and Company, involving a tangled Russian matrimonial situation, which is handled with a considerable degree of cleverness. Phil Percival raised a hearty laugh by his burlesque ongoings, and some daring features characterise the trick cycling of the Daunton Shaw troupe. Others contributing to a well-sustained programme were Sam Kelly, a Scotch comedian and clever conjurer; Miss Gracie Graham, a singer of attractive songs; Fred Keeton, an eccentric comedian; Bissett and Scott, American freak dancers; and the Robin Collier Trio of singers and dancers.

The *Edinburgh Evening News* of 8 April reported:

In the realm of stage mystery and illusion there are a number of clever artists, but with all their versatility and imposing array of attendants and appurtenances, there is something unconvincing about the show. Not so Houdini, who is the leading figure at the Empire Palace Theatre this week. He performs two feats, one the 'Water Torture Cell' and another the 'East Indian Needle Mystery'. This latter trick – for one has to assume it is a trick – properly comes under the category of things wonderful. On Wednesday night, Houdini proposes to implement a challenge from the employees of a local firm to get out of a box constructed by them.

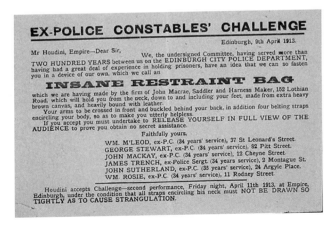

Ex-police constable challenge Houdini to escape from an insane restraint bag on Friday, 11 April 1913 at the Empire, Edinburgh.

Harry Handcuff Houdini.

HOUDINI

PRESENTS HIS OWN ORIGINAL INVENTION
THE GREATEST SENSATIONAL MYSTERY
EVER ATTEMPTED IN THIS OR ANY OTHER AGE!!!

£200 REWARD TO ANY ONE PROVING THAT IT
IS POSSIBLE TO OBTAIN AIR IN THE UP-SIDE-DOWN
POSITION IN WHICH HOUDINI RELEASES HIMSELF
FROM THIS WATER-FILLED-TORTURE-CELL.

A photo signed by Houdini on 25 April 1913 while he was appearing in Sheffield. (*Image courtesy of Kevin Connolly http://houdinihimself. com/*)

A poster showing Houdini in the Water Torture Cell.

Houdini was challenged to escape from an 'insane restraint bag' on 9 April by members of the Edinburgh city police department.

From Edinburgh, Houdini travelled to Glasgow to appear at the Coliseum between Monday 14 and 19 April. He also appeared at the Hippodrome in Hall Craig Street, Airdrie in April although the exact date is unknown. It would have had to have overlapped with one of his other shows so it's probable that he put on a show there while appearing at the Coliseum in Glasgow.

Thousands of people wanted tickets to see Houdini's performance in Airdrie in 1913 but it very quickly sold out. Because of this Houdini put on an extra free show outside. Over 7,000 people turned up to watch a local police sergeant chain and handcuff Houdini on the front steps of the theatre. He soon escaped. Sacks and crates were also produced which he was either tied or nailed inside but again, he soon made his escape.

At the end of the show, Houdini's infamous Water Torture Chamber was produced and filled up by the local fire brigade. As the crowd watched enthralled, Houdini once more made his escape to much applause from everyone who had turned up.

There is a record of the 'Houdini company' travelling by the north-eastern railway from Glasgow to Sheffield on Sunday 20 April.

Houdini next appeared at the Empire Palace in Sheffield between 21 and 26 April. While there, he was challenged by three employees of Sales and Teather of Eyre Street Saw Mills. The challenge involved the employees making a full packing case in front of the audience, for Houdini to get in, the lid to be nailed down and the case secured with ropes. Houdini accepted the challenge and the escape took place during the second house on Friday 25 May.

The *Sheffield Evening Telegraph* of Tuesday 22 April reported:

Anything more mysterious than the astounding feat being performed by Houdini at the Empire this week it is hardly possible to conceive. With his feet in stocks, he is placed, head downwards, in a cell full of water and is secured with locks, but succeeds in escaping in a very short time. He also mystifies the audience with a remarkable East Indian needle trick.

Houdini's next venue was the Birmingham Empire where he appeared between 28 April and 3 May. Clayton Hutton challenged Houdini to escape from a packing case which he insisted was built on stage in front of the audience. Hutton's uncle owned a timber mill at Saltley. Hutton had seen Houdini's act and had gone back stage to meet him. At the time, Houdini was offering £100 to anyone who could produce a case from which he couldn't escape. After hearing Hutton's terms, Houdini agreed as long as he could visit the mill and meet his uncle's carpenter, who was to construct the case.

Houdini arrived at the mill in a Hansom cab complete with a fur-lined coat, carpet slippers and a big cigar. He talked with the carpenter, Ted Withers, before leaving. On the night, the wood to make the box was taken on stage and the box was constructed in front of the audience by Withers. Houdini was then handcuffed and placed in a sack before being put in the box. Withers nailed the lid shut and the rope was then tied tightly around the box. It took 15 minutes for Houdini to escape.

Houdini was meant to have revealed to Hutton in 1920 that he'd paid Withers £3 to hammer only two nails where his feet were so that he could have an easier escape.

Also on the bill at the Birmingham Empire were the Great Weiland, May Henderson, Chris Baker, Gerald Griffin, J.H. Scotland, Bissitt and Scott, the Bioscope, Rich and Rich and Bert Errol.

Supporting the chairman, Harry Houdini, at the Magicians Club Ladies' Night, during May 1913, are Horace Goldin, Will Goldston, Chung Ling Soo, Harry Day, Stanley Collins, Jules Inger, W.C. Zelka, Bennett Scott and others.

The *Dundee Evening Telegraph* of Tuesday 29 April carried a story under the headline *A MAGIC NIGHT WITH FAMOUS CONJURERS* about a meeting of the Magic Circle of which Houdini was president. It read:

How do conjurers spend the one night in the week when they are not busily producing rabbits from opera hats and yards of ribbon from the pockets of unsuspecting members of their audiences?

That was the first question which suggested itself to a press man when he received an invitation to spend Sunday evening at the 'First Ladies' Night' of the Magicians' Club, the one club whose members are all proficient in the black arts.

The answer is that they spend their holidays conjuring to each other and the novices in the magic world watch with awe the successful feats of the experienced adepts, applauding vigorously when coins appeared suddenly in the air, to fall jingling into the magician's hat, or when cards mysteriously appear and disappear all over the artist's body.

When the press man reached the Veteran's Club in Bedford Row, where the evening's entertainment was being held, he found that the room itself was a miniature baronial hall, whose heavy rafters and great fireplace gave quite the medieval touch to the performance. But, instead of the black hat and magic wand, the wizards were charming gentlemen in evening dress and lounge suits, who thoroughly enjoyed the programme.

And, indeed, the programme for the evening was a sufficiently remarkable one, for rarely, if ever, has any audience before been so favoured as to see Harry Houdini doing his tricks under the eye of Horace Goldin or to find Horace Goldin producing vanished biscuits from Harry Houdini's pocket.

Once it even happened that, when Houdini was performing his masterly trick of swallowing separately two needles and thread and producing them from his mouth again threaded, one of the committee on the platform who watched him had himself given a demonstration earlier in the evening but even he failed to detect any hidden contrivance.

One of the best turns was given by a young conjurer, Mr Claude Chandler, whom Mr Houdini, the president of the club, introduced as one of the most dexterous magicians of the future.

The Era of Saturday 3 May went into more detail about the Magicians Club Ladies' Night:

The recently-formed Magicians' Club – the only club of its kind in existence, and which will doubtless soon become the headquarters of magic for England and indeed the whole world – held their first ladies' night on Sunday last. Through the hospitality of the Veterans' Club this highly successful and most enjoyable function took place at their premises, 47 Bedford Row, London and magicians and their friends to the number of over 300 spent a most delightful evening. Every lady present received a scent bottle, 'with the compliments of the Magicians' Club', a gift that was much prized; and many of the lady artistes were handed beautiful bouquets.

A unique feature to the evening's entertainment was the appearance on the stage together of those three famed men of magic, Harry Houdini, Horace Goldin and Chung Ling Soo and their humorously worked and clever biscuit trick afforded keen delight to all present. Individually, Harry Houdini did his wonderful needle trick; Chung Ling Soo, ring tricks; and Goldin, knot tricks; and among others who 'magished' were Mr Stanley Collins, in humorous conjuring, Zelka, in the bird trick, Mr Claude Chandler and Mr Wellesley Pain, cord trick. Miss Lena Kent sang 'My rosary'; Miss Mabel Godfrey, 'Joshua'; Miss Lee Laurie, 'Italian eyes'; and Miss May Beatty and Miss May Fairclough's contributions were keenly enjoyed. Mr Harry Claff's fine voice was heard to advantage in the 'Toreador' song and others who appeared were Ed E Ford, Ralph Stanley, Little Else Prince, Mr Henderson White, Mr John E Nestor and Mr George Adams. Mr Ed Lauri stage-managed and among those present were Mr Harry Day, Mr Will Goldston, Mr Leslie Harris, Mr Sydney Lee and many other prominent in the world of variety and magic.

Houdini next appeared at the Empire Theatre in Nottingham between 5 May and 10 May.

The *Nottingham Evening Post* of Tuesday 6 May wrote:

Houdini was ever a master-hand in the exploitation of sensational feats and his latest invention is the most thrilling of them all. Tightly manacled by the feet to a solid mahogany top, which is itself bound round by a steel frame and securely fastened, he is lowered head-first, in a steel cage, into a water-filled tank and succeeds in liberating himself within the space of two minutes. Both houses at the Empire last night were amazed as they were mystified by his remarkable feat and not less so by the East Indian needle mystery which he has only introduced comparatively recently.

HACKNEY.

E M P I R E

Managing Director, Oswald STOLL.
Acting Manager, Chas. MARTE.
MONDAY, MAY 8, 1911.
Twice Nightly during week, 6.45 & 9.
HOUDINI.
The Handcuff King.
MADAME DIANA. With
Dogs, Cockatoos and Monkeys.
LUDWIG AMANN.
EIGHT COLLEGE GIRLS.
ERNIE MAYNE.
SYD MAY.
J. H. MILBURN.
The DANDINIS.
JENNIE JOHNS.
The Bioscope.
All artistes appear at each Performance, and BOTH Performances are alike
PRICES of ADMISSION: 2d. to 1/6
Boxes 5/- and 7/6 for four persons.
BOX OFFICE OPEN DAILY from 1 to 4. 7 to 8 30. 9.30 to 10.30
Seats may be booked by Post or 'Phone; No. 8 Dalston.

An advert for Houdini's show at the Hackney Empire where he played during May 1911.

Houdini wrote in his diary: 'After the show (Nottingham Empire) Anna Eva Fay and her husband Mr Pingree came and had supper with Bess and myself at our digs. Had a long chat with them. She grieves over son John and calls his suicide his accident. She will never recover from the blow. I took them to the Hotel Vic at about 2 in the morning.'

The Era of Saturday 10 May wrote about Houdini's appearance at Nottingham Empire:

There is no lack of genuine enthusiasm when Houdini succeeds in liberating himself from seemingly impossible situations and packed houses give him the heartiest of receptions.

From Nottingham, he travelled to the New Cross Empire, London where he

The Hippodrome at Devonport where Houdini appeared between 24 March and 29 March 1913.

appeared between 12 and 17 May. On the bill were the Viennese trio, Ida Barr, the Juvenile American Rag-timers, Brett and Orford, Mildred Bryann, Stacey and Williams, Cavalieri, the Six Ceylons and pictures.

The *Western Times* of Saturday 17 May carried an interesting story about a case heard at the Plymouth Bankruptcy Court on the previous day. Before them appeared Charles Lyons who gave his profession as a tailor but was better known as the music hall artiste, 'Soldini', the man who made a nightly escape from a tank of water unobserved by the audience at the Hippodrome, Devonport. There was a suggestion of fraudulent removal of assets at the case.

Mr Goodman prosecuting stated, 'He had been a barman and a tailor and also a music hall artiste. His trick was to get out of a chamber of death without the aid of a tin opener.' There was laughter in the court.

Mr Goodman asked, 'You call yourself Soldini, I believe?'

Lyons replied, 'Yes.'

'Was that business a success?' asked Goodman.

'No.' replied Lyons.

'You had a tank made?' inquired Goodman.

'Yes, a cylinder.' answered Lyons.

'And your liabilities are in connection with the floating of that tank, while as a matter of fact the tank sank?' continued Mr Goodman.

'Yes.' replied Lyons.

'How much did you get for your week's engagement at the Hippodrome?' inquired Mr Goodman.

'£12.' answered Lyons.

'You ought to have done very well on that,' continued Mr Goodman.

'I had to pay Voss £6,' replied Lyons.

'Who is that, the gentleman who comes to the front in a dress suit and diamond studs and announces the turn?' asked Mr Goodman.

'Yes,' continued Lyons. 'Voss was my manager and those were the terms, that he was to have half.'

'What has become of the tank now?' inquired Mr Goodman.

'I sold it to Houdini who ran a similar business and received £10,' answered Lyons.

'What have you done with the money?'

'£4 was used to file the petition and I had to make several repairs to the tank before I handed it over to Houdini.', answered Lyons.

Houdini at Southampton Docks prior to his departure for New York on 21 May 1913. Pictured with him are the Associated Wizards of the South. Houdini had become a member of the group while appearing at the Southampton Hippodrome in 1911. Professor Woodley, the AWS chairman, is pictured behind Houdini's left shoulder wearing a cap.

The Era of Wednesday 16 July reported:

> *Mr Harry Houdini, self-liberator and necromancer, and real good fellow, was the chief attraction in a special mid-ocean performance given on board the Norddeutscher Lloyd liner,* Kronzprinzessen Cecilie – *Captain Charles Polack. He had as companion artistes, Mrs Clara Braatz, operatic whistler and*

Houdini on board the SS *Imperator* on 5 September 1913. (*Image courtesy of Library of Congress http://www.loc.gov*)

Miss Selma Braatz, the famous lady juggler. Houdini freed himself from leg-irons belonging to the ship and secured by a hardy sailor. The performance, which was a great success, was for the benefit of the Sailors' Widows' and Orphans' Fund. Houdini sends me a most artistically-printed programme.

Houdini on the SS *Imperator* in 1913. (*Image courtesy of Library of Congress http://www.loc.gov*)

Houdini returned to America and in July, his mother, Cecilia died. Deeply affected by this, he could not work again until September when he appeared at the Apollo Theatre in Nuremberg.

A show had been scheduled for the Sheffield Hippodrome but this was cancelled because of the death of his mother.

Houdini was at the Paris Alhambra between 1 and 15 November.

It's recorded that the Palace Theatre in Oxford Street, Manchester reopened in December 1913 with a reduced capacity seating of 2,600, and that the first act to appear there was Harry Houdini.

On Christmas Day, 1913, Houdini was back in London after a short holiday with Bess in Monte Carlo.

Chapter Thirteen

1914 – The Grand Magical Revue

In the year that the First World War broke out, Houdini began his engagements in the UK at the Tivoli in Barrow in Furness between 12 and 17 January. A challenge was issued by local shipwrights which read:

We, the Shipwrights employed at the yard of Vickers Ltd having heard of your ability to escape from apparently impossible and peculiar places, challenge you, Houdini, to allow us to construct a strong timber packing case into which we will rope and nail you.

From Barrow in Furness Houdini travelled to Birmingham to appear at the Grand Theatre between 26 and 31 January. Before Houdini went on stage, a series of films were shown showing his dexterity in freeing himself first from a straitjacket and then from several pairs of handcuffs whilst swimming in the Seine.

The *Birmingham Daily Gazette* of Saturday 31 January reported: '*The challenge held out to Houdini, who is appearing at the Grand Theatre this week, was accepted at the second performance last evening.*'

Four workmen engaged at the City Saw Mills, King Edward's Road, challenged Houdini to make his escape from a strong wooden packing case without demolishing the box and the popular performer was promised the 'finest fixing-up' he had ever had.

It was not until 11.10 that Houdini entered the case in the presence of a large audience and the challengers then fastened on the lid with countless nails, completing the 'fixing up' with a stout rope tied securely round. Eight minutes later Houdini was out and the packing case was in exactly the same condition as when it was fastened, the rope still being knotted around it. He showed evident signs of strain after the event and in order to satisfy the curiosity of one or two onlookers, he split the case to show there were no traps, sliding panels etc. For the feat, Houdini was loudly cheered and also congratulated by his challengers.

Will Goldston mentions in his book *Sensational Tales of Mystery Men* that Houdini wanted to feature more magic in his shows:

In spite of his wonderful success as an escape artist, Houdini was always very keen to build and present a number of ordinary magical illusions. It was with this end in view that he called at my office one morning about twenty years ago, and told me of his secret ambition. 'What do you think of it, Will?' he asked, finally.

'Your escapes are good and the public like them,' I replied cautiously.

'I know that, but I'd like a change. Can you tell me the name of an illusion inventor who can keep a secret?'

'Yes. Why not try Charles Morritt who has built stuff for Maskelyne and Devant Ltd.?'

Houdini took my tip and paid a visit to Morritt's workshop. After some discussion he agreed to buy several of Morritt's own tricks and commissioned the inventor to build them for him.

Harry decided to give his new show a trial run in the provinces. For some reason best known to himself, he left me definite instructions not to be present at the first night. Naturally I respected my friend's wishes, but I had a full account of the performance from another magician who was present.

One of Harry's best tricks consisted of producing five hundred gold sovereigns from an apparently empty bag. The audience received the programme well enough, but, in order to give it an extra fillip, Houdini thought out an extraordinary publicity stunt.

On the following day he hired a number of detectives to accompany him to the local bank. There, with a good deal of unnecessary ceremony and palaver, he paid in the five hundred sovereigns. Of course, the money was drawn out again for the next performance. This strange proceeding naturally caused a stir in the provincial town which was just what Houdini wanted. There was a long account of the affair in the newspapers next morning, and no doubt the magician felt his trouble had been worth while.

He was wrong. The magical show was an utter and complete failure. After a week's trial he wisely decided to return to his escapes. 'If the English want escapes, they can have them,' he explained to me afterwards. 'But I'm determined to give a good magical show before I die.' So he shipped all his apparatus to New York to be stored for use at some later date.

Houdini's next appearance was at the Sheffield Empire between 2 February and 7 February. On 6 February 1914, Houdini escaped successfully after being tied to a plank on the stage of the Empire Theatre in Sheffield.

The Era of Wednesday 4 February reported on the first anniversary of the Magicians' Club:

There was a large and festive gathering in the Grand Hall of the Hotel Cecil on Sunday evening, when the first annual dinner of the Magicians' Club was held.

The club, which it will be remembered, was only opened in March last, is, we believe, the only one of its kind in existence and it has rapidly become the headquarters of magic, not only as regards England, but for the whole world. New members are coming in weekly and there can be no doubt that this pleasant rendezvous in the Gray's Inn Road has satisfied a long-felt want. Anyone interested in magic may join, the subscription is very moderate, and Mr Harry Houdini, its president, Mr Will Goldston, one of the prime movers in its foundation, and others who have worked untiringly for its success, must be well satisfied with the result of their efforts.

The popular president, Mr Harry Houdini, was in the chair on Sunday, on the left being Mrs Houdini, and on his right, Mr Horatio Bottomley. Amongst many others present well-

A portrait shot of Will Goldston.

Carl Hertz, the well-known illusionist from San Francisco, attended the first anniversary of the Magicians' Club during February 1914.

Emilie D'Alton, wife and stage assistant to Carl Hertz. D'Alton appeared in many of Hertz's illusions including one where she appeared to be suspended in mid-air with no visible support.

known in the world of entertainment were Mr and Mrs Will Goldston, Mr and Mrs Stanley Collins, Mr and Mrs Harry Day, Mr and Mrs Charles Morritt, Mr and Mrs Carl Hertz, Mr and Mrs David Devant, Mr Arthur Prince, Mr and Mrs Joe Hayman, Mr and Mrs George Wetton, Mr and Mrs Edward Lauri, Mr and Mrs Ernest Wighton, Mr and Mrs Alfred Barnard, Mr and Mrs Sydney Lee, Mr Bennett Scott, Mr R H Douglas, Miss Bessie Slaughter, Professor Alberto and Mr C B Fontaine.

The dinner was an excellent one and the disappearing trick having been accomplished to everyone's satisfaction, the toast list, which was a brief one – all the speeches being short and to the point – was proceeded with. After 'The King' had been heartily honoured.

Mr Charles Morritt proposed 'The Magicians' Club', and said that, though he was sure many gentlemen present could have done so more eloquently, none would have been more sincere. A Magicians' Club had been a long-felt want and, with the aid of their worthy president, Mr Harry Houdini, assisted by Mr Will Goldston and Mr Stanley Collins, he was glad to say that at last it was an accomplished fact.

There were many other speeches and enjoyable entertainment followed.

Houdini's next venue was the Empire Theatre in Glasgow where he played between 9 and 14 February.

Houdini was filmed while in Glasgow and the shots were later used as part of his movie, *Haldane of the Secret Service*.

While at the Empire, Houdini was challenged by the men of Fairfield Shipbuilding Yard. Once again, he was to be nailed into a packing case. His escape took place at the second house on Friday 13 February.

From Glasgow, Houdini travelled to Leeds. There, he appeared at the Empire Theatre, between 16 and 21 February. He is recorded as jumping off Leeds Bridge in a milk can during his week at the Empire.

The *Yorkshire Evening Post* of Tuesday 17 February noted:

Of Houdini, it suffices to say that he left every person in the audience hopelessly bewildered by the neatness and dispatch of his tricks.

Houdini was filmed while in Glasgow in 1914. The shots were used in his movie, 'Haldane of the Secret Service'. (*Image courtesy of John Cox http://www.wildabouthoudini.com/*)

He still stands alone in his particular line. And the needle-threading trick in full view of the audience: It borders on the uncanny.

The Leeds date was followed by an appearance in Manchester where he performed at the New Palace between 23 and 28 February. On Saturday 1 March, he attended the annual dinner of the Manchester Press Club. He formed part of the musical programme which also included artistes who were playing at other venues in the city.

Houdini escaped from a packing case made by Messrs Lucy and Sunderland while appearing at the Palace Theatre in Manchester. The case was nailed shut and roped around. After the escape in five minutes, he said to an enthusiastic and crowded audience, 'The only difference is that I was then inside and now I'm outside.'

A poster advertising Houdini's appearance at the Empire, Leeds during February 1914.

From 3 to 8 March Houdini played at the Empire in Swansea.

Between 16 and 21 March, he appeared at the Empire in Newport. While there, he was challenged to escape from an iron bound cask by a Newport inventor.

A challenge from a Newport inventor to Houdini which took place on Friday, 20 March 1914.

An advert for the Grand Magical Revue at the Empire and Hippodrome, Bristol during March 1914.

From 23 to 28 March, Houdini appeared at the Empire and Hippodrome in Bristol.

The *Western Daily Press* of Tuesday 24 March wrote:

Houdini never fails to attract generous patronage when he visits Bristol and, as he announced the presentation of new mysteries at the Empire and Hippodrome, Old Market Street, there were large companies present last night to enjoy the programme in general and Houdini's feats in particular. Houdini, in his usual explanatory address, stated that an Indian that morning informed him it was impossible for a white man to do the Indian needle trick, while regard to the burnt turban trick, he said nobody was supposed to perform it except a Hindu, yet in the course of his travels he usually gave the performance. Proceeding with the turban feat first, the usual committee from the audience appeared and decided that the long strip of calico used was without cut or joint. Houdini cut the calico in half, tied the ends, which were then burnt, the committee tugged at the calico, the knot disappeared and the strip of material was intact. The deep sense of mystification was increased immediately after, for Houdini placed the needles from two packets on his tongue, apparently swallowed a quantity of thread, and when the latter was withdrawn, the needles were found to be neatly threaded at short distances.

At the same show he performed Metamorphosis 'in which a human being is transported through space with the rapidity of thought, having been roped, bound, gagged, chained and fettered under the supervision of a committee', Hypnotic Manipulation of Cards 'proving conclusively the power of mind over matter' and The Egg and Bag Mystery 'an improvement on this trick as originally by Fawkes, Bartholomew Fair Conjuror, who performed this in the year 1712.' There was also a straitjacket escape.

The tricks were followed by the water torture cell and, after Houdini made his escape, he received tremendous applause.

On Thursday 26 March, Houdini accepted a challenge from the employees of the British American Tobacco Company Ltd. The challenge read:

We challenge you to allow us to bring battens, ropes and wire nails and, on the stage, in full view of the audience, we will construct a strong packing case. You must enter it immediately to prevent any preparation on your part. We will nail down the lid, securely rope up the box and defy you to escape there from without demolishing the box.

Houdini accepted the challenge but stipulated that the box must not be airtight. During the second house, he was nailed into a crate and escaped in less than quarter of an hour. His challengers gleefully shook his hand and there was much applause from the audience.

On Saturday 28 March, he appeared in his Magical Revue at the Empire and Hippodrome, Bristol.

The *Western Daily Press* of Saturday 28 March carried a story under the headline *A NIGHT OF MYSTIFICATION*:

Last night Houdini varied his usual performance and gave a mystification evening. The crowded houses testified to his popularity. He said that, as a variation to his regular performance, he would make a desperate attempt to entertain and mystify his audience by a number of peculiar experiments in sleight-of-hand and mechanical problems. It is almost 20 years since he gave a full magical performance and in case some of the tricks did not act he hoped that they would at least entertain. Needless to say, all Houdini's tricks 'acted' and his feats were a matter of wonderment and speculation.

He first of all showed with the greatest of ease how to escape the hangman and then proceeded to display the delightful trick of extracting coins from the air and causing them to settle in an empty glass. The disappearing egg was all the more interesting, as members of the audience held Houdini's arms and still failed to prevent the reappearance of the popular commodity. Finally, he gave the trunk performance. As a preliminary, he bewildered the audience by the way in which he disdained the knots with which his hands were tied and then he was effectively sealed and tied up in a locked trunk. The curtains were drawn aside and not only had he escaped, but his sister was found in the trunk, sealed and tied just as Houdini had been. As one of the audience remarked, 'If the trunk had been open and Houdini had changed places in full view of the audience the feat would have been remarkable in the time occupied.'

The article mentions his sister but probably refers to his wife, Bess.

Houdini next played at the Newcastle Empire between 30 March and 4 April. The *Newcastle Journal* of Saturday 4 April reported:

There was a very large second house at the Empire Theatre last night when Houdini accepted the challenge of Mr George Coulthard, cooper, of Monk Street, and added still further to his reputation as a lock-picker and self-liberator. The challenger produced a specially-invented cask, from which he defied the artist to escape, after it had been filled with water and hermetically sealed. Houdini was duly confined in the cask, which was moved under cover, and after the audience had spent a few thrilling moments of expectation, they were relieved to see him emerge safe and sound. Their relief was expressed in enthusiastic applause as he 'drippingly' bowed himself off the stage.

From Newcastle, Houdini travelled to Edinburgh to appear at the Empire Palace Theatre between 6 and 11 April. Whilst there, he celebrated his 40th birthday.

An advert from *The Scotsman* from April, 1914 stated:

Houdini has accepted a challenge from four employees of Mr Adam Currie, Building Contractor, Newington Works, Edinburgh, to escape from a strong box. Constructed in full view of the audience, the lid will be nailed down, and the box roped up, also in full view of the audience.

EMPIRE PALACE THEATRE.
6.40.   TO-NIGHT.   9.
ENORMOUS ATTRACTION.
HOUDINI.
The World-Famous Self-Liberator,
CHALLENGE.
Houdini has accepted a challenge from four Employees of Mr Adam Currie, Building Contractor, Newington Works, Edinburgh, to escape from a Strong Box, constructed in full view of the audience, the lid will be nailed down, and the Box roped up, also in full view of the audience. The only condition stipulated by Houdini is that the Box must not be air-tight.
IRMA   LORRAINE,
The Famous Poseuse
PARK'S ETON BOYS. | SMARTE BROS.
CRYSTAL AND SAVILLE. | FRANK POWELL.
FLORENCE TURNER,
The World-Famous Cinema Actress,
On the Bioscope
(Next Week Florence Turner will Appear in Person.
CARL   DE   MAREST,
Novelty Violinist.
RAY   WALLACE,
Mimic at the Piano.

An advert for the Edinburgh Palace Theatre where Houdini appeared between 6 April and 11 April 1914.

The Scotsman from Tuesday 7 April carried the following story:

Houdini, who has spent an arduous career on the stage making seemingly impossible escapes from a variety of captive contraptions, is the principal performer on a splendid programme at the Empire Palace Theatre this week. He is featuring his water cabinet invention, which, though not new to Edinburgh audiences is, if anything, more interesting and mystifying at the second time of seeing. Houdini's ankles are clamped and locked in a polished and modern sort of stocks, and he is lowered head first into the narrow cell which is filled with water, and so banded about with steel and iron bars as to make it appear impossible or superhuman for him to do anything at all, much less make his way out. The cabinet is surrounded by a tent, and in less than two minutes Houdini is out and smiling to an astonished audience. Moreover, the water cell stands intact, locks and steel bands and all, so that Houdini, even in the mere physical sense, seems almost to demonstrate that iron bars do not make a cage. With a winning way, he also performed a couple of baffling tricks, including a curious one with needles, and his 'turn' altogether was much enjoyed.

An exceedingly well-staged performance is that of Irma Lorraine, who, with her lady assistants, presents a number of striking and artistic poses, some in attractive colours and others after the style of the marble medium. Crystal and Saville give a crisp little sketch, in which they work upon an amusing little misunderstanding, giving them opportunity for some smart dialogue and one or two character impersonations; and Park's Eton Boys and Girton Girls submit an attractive vocal and dancing item in which a small boy singer scored a success. Carl de Marest gave a popular instrumental performance on very modern lines, a speciality being ragtimes on the violin with appropriate dance movements at the same time. Miss Ray Wallace drew upon her clever repertory of imitations of well-known performers; the Smart Brothers succeeded in being funny as well as capable acrobats; and Frank Powell, as a comic postman, and the Bioscope rounded off the entertainment.

The Easter holidays brought tourists from other parts of the country and Houdini was a keen attraction for them. The *Edinburgh Evening News* from 7 April also carried a report of the show:

Holiday-makers from Fife swelled the attendance at the Empire Theatre last night to such an extent that even the standing accommodation was fully occupied. There was a holiday spirit pervading the atmosphere, and the various turns in the programme of a standard well above the average were received with acclamation.

Houdini's next venue was at the Olympia Theatre in Liverpool between 13 and 18 April.

He first performed the trick, 'The Expanding Die', in England in the spring as part of his Grand Magical Revue. The Revue was not popular with audiences and only lasted for about twelve performances. The Expanding Die trick was disappointing and Houdini only incorporated it within the show a few times. Chung Ling Soo's version was more successful but not used much.

Chung Ling Soo and Houdini were great friends for many years. Unknown to audiences and journalists, Soo wasn't Chinese at all and was born William Ellsworth Robinson in 1861. He was accidentally shot on stage at the Wood

An advert for Houdini's Grand Magical Revue at the Olympia, Liverpool, which appeared in the *Liverpool Echo* of Thursday, 16 April 1914.

Houdini and a little girl with the pony he bought while at the Olympia in Liverpool in April 1914. (*Image courtesy of Library of Congress http://www.loc.gov*)

A portrait shot of Chung Ling Soo.

A theatre poster advertising Chung Ling Soo.

Green Empire in London on 23 March 1918 while performing a trick where he supposedly caught a bullet in his teeth. To keep up the deception that he was Chinese, he had never spoken on stage but uttered the words, 'Oh my God. Something's happened. Lower the curtain!' when he was shot. He was taken to hospital but died the next day aged 56.

While in Liverpool, Houdini placed an advert in the wanted section of the *Liverpool Echo* of Tuesday 14 April. It read: *Pony wanted. I wish to buy a small pony, light-coloured preferred; must be under 10 hands, docile and one any child can drive. Houdini, Olympia.*

There's a photo of Houdini and the said pony together with a little girl on its back. It's unclear who the pony was bought for. It's been said that Charles Morritt suggested Houdini purchased the pony to emulate his own 'Disappearing Donkey illusion' which would later lead to the vanishing elephant trick. However, there's no record of the pony trick ever being displayed in the UK by Houdini.

The *Liverpool Daily Post* of Tuesday 14 April 1914 wrote:

In harmony with the prevailing holiday spirit, the Olympia furnished a full and attractive programme for the Bank Holiday. The attendance at both houses last evening was of the bumper order, the entertainment being thoroughly enjoyed. The programme commenced earlier than usual, in order to work off all the items in good time. The presence of Houdini is always a draw in Liverpool, for one reason – because he has done some extra al-fresco turns on the Mersey, which at the time caused a sensation. His clever performance on the stage never fails to concentrate attention. Houdini is, of course, the man of the evening. His water torture cell is a new form of display and is quite as sensational as anything hitherto introduced.

The *Liverpool Echo* of Thursday 16 April reported:

Houdini is a man with a remarkable career for no matter how tightly he may be manacled, handcuffed or tied he can effect his escape.

One of his most interesting feats was performed near the landing-stage at Suva in the Fiji Islands. A number of tribal chiefs were mystifying the crowds by diving into the water and bringing up in their mouths golden coins and, at the same time, endeavouring to convey the impression that they caught them in their mouths without using their hands in any way.

Houdini challenged one of the chiefs to dive with his hands tied behind his back whilst he himself should dive with his hands handcuffed in the same position. The challenge was accepted and, needless to say, Houdini was able to stagger the chief and his friends with a marvellous performance.

Speaking of handcuffs, Houdini described the English handcuffs as the easiest to obtain release from in the world; a sharp knock and they would spring open. The American and German handcuffs, he declares to be the most secure and the French most complicated in make.

Houdini next appeared at the Palace Theatre in Oldham between 20 and 25 April. The *Oldham Chronicle* of 21 April 1914 reported:

Last night two large audiences assembled at the Palace Theatre of Varieties to witness the remarkable feats of Houdini, the world-famed self liberator.

Houdini was born in Appleton, Wisconsin, in 1874. From childhood he showed an insight into mechanics. He left home at an early age, and in exploiting his wits to amuse and entertain audiences, he hit upon the idea of escaping from ropes, handcuffs, leg irons, shackles etc. He has dived, heavily manacled, into rivers, releasing himself in the water and has escaped from the straitjacket. Since 1908, Houdini has dropped handcuffs, and has made his performance replete with new mysteries, escaping out of an air-tight galvanised iron can filled with water after it has been locked in an iron-bound chest. He has been confined in prison cells that were supposed to be so constructed that a breakout was impossible, but he has managed to get free, and at one time released all the inmates of one of the American prisons, and transferred each into some other cell than the one to which he was originally committed.

Last night he started with the burnt turban trick, knotting a long length of calico in the centre, having it cut in two and burning the edges, and afterwards showing the audiences the whole piece complete as it was originally. His next was a needle affair. Houdini placed a number of needles in his mouth, along with some silk thread, and the needles were extracted threaded complete, a truly wonderful affair. But his water torture cell concoction was most outstanding. A large case was brought on to the stage, fitted with a grill and a glass front. The case is filled with water, and Houdini is placed inside, head downwards, his ankles locked above in the centre of a massive cover. It seems impossible to obtain any air whatever in the upside-down position, or even escape, but in about one and a half minutes he was standing on the front of the stage. He

PALACE, OLDHAM

A tip-top programme has been arranged at the Palace this week which we feel sure will please all comers. In spite of the beautiful weather which prevailed out of doors, the house was well filled last night, which for a Monday night is a sure sign of an attractive programme. Houdini, the world famous self liberator, gave a marvellous display of his power. Although ten of the audience were allowed upon the stage they were unable to fathom the mystery of his wonderful tricks. It was most amusing to notice how awestruck they were when, after swallowing about half a dozen needles and then swallowing about a yard of cotton, Houdini brought the needles threaded on the cotton out of the mouth. His feat of liberating himself from a water torture cell (Houdini's own invention) borders on the miraculous and is one that must be witnessed to

THE GREAT HOUDINI.

be full appreciated. As usual Florrie Gallimore takes the house by storm. She has a way and a charm of her own that defies description. Her songs went with a swing, and her song "Leaving the west for home" touched the hearts of all, but it was her last song 'Oh! Let it be soon,' which captivated and amused the audience most. Brothers Huxter, the successful and refined æro pantomimic humorists, in languid energy were clever and performed some wonderful feats. A singer whose sweetness of tone could not fail to charm the ear is Bertha Smillie. She sang "When love creeps in your Heart" with feeling and apparently without effort. It is a pleasure to see and hear so natural and charming a singer, and one naturally feels glad that she left the loom to grace the boards with her presence. Two Canadians, "Canada's expert instrumentalists" showed great talent and proved a delightful treat. An eccentric dancer of no mean order is Harold Heath. He is so light and neat and clever that his dancing is pleasing to all, and was well applauded. Kitty Clayton as the Duchess in the sketch entitled "The Duchess of Dishwater" provoked roars of mirth, and kept all in smiles from start to finish. Tom Reno delighted the audience with his eccentric patter. The Palace programme is one of star artistes, many of whom are well known to Oldhamers, and need no special commendation.

A newspaper review of Houdini's show at the Palace in Oldham where he appeared between 20 and 25 April 1914.

was the recipient of great applause. A committee of local gentlemen went on stage and scrutinised everything very keenly.

Florrie Gallimore is an old favourite here, and her reception last night was great. Her first effort was 'Where did you get that girl!' which she manipulated a looking-glass on the audiences in an amusing manner.

The article on the previous page from the *Oldham Standard* of 21 April 1914 read:

A tip-top programme has been arranged at the Palace this week which we feel sure will please all comers. In spite of the beautiful weather which prevailed out of doors, the house was well filled last night, which for a Monday night is a sure sign of an attractive programme. Houdini, the world famous self liberator, gave a marvellous display of his power. Although ten of the audience were allowed upon the stage they were unable to fathom the mystery of his wonderful tricks. It was most amusing to notice how awestruck they were when, after swallowing half a dozen needles and then swallowing about a yard of cotton, Houdini brought the needles threaded on the cotton out of the mouth. His feat of liberating himself from a water torture cell (Houdini's own invention) borders on the miraculous and is one that must be witnessed to be fully appreciated.

As usual Florrie Gallimore takes the house by storm. She has a way and a charm of her own that defies description. Her songs went with a swing, and her song 'Leaving the west for home' touched the hearts of all, but it was her last song 'Oh! Let it be soon' which captivated and amused the audience most. Brothers Huxter, the successful and refined aero pantomimic humorists, in languid energy were clever and performed some wonderful feats. A singer whose sweetness of tone could not fail to charm the ear is Bertha Smillie. She sang 'When love creeps in your Heart' with feeling and apparently without effort. It is a pleasure to hear and see so natural and charming a singer, and one naturally feels glad that she left the loom to grace the boards with her presence. Two Canadians 'Canada's expert instrumentalists' showed great talent and proved a delightful treat. An eccentric dancer of no mean order is Harold Heath. He is so light and neat and clever that his dancing is pleasing to all and was well applauded. Kitty Clayton as the Duchess in the sketch entitled 'Duchess of the Dishwater' provoked roars of mirth and kept all in smiles from start to finish. Tom Reno delighted the audience with his eccentric patter. The Palace programme is one of star artistes, many of whom are well known to Oldhamers, and need no special commendation.

From Oldham, Houdini travelled to the Palace Theatre in Hull where he appeared between 27 April and 2 May. The Magical Revue continued at the Palace Theatre and included six illusions including, The Crystal Casket, Good Bye Winter, Money For Nothing, The Arrival of Summer, Calico Conjuring and Metamorphosis.

The *Hull Daily Mail* of Monday 27 April reported:

> *The immense crowd that assembled on the Corporation Pier and jetty yesterday afternoon to witness the daring feat of Houdini, who is appearing at the Palace this week, suggests that many Hull people feel monotony gnawing at them on Sundays. There would be about 8,000 people around and near the Pier and all sorts of points of vantage were secured. Numerous rowing boats were requisitioned by the more speculative ones; the scene under the sun rivalled that of Henley during regatta week. Numerically it equalled both. With Mr S J Barnett, the resident manager of the Palace, and members of the press, Mr Houdini arrived by motor at the Pier shortly before five o'clock. The reception had cheered him but the fight through the crowd to the tug tried his patience severely.*

> *Press representatives examined the handcuffs, chains and elbow irons before fastening them upon Mr Houdini. His hands were manacled behind his back with handcuffs that when locked bit into the skin. The elbow irons weighing 19½lbs, bound his arms, and a massive chain, worn around his neck, was locked to the handcuffs at the back. There could be no flaw in the cuffs; they fitted tightly and were regulation irons. The chain around his neck was certainly much tighter and far more painful than the black velvet neckbands that so many girls are fond of wearing. There could be no doubt that all the time Mr Houdini was in the cuffs and chains he felt them. They bit into his skin and it was impossible for him to bend his head back. At the last moment, his only misgivings came from the visible signs of a strong current. A few deep breaths, a clean dive and he was out of sight. But only for a few moments! He quickly re-appeared above the water smiling, and holding up the irons – broken*

PALACE THEATRE,

FRIDAY, APRIL 24th, 1914.

GRAND SPECIAL NIGHT.

The World-Famous Self-Liberator,

HOUDINI,

The Supreme Ruler of Mystery,

WILL PRESENT A

GRAND MAGICAL REVUE

In which he will prove himself to be the Greatest Mystifier that History Chronicles, introducing a number of problems from his inexhaustible repertoire.

WHICH WILL BE SEEN FOR THE SECOND TIME ON ANY STAGE.

1. **THE CRYSTAL CASKET.**
2. **GOOD-BYE, WINTER.**
   Vanishing a living, breathing human being in mid-air, in centre of stage away from all curtains, and in full glare of the light, in less than One-Millionth of a Second.
3. **MONEY FOR NOTHING.**
   In which HOUDINI solves for humanity that which has been the ambition of millions who try to get "Something for Nothing," obtaining £1,000 in genuine Gold and Silver in the midst of the audience in a manner never before shown by any performer past or present.
4. **THE ARRIVAL OF SUMMER.**
   Materialising in a most inexplicable manner a FAIRY QUEEN GARDENER under strictest conditions possible. Everything open and above board, defying the Five demons at his toil away.
5. **CALICO CONJURING.**
   An Object Lesson for the Ladies
6. **METAMORPHOSIS.**
   Continuous being transported through space and walls of steel-bound oaken boards, outstripping the rapidity of thought, after being bound chained, roped, gagged, and sealed by a committee selected from the audience.

Houdini performed his Grand Magical Revue at the Palace Theatre, Oldham on Friday, 24 April 1914.

open – and a little mud. The crowd was nothing if not enthusiastic. An act such as that given by Houdini invariably excites scepticism but yesterday there was practically nobody who could doubt the genuineness of Houdini's cleverness. As the popular music-hall artiste remarked, 'there was nobody underneath the water to free him'. The aquatic display terminated in a fight through the crowd – an excited crowd – to the waiting motor car.

He was besieged by autograph hunters and admirers but he could only favour one. That was a little girl who was feeling the effects of the buffeting among the crowd. She wailed out, 'Save me, Mr Houdini' and that worthy found the task of carrying the girl to a place of safety as difficult as his 'submarine struggle'.

The Mail had a talk with Mr Houdini once he was once more in presentable attire. He was the most serious man in all the great crowd yesterday. Nobody realises better than he how he is flirting with death and yet he continues to do so. He has had many narrow escapes. Naturally reserved, he neither smokes or drinks and believes that abstinence from these things has been a help.

He has tried to settle down but he cannot; he must be surrounded with tingle and excitement.

He has proposed many things and although reverses – domestic and otherwise – have been many he still triumphs. His nerves are as 'steely' as the manacles that bind him which will, he feels, bind him some day in a vice-like grip that even he will have difficulty in relaxing. It will be a long time, however, before he attempts another manacled dive.

Shortly after Houdini had accomplished his amazing feat an exciting scene was enacted. A little boy named Moore was pushed by the swaying crowd into the water and the current was carrying him rapidly away when he was pluckily rescued by a boatman named Thomas Ellison of 14 Finkle Street, Hull. He was rowing a small boat containing several people when he saw the boy in the water. Without divesting himself of any clothing, he sprang into the water and swam with the boy to the landing steps. He was warmly applauded for his pluckiness.

Although Houdini continued with his daring and exhausting stunts, he wasn't getting any younger and the tasks must have seemed a lot harder than they were when he first tackled them years before.

The *Hull Daily Mail* of Thursday 30 April carried a story about how the act was affecting Houdini's health:

The wear and tear of such a life is now making itself felt in Mr Houdini's health. Although only forty years of age, in many respects he feels lamentably older. He was a born pessimist, but now he is experiencing the dawn of optimism.

The trend of his work must be altered. He is not so indefatigable as he formerly was. It is only pluck and genuine indomitable courage that has supplemented one of the finest human frames and faultless constitutions any man could wish, and this combination has only safely carried him through a vortex of troubles. But we are glad that optimism is triumphing even at this part of his notable career. His brain and his brawn are jointly at work daily concocting and manufacturing new illusion tricks with which he hopes to smooth the rugged path that his strenuous career has always found for him.

He came into the life of the music hall world like a lion and is he going to leave it like a lamb? Whatever he does, there will be genius in his action. He is a master of illusion and we can predict with due regard to truth that he will be one of the best illusionists just as he is the best self-liberator from handcuffs. We are unanimous in expressing 'Let the 'Handcuff King' be the 'Illusion King' and the sooner the better.

His whole performance at the Palace last night was to combat the challenge of the Hull Seamen's Union. A committee of that body avowed that they would bind him with ropes to a broomstick and afterwards to a seven-foot plank, in such a manner that in their opinion, it would be impossible for him to release himself. The theatre was filled in every available corner and hundreds were unable to obtain admission. The stalwarts of the sea arrived and it was apparent they meant business. If rumour is to be considered at all, then the confidence of the seamen in their powers of trussing were so sure that, it is stated, money changed hands at the docks concerning the result of the challenge. However, King Neptune must have turned over in his watery bed with interest to know that the sea was so well represented on the Palace stage last night. There were several seamen comprising the challengers, and their combined sea-going experience equalled 300 years. And poor Houdini's stage career only 30 years – just one nought less! Anyway, he is in his element when fighting against tremendous odds. An independent committee also went upon the stage and the lashing commenced. One seaman took his coat off, another spat on his hands and all took their hats off.

Mr McKee, the well-known local secretary, was the head of the committee. A broomstick was passed under Houdini's knees, to which his wrists were secured in no gentle manner. With his knees and wrists in the air, a truly awkward position, he was lifted on to a seven-foot plank. Yards and yards of rope were used in lashing him tightly to the wood. Some of the most difficult of sea knots were used and, when finished, a whole network of ropes encircled his body. His neck, wrists and feet were especially tightened, and Houdini stated that the blood circulation in his arms had ceased. The tying up business occupied more than quarter of an hour and then a grim struggle began. The rope round the neck was a source of great trouble and for ten minutes, Houdini could make little headway. And then he used his feet just the same as another man would use his hands and the result was that his feet slipped the ropes. He managed by dint of skilful struggling to get one of his hands free and then he moved in brisk style. To him the rest was easy. Even the complicated sea knots were little trouble and he was free, but the seventeen minutes struggle showed itself upon him and he was glad to get away from the vociferous cheering of the audience. Later, the Mail representative saw Mr Houdini being rubbed down with alcohol by an athlete and from the trend of the conversation was able to extract the foregoing from him.

Mr G McKee, secretary of the committee that lashed Mr Houdini, told the Mail that he was amazed at Mr Houdini's triumph. He would have laid any odds last night when he saw him tied up that escape was impossible. But nobody was more pleased than he that success had attended this great artiste's fight. He wished to pay tribute, on behalf of all their members, to the extraordinary strength and remarkable prowess displayed. Continuing, Mr McKee said that years ago when working on a Wilson liner, one of the crew, a German, went mad. He became worse, a raving maniac, and his arm was fastened and locked into the woodwork of his trunk. During the night, however, he tore the woodwork away and stripped the cabin of everything, displaying extraordinary strength. About nine of his fellow seamen tried to hold him but he bowled them over like ninepins. Eventually he was captured and lashed to a plank in a similar manner to which Mr Houdini was subjected last night but no broomstick was used. The knots were almost identical as those used on Houdini last night. The maniac raved and tore but never released himself. He converted himself into a bleeding mass, nothing more. The knots used last night were also identical with those used on the maniac, a clubhitch round the neck so that when the cord was slackened the other tightened. There were hitches round the knees which secured them firmly to the broom shaft. All the hitches and turns round the wrists, ankles and body were independent to each other. The task and the success is all the more credible.

As we state above, Mr Houdini is a great illusionist and to verify our contentions, he will present at both houses tomorrow night a grand magical revue, in which he will introduce a number of problems from his inexhaustible repertoire. Among the items he has selected are the crystal casket, goodbye winter, money for nothing, the arrival of the summer, calico conjuring and metamorphosis. These are nothing if not versatile and the greatest remark we can make on their favour will be able to bear favourable comparison, with the performance of Mr Houdini's late colleague Lafayette's.

Houdini's next venue was the New Cross Empire in London between 4 and 9 May 1914.

At the Hotel Cecil on Sunday 10 May, the Magicians' Club held their first annual supper and ball. *The Era* of Wednesday 13 May wrote:

The layman entered the banqueting hall apprehensive that strange things would happen at the festive board and his misgivings were not entirely unfounded. At least one puzzling trick was accomplished, the Three Rascals occupying one chair at the supper table. The writer did not see the feat performed but that's how it was shown on the table plan. There was, moreover, a manifestation on the part of Mrs Houdini who caused to appear before each guest a daintily arranged doll dressed by her own hand.

The spirit of illusion was also present in the after-supper oratory, for when one expected the chairman, Mr Harry Houdini, to propose the toast of 'The Magicians' Club', lo! there rose Sir William Bass in his place. Sir William, who was received with warm applause,

An advert for the Magical Revue at the Palace Theatre, Hull on Friday, 1 May 1914.

said he had been asked by the president to propose what he believed was the most important toast of the evening – that of 'The Magicians' Club'. When he was invited to the supper, he had no idea he would be asked to speak; in fact had he though, so would he have gone 150 miles in the opposite direction. (Laughter.) He did not profess to be an orator, so they must forgive him if he made a bad speech. He must confess that he really knew nothing about the Magicians' Club. Until the beginning of the week he regretted to say that he had never even heard of it. That was a calamity for him but influenced by the excellent attendance and the bevy of beauty he saw around him, it would be his earnest endeavour to learn a great deal more about the club in the near future. (Applause.) He was sure they would rather listen to the entertainment and dance at the ball then hear him speak and he, therefore, had great pleasure in proposing the toast of 'The Magicians' Club' coupled with the name of Mr Alfred Barnard.

The chairman called upon Stanley Collins who was presented with a diamond collar-stud and a diamond ring in appreciation for his services to the club. Houdini thanked all the members of the club who had contributed to its success.

After the event, the members withdrew to the Victoria Hall where they were entertained by various acts including Houdini, performing the egg and bag trick; Maurice showed his expertise as a card palmer; Zomah impressed all with his mind-reading act and Miss Mabel performed conjuring tricks. Various other acts took part before the ball began at midnight and continued well into the morning.

Houdini's next venue was the Empire Theatre in Cardiff where he played between 25 and 30 May.

Included in Houdini's act was the stunt performed the previous year, the Water Torture Cell. The *Cardiff Review Western Mail* of 26 May 1914 quoted Houdini as saying that he started work on the trick in Cardiff about two years previously and that the rough timber used to build the cell had been bought in the city.

The story was told by Milbourne Christopher (illusionist and biographer of Houdini) who said that the stunt was perfected in 1911 and performed before the Lord Chamberlain. It was then put into storage in London and used on his next visit to the Continent.

The *Western Mail* of Friday 29 May reported:

'He is marvellous!' This and similar expressions have been heard from the big crowds who have witnessed the escape of Harry Houdini from his water torture cell at the Cardiff Empire this week but the gentleman who has held enthralled audiences all over the world with his magic is an amicable person off stage.

He was bubbling over with good spirits when a Western Mail *reporter was ushered into his dressing-room at the Empire. He was the originator of the 'escape' performance but this he now considers antiquated and has practically given it up.*

With regard to the 'water torture cell,' Mr Houdini commenced to work on it in Cardiff two years ago and bought the rough timber in the city and a Cardiff audience in January, 1913, was the first to witness it in the United Kingdom.

Mr Houdini is never satisfied with his work, no matter how 'taking' it is with the public, and he is always at work on a new idea. Thus, although the 'water torture cell' is received everywhere with great enthusiasm, he finds time for securing material for a fresh sensation.

This evening, Mr Houdini will give a magical revue and in a week's time will sail for America. On the way out, he hopes to get permission to dive overboard manacled and release himself before returning from beneath the waves.

KING'S HALL

BIGGIN STREET, DOVER.

Proprietors ... ... HARRY DAY'S AMUSEMENTS, LTD.
General Manager ... ... Mr. HARRY DAY.

6.50 : TWICE NIGHTLY : 9.0

MONDAY, JUNE 1st, 1914

POSITIVELY THE FIRST APPEARANCE IN DOVER OF THE
WORLD-FAMOUS SELF LIBERATOR

HOUDINI

THE SUPREME RULER OF MYSTERY

At the Most Fabulous Salary ever paid to any Mystifier. HOUDINI'S last week but one in Great Britain, sailing on the "Imperator," June 18th for a Tour round the World.

Two totally different Programmes will be presented during the week:—

MONDAY, TUESDAY AND WEDNESDAY HOUDINI will liberate himself after being locked in a **WATER TORTURE CELL**

(HOUDINI'S OWN INVENTION) whilst standing on his head, entirely submerged in water, his ankles clamped and locked above in the centre of the massive cover. A Feat which borders on the Supernatural. **£200** HOUDINI offers this sum to anyone proving that it is possible to obtain air in the upside-down position in which he releases himself from this Water Filled Torture Cell. Also introducing the EAST INDIAN NEEDLE TRICK.

THURSDAY, FRIDAY AND SATURDAY **GRAND MAGICAL REVUE** In which he will introduce a number of his Original Illusions which will prove HOUDINI the Greatest Magician that History chronicles, including:—

1. **THE CRYSTAL CASKET.**
2. **GOOD-BYE WINTER.** Vanishing a living, breathing human being in mid-air, in the centre of the Stage, away from all curtains and in full glare of lights in less than ONE MILLIONTH OF A SECOND.
3. **MONEY FOR NOTHING.** In which HOUDINI solves for humanity that which has been the ruination of millions who try to get SOMETHING FOR NOTHING, obtaining £1,000 in genuine gold and silver in the midst of the audience in a manner never before shown by any Performer, past or present.
4. **ARRIVAL OF SUMMER.** Materialising in a most inexplicable manner a FAIRY QUEEN GARDENER under the strictest conditions possible. everything open and above board, deceiving the FIVE SENSES at one fell swoop.
5. **CALICO CONJURING.** An object lesson for the Ladies.
6. **LADY GODIVA.**
7. **DE KOLTA'S MARVELLOUS CUBE.** This HOUDINI purchased with all original apparatus, rights and everything appertaining to the trick from the Legatee. This was invented and constructed by the Famous French Inventor.
8. **METAMORPHOSIS.** TWO HUMAN BEINGS transported through space and walls of steel-bound oaken board, outstripping the rapidity of thought, after being bound, chained, roped, gagged and sealed by a Committee selected from the Audience.

BESSIE SLAUGHTER Phenomenal Contralto	**CLOWN ARGO** The Circus Mimic
	NELL CALVERT Comedienne and Burlesque Actress
THE FOUR MIRADORS In Wonderful Pot-Pourri	**HARRY HALSEY** London Star Comedian and Mimic
	BIOSCOPE : ESSIE Topical Budget Gipsy Violinist

Houdini's appearance at the King's Hall, Dover between 1 and 6 June 1914.

MARINE PORTERS CHALLENGE HOUDINI

HOUDINI, Esq.—Dear Sir,

We, the undersigned, a Committee selected from our Members, CHALLENGE YOU to escape from a lashing we propose to give you, after the system used years ago on slave and sailing vessels.

We will tie a broomstick behind your knees, your hands lashed to each side. In this trussed up condition we will lay you on your back on to a seven foot plank to which we will secure you in a network of cords and ropes, and finish up by tying your neck off at one end of plank and your ankles at the opposite end.

If you accept challenge, you do so at your own risk, and you must make the attempt to escape in full view of the audience to prove you have no concealed assistants.

Yours faithfully,

P. Hudson, 70, Balfour Rd. M. Pearce, 13, George St.
P. Hatton, 15, Monins Rd. W. Mundy, Albany Place.

Houdini accepts the above Challenge

for SECOND HOUSE, at the KING'S HALL, on FRIDAY NIGHT, JUNE 5th, 1914, under the condition that **there must be no danger of strangulation** from ropes encircling his neck and that he has the right to have a physician present.

Marine porters challenge Houdini during his show at the King's Hall, Dover on Friday, 5 June 1914.

Houdini next made an appearance at the Kings Hall in Dover where he played between 1 and 6 June.

On Whit Monday, the re-decorated Kings Hall, with its increased seating accommodation, was re-opened as a variety theatre under the proprietorship of Harry Day, with Mr E.W. Howard as the manager, crowded houses were the rule. The opening show featured Houdini with an array of attractions. On Monday, Tuesday and Wednesday, he liberated himself from the water torture cell. He also performed the East Indian needle trick as well as the Burnt Turban trick.

On Wednesday night, during the second house, he made a rapid escape from a box constructed by the men of Tolputt's Timber Yard. During the second house on Friday evening, he was again lashed to a plank, this time by the Dover Marine Porters. It was stated that this method was used years ago on slave vessels.

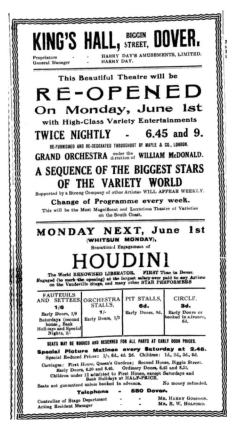

An advert announcing Houdini's forthcoming show at the King's Hall, Dover.

Houdini in Dover during June 1914.

There were two separate shows and on Thursday, Friday and Saturday, the show included Houdini's Grand Magical Revue. Eight illusions were performed. The first, The Crystal Casket, had no description mentioned on the flyer for the show. The second, Good-Bye Winter, involved the vanishing of 'a living breathing human being in mid-air, in the centre of the stage, away from all curtain and in full glare of lights in less than one millionth of a second.'

The third illusion was called Money For Nothing. The description read, 'Houdini solves for humanity that which has been the ruination of millions who try to get something for nothing, obtaining £1,000 in genuine gold and silver in the midst of the audience in a manner never before shown by any performer, past or present.'

The fourth illusion was entitled Arrival of Summer, described as 'Materialising in a most inexplicable manner, a fairy queen gardener, under the strictest conditions possible, everything open and above board, deceiving the five senses at one fell swoop.'

The fifth illusion was Calico Conjuring which was described as 'an object lesson for the ladies.'

This was followed by Lady Godiva, an act which featured no description.

The seventh illusion was De Kolta's Marvellous Cube. This was the act known as The Expanding Die and was the cause of disagreement between Houdini and his friend, Chung Ling Soo. The advert for the illusion read, 'This Houdini purchased with all original apparatus, rights and everything appertaining to the trick from the Legatee. This was invented and constructed by the Famous French Mystical Inventor.'

The eighth and final illusion was entitled Metamorphosis. The act was described as 'two human beings transported through space and walls of steel-bound oaken board, outstripping the rapidity of thought, after being bound, chained, roped, gagged and sealed by a Committee selected from the Audience.'

Also on the bill were Bessie Slaughter (Phenomenal Contralto), The Four Miradors (In Wonderful Pot-Pourri), Clown Argo (the Circus Mimic), Nell Calvert (Comedienne and Burlesque Actress), Harry Halsey (London Star Comedian and Mimic), the Bioscope (Topical Budget) and Essie (Gypsy Violinist).

Shows were twice nightly at 6.50pm and 9.00pm. This was Houdini's first and last show in Dover.

On Tuesday 2 June, Houdini jumped from a motor-boat into the Admiralty Harbour between the Prince of Wales and promenade piers at Dover at 12.30pm.

The *Dover Express* of Friday 5 June covered the event:

On Tuesday, at mid-day, Harry Houdini gave another extraordinary display when he dived into the bay at a considerable distance from the shore, manacled, and freed himself and rose to the surface in 22 seconds. The performance, having been previously announced, a huge crowd gathered on the beach and a number of boats flocked round the 'Argus', Messrs Friend and Co's motor boat, from which Houdini entered the water. He was manacled with elbow irons, which were attached to a chain which was passed round his neck and was padlocked at the point where it crossed on his chest. A pair of handcuffs bound his wrists together behind his back and these were attached by a padlock chain to the chain round his neck. The operation was carried out by a pressman. After taking several deep breaths, he shouted, 'I'm ready,' and dived head first into the water and after 22 seconds re-appeared at the surface holding the chains and handcuffs at arms length above his head. He was picked up by a waiting boat and taken ashore where a huge crowd flocked after him until he reached a taxi and drove away.

Houdini was delighted by the reception that he received at Dover and wrote, 'Said by all great English critics to be the Best Mystery Show Ever Presented. An almost original programme.'

HARRY HOUDINI.
(Empire.)

A photo of Houdini which appeared in the *Nottingham Evening Post* of Tuesday, 9 June 1914.

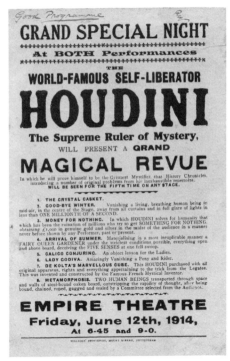

An advert for Houdini's show at the Empire, Nottingham where he appeared between 8 June and 13 June 1914.

A handbill advertising Houdini's Grand Magic Revue at the Empire Theatre, Nottingham, on Friday, 12 June 1914. (*Image courtesy of Kevin Connolly http:// houdinihimself.com/*)

Theatre owners who saw his shows in Dover and Nottingham disagreed with his praise of the show. They wanted to book Houdini the world famous escapologist rather than a master of illusion, which, they said, were ten a penny.

Houdini next appeared at the Empire Theatre in Nottingham between 8 and 13 June which was thought to be his last performance in Great Britain in 1914.

Also appearing in the show were the Three Aeros, Madge Clifton, Dorane Sisters and Wood, Chas Norton, George Tawde and Eva McRoberts, Ed Crossland's Melody Makers, Barton and Ashley and the Bioscope.

The young Randolph Osborne Douglas better known as Randini.

Houdini escaping from a strait jacket while suspended by a rope and pulley.

The *Nottingham Evening Post* of Saturday 13 June stated:

The turn had a fine spectacular finish in the exchange of places between Houdini and his assistant, in a sealed sack, placed in a locked and roped oak chest.

The *Evening Despatch* of Saturday 13 June reported:

Harry Houdini is fulfilling his last week's engagement this week in Great Britain at the Nottingham Empire. He sails for America on the Imperator *on the 18 June opening at Hammerstein's Roof Garden, New York City on 6 July. He is booked in America and foreign countries for a number of years.*

On the day after the last show, Houdini travelled to Sheffield to visit 19-year-old Randolph Osborne Douglas. Douglas had a short career as Randini and had known Houdini for some years. His first meeting with Houdini was at Sheffield in 1904 and is recorded earlier in this book. During the visit, Douglas showed Houdini a trick that would later be adopted and performed by him. After tea, Douglas

An advert stating that the 'Walking through a solid wall' trick has been sold to Houdini by S.E. Josolyne dated 16 June 1914.

and his mother Kitty took Houdini to the attic room of the house. There, Douglas put on a straitjacket and his mother tied rope around his legs before hoisting him up by his feet on a winch into the air. As Douglas dangled upside down, he escaped from the straitjacket with his arms outstretched. Houdini was amazed by this and used the stunt in many future performances.

Houdini pictured on board the SS *Imperator* with Theodore Roosevelt in June 1914. (*Image courtesy of Library of Congress http://www.loc.gov*)

An advert in *The Era* of Wednesday 17 June announced that S.E. Josolyne had sold his 'Walking through a solid wall' trick to Houdini. Josolyne reserved the right to perform the act in England though and his show was due to begin on 6 July under the management of Day's Variety Agency.

Houdini sailed onboard the SS *Imperator* on 18 June to commence a tour around the world. Also on board was former president, Theodore Roosevelt, and the photo shown was taken on 23 June. While on board, Houdini entertained fellow passengers.

The Era of Wednesday 15 July wrote:

Houdini gave a performance that made Colonel Roosevelt rock with laughter. The audience were asked to write down questions which were placed in a sealed envelope and then fastened between two slates and tightly bound. The first question drawn out read: 'Can you draw a map tracing the recent journey made by our most famous passenger?'

When the slates were untied, there appeared a general map of Brazil and its wilds with the Colonel's famous river clearly indicated. This was greeted with screams of laughter and the Colonel jumped up, waving his arms and laughing till the tears rolled down his cheeks. 'By George, this proves it!' shouted the Colonel as the passengers renewed their applause.

On 15 July 1914, Houdini famously performed his overboard box escape off New York's Battery Park. A crowd of 15,000 gathered to watch him.

In Milbourne Christopher's biography, Houdini was said not to have appeared in Britain during the war years of 1914 to 1918. However, a letter sent to the 'postbag' section of the *South Wales Echo* published on 11 August 1978 stated that Houdini jumped off Canton Bridge in Cardiff in either 1916 or 1917. However, this can't be verified.

Houdini raising money for the British Red Cross during 1914.

While away from the UK during the war, Houdini successfully raised money for the British Red Cross. He wrote in his diary on 20 October 1916 while performing in Canada: 'Toronto, Canada. No challenges as paper does not notice the house as they do not advertise in them. I helped Red Cross and recruiting drive with an outdoor stunt. After the street show 12 boys of the Red Cross, I am told, collected $2796.12 – a neat sum. No one even thanked me.'

Christopher's biography states that Houdini did not return to Britain until December 1919.

Chapter Fourteen

1919 – Houdini's Highest Earnings

Houdini's fifteen-episode serial, 'The Master Mystery' played to audiences at picture houses all over Great Britain from September. It was greatly praised by all of the newspapers.

The *Star* of 29 January wrote:

Houdini, the Handcuff King, has been filmed. He has embodied in one long 15-episode film all the best of his tricks. Around him has been woven the usual 'strong' drama but throughout it all, Houdini is the centre-piece. He himself is very pleased with the film, which is certain to be of immense interest to the cinema-going public.

For instance, when he was thrown manacled and in a barrel off Clifton

A hypnotic photo of Harry Houdini.

Houdini is attacked by a robot in the movie, 'The Master Mystery'.

A poster advertising an episode of 'The Master Mystery'.

A poster advertising 'The Master Mystery'.

An advert for 'The Master Mystery' which appeared in The Era of Wednesday 12 February 1919.

A thoughtful portrait of Houdini.

An advert for a Houdini movie which appeared in the *Burnley Express* of Wednesday, 5 November 1919.

Bridge, all the public then saw was his disappearance beneath the water and his reappearance. In this film, we have actually secured photographs of every movement while he was in the barrel. In fact, the public see him all the time.

Houdini also is a first-rate actor and a 'strong' man. In one scene, he is 'crucified' – arms tied out above him and his feet resting on two pegs six inches above the ground.

While he is thus strung up, one of the villains strikes him. With a sudden spring, Houdini gets his legs away, kicks the man under him and overpowers him. Then, standing on his body, with his feet alone he extracts from his pocket a key which opens the door of the room.

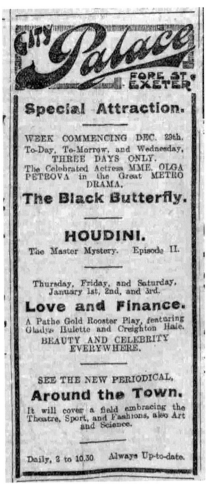

An advert for Houdini's silent movie, 'The Master Mystery', which was showing at the City Palace, Fore Street, Exeter during December 1919.

Holding this in his toes he unlocks the door, opens it, and by an acrobatic trick – he is no mean acrobat – gets his legs over the top of it. He is then able to release his hands.

The remarkable thing about it is the scene is continuous, there are no breaks to enable the film to be 'faked'.

The article stated that Houdini leapt from the Clifton Suspension Bridge, presumably while at Bristol. However, there seems to be no record of this and it seems likely that, with the great height of the bridge, the fall would have

Houdini driving his car with his wife Bess (left) and his sister Carrie Gladys Weiss in the back seat. (*Image courtesy of Library of Congress http://www.loc.gov*)

Houdini with hands chained and padlocked.

quite probably killed him. Perhaps the footage was just mocked up for Houdini's movie.

Houdini headed back to Britain in December 1919 to fulfil dates that had been postponed because of the First World War. His first appearance was on 19 December at the London Palladium where he was reported to have been paid $3,750 a week, which would have been an absolute fortune at the time. This was the highest salary that the theatre had ever paid to a performer.

Will Goldston recalled an incident with Houdini in his book *Sensational Tales of Mystery Men*:

> Houdini was a great man in many ways. He had courage, determination, and infinite patience. In other things he was often unscrupulous and dishonest.
>
> On one occasion I asked him to dine with me at my flat. At that time my hobby was collecting pictures of which I was said to be no mean judge: I was especially proud of one that I had recently bought, a small watercolour of a handsome woman. It was a real work of art, and occupied an important position on my drawing room wall.
>
> 'How do you like that, Harry?' I asked, pointing with the stem of my pipe at my latest acquisition. 'Pretty good, eh?'
>
> 'Good heavens, Will, that's mine!' came the startling reply.
>
> 'Yours?' I returned, puzzled. 'What do you mean?'
>
> 'Of course it's mine. It was promised to me.'

'Don't talk such rubbish. I can show you the receipt for it.'

'I can't help that. It was offered to me, and I said I would consider the matter. I must have it.'

'But I've paid for it.'

'What you have done is no concern of mine. I claim that picture.'

'Harry,' I said, gently. 'Your friendship is worth more to me than that picture. Don't let's have words over it.'

'No. Don't let's. I'll take it.'

Houdini removed the picture from the wall. I watched him in silence, wondering at the incredible smallness of the man's character. The next time I saw my watercolour, it was hanging in the bedroom of Harry's New York home.

Houdini wrote in his book *A Magician among the Spirits*:

During my last trip abroad, in 1919, I attended over one hundred séances with the sole purpose of honest investigation; these séances were presided over by well-known mediums in France and England.

Chapter Fifteen

1920 – The Final Tour

Houdini's last tour of Britain took place in 1920. The shows regularly began with Houdini showing scenes from his latest Hollywood films. He would then stroll on stage, to much applause, and begin his act.

The films *The Master Mystery* and *The Grim Game* showed throughout the year. Houdini's first show in the UK was at the Alhambra Theatre in Bradford between 12 and 17 January.

He performed his Water Torture Cell escape and offered £200 to any member of the audience who could prove that it was possible for him to get air while performing the stunt.

He next appeared at the Finsbury Park Empire between Monday 26 January and Saturday 31 January.

On Sunday 1 February, Houdini's fellow members of the Magicians' Club presented him with a scroll of welcome encased in a

An advert for Houdini's movie 'The Grim Game' which was showing at St George's Theatre in Canterbury during October 1920.

silver casket at a dinner held at the Savoy Hotel. The Great Raymond presided over the event which included performances from many well-known artists. Raymond had annoyed Houdini by ordering a Water Can for his act without Houdini's permission. Raymond apologised and admitted that Houdini was the founder of the escape. Tickets for the dinner were one guinea each.

Houdini was more interested talking about the movies he was currently making than about his magic. He had filmed scenes in various cities around Britain which he planned to incorporate in a later movie. He stated that he planned to concentrate more on movies than stage work.

Will Goldston recalled the event in his book *Sensational Tales of Mystery Men*:

A movie poster advertising 'The Grim Game'.

'The Grim Game' showing at the Royal Electric Theatre in Hartlepool during November 1920.

I have already made some reference to the weaker side of Harry Houdini's nature, his childishness, his irritability, and his quick temper. While it is not my intention to stress the faults of one who for many years was a friend, I feel it is my duty to present to the public a true pen picture of the man as I knew him.

The weakness of Houdini's character was never better illustrated than at an annual dinner of the Magicians' Club, eight or nine years ago. We had decided that the gathering would provide a splendid opportunity of making him a presentation, for he had been our President since the inauguration of the club.

It so happened that the only available magician of any repute willing to occupy the chair and make the presentation was The Great Raymond. And Harry detested Raymond. 'I won't accept anything from that --,' he declared hotly. 'Why, he pinches my ideas,' and then he went on to tell me in a few well chosen words just what he thought of Raymond's capabilities.

I felt the position very keenly, but, to my relief, I managed to talk Harry over. I was a happy man when he finally agreed to allow Raymond to officiate.

An advert for a Houdini movie which was shown at George's in February 1920.

'The Grim Game' showing at the Miners' Theatre, Ashington during November 1920.

We had several hundred cards printed for distribution amongst our members. But they didn't please Houdini.

'These are all wrong,' he said, when they arrived back from the printers.

'What's the matter with them?' I inquired wondering what my friend had at the back of his mind.

'You've got here 'In the Chair – The Great Raymond.' He's not great at all.'

'I shouldn't let that worry you. It's only a professional name.'

'Well it'll have to be altered. Call him just 'M. F. Raymond.' Even that's a damn sight too good for him. Don't let's argue about it, Will. Either you have these cards reprinted as I like them or I'll refuse to attend the dinner, and resign the presidency of the club in the bargain.'

There was no argument. The cards were reprinted.

After Finsbury Park, Houdini appeared at the Empire Palace in Liverpool between 2 and 7 February before heading back to Edinburgh to appear at the Empire Theatre, from 23 until 28 February.

While in Edinburgh, Houdini took Bess to the grave of the Great

The Great Lafayette with his dog, Beauty.

Lafayette. At the grave, he asked Lafayette to give him a sign of life after death. Pots with flowers that Houdini brought fell over and smashed. Rather than putting it down to anything spiritual, Houdini decided that it had just been caused by the strong wind.

At the beginning of March, Houdini injured his right ankle while performing the Water Torture Cell stunt and his doctor ordered him to rest for a week. It's unknown at which venue this took place. While he was laid up, he decided to collect together the notes he had written regarding fraud and trickery during the many séances that he'd attended. He wrote at the time, 'The more that I investigate the subject, the less I can make myself believe.' Houdini decided to write a book debunking spiritualists and contact with the dead.

A movie poster advertising 'Haldane of the Secret Service'.

Film sequences were shot in and around Edinburgh for Houdini's movie *Haldane of the Secret Service*. These involved fight scenes near to Waverley Station as well as shots of Haldane meeting two kilted soldiers in the city. This part of the film was edited out of the final version and appears to be lost although it could be in a private collection somewhere. Glass negatives showing some of the action have been sold at auction in

A later studio portrait of Harry Houdini.

the past and have raised hundreds of pounds each.

While in Edinburgh, in his quest for rare books, Houdini took Bess to the Knox House Old Curiosity Shop where the William J. Hay Bookseller shop was located.

Speaking in later years, Houdini stated, 'I once walked into a bookshop in Edinburgh and bought out the entire stock on the fourth floor, mostly books and manuscripts on spiritualism. I spent a whole day doing it.'

He next played at the Coliseum in Glasgow between 1 and 6 March. On the bill with Houdini were Maudie Ford, the Benedetti Brothers, Hughie Ogilvie, Moss and Maachah, George Morton and the Four Swifts.

The next venue was at the Empire in Leeds between 8 and 13 March. The *Yorkshire Evening Post* of Saturday, 13 March noted:

A poster advertising one of Houdini's shows during 1920.

There has probably never been anything in Leeds quite like the youngsters' nightly welcome to Houdini at the Empire this week. Some people believe the 'movies' are educating a new race of playgoers, who will tend to turn, in their time, from photographed players to real people. However that may turn out, there is no question that when an artist has attained popularity with the picture-going public, theatres are not big enough to hold those who went to see him on his appearance in the flesh.

Houdini has a good deal of affection for this part of England. 'A genuine affection,' he said. 'Don't think I tell this yarn everywhere I go. I don't.'

It was in Bradford that he made his first appearance in this country, just over 20 years ago. The big variety syndicates were shy of his turn and he went to the Bradford Palace on the offer of a trial week. That was why,

The Knox House Old Curiosity Shop where the William J. Hay Bookseller shop was located.

when he returned to this country a few weeks ago, after an absence of six years, he arranged his tour to begin at Bradford, at the Alhambra. Bradford gave him such a good start on the original venture that he did not hesitate to try it again.

It was in Leeds, just after his early start, that he got one of his first large salaries – at the City Varieties. He was paid the biggest sum ever paid there to any performer, up to then. The next best record was held by Jenny Lind.

Why does not Houdini do some of his original work as a defier of locks, bolts and bars, if only as a prelude to his water feat? His own answer is that people know all about that and want something fresh. Hammerstein, of New York, no mean showman, wanted him to do so and Houdini says he did, for one performance, after which Hammerstein gave in.

How did he first develop his extraordinary powers? He was about nine years old, he says (he is now 45), when he found a means of opening the lock of the cupboard in which his mother put pastry out of his reach and by that means, he had many a surreptitious feast. But though his mother never found out how it was done, she found a way of beating him. She hid things where he never thought of looking – in his own bedroom.

Houdini's next appearance was at the Empire Theatre in Sheffield between 15 and 20 March.

Houdini had sent Sir Arthur Conan Doyle a copy of his book, *The Unmasking of Robert-Houdin* to which Conan Doyle had shown great interest, particularly in a section which mentioned the Davenport Brothers who were American mediums and magicians. Conan Doyle was a devout spiritualist and believed in the work of mediums while Houdini realised that all the results were achieved by trickery.

While appearing at the Empire in Sheffield, Houdini wrote a letter to Conan Doyle which read:

Empire, Sheffield
17.3.20
Dear Sir Arthur Conan Doyle,
Pleased to hear from you and that you were interested about some of the points in my book.

Regarding the Davenport Brothers: It will interest you to know that I was an intimate friend of Ira Erastus Davenport, and was the last man outside his family circle to visit him in Maysville, Chautauqua County, New York. In fact he was waiting for me and passed away the morning I was leaving to pay him my annual visit.

I can make the positive assertion that the Davenport Brothers never were exposed. Their first trouble at the Salle Herz, in Paris, came about through the fact that one of the legs of the cabinet was dislodged, and the cabinet tripped over, and this happened only a short time after the arrival of the brothers in Paris.

The trouble they had in Leeds and Liverpool did not arise from the fact that they were exposed. Mr. Ira Davenport told me they were bound so inhumanely that Dr. Ferguson cut the rope before the séance started in Liverpool.

I know for a positive fact that it was not essential for them to release these bonds in order to obtain manifestations.

The reason why Mr. Ira Davenport became so friendly with me was that, during my tour around the world, I visited the cemetery where his brother, William Henry Harrison was buried near Melbourne, Australia. His grave had not been visited for many years and I had it put in order.

I have all the Davenport Brothers' scrapbooks, and intend, some time in the future, to write a biography about their career from a different 'angle' than any which have hitherto appeared.

I trust you will not think I am egotistical in making this statement; that I know more about the Davenport Brothers than anyone living. The widow is still alive and there are two sons and a daughter in this 'vale of tears'.

I remember distinctly, in talking to Mr Davenport, that he was astonished at my knowledge of their tours, and he remarked, 'Houdini, you know more about myself than I do.'

Regarding my own work, I never claim spiritualistic or supernatural aid, always informing the public that it is accomplished by natural means, or as you suggest by 'art and practice'.

I don't want to write a long letter, so will close.

Sincerely yours,

Harry Houdini.

Conan Doyle later wrote to Houdini: 'I've been reading the Davenport book you gave me. How people could imagine those men were conjurers is beyond me.'

Houdini's next performances were at the Palace Theatre in Hull between 22 and 27 March. The *Hull Daily Mail* of Tuesday 23 March reported:

PALACE THEATRE (6.45 and 8.45).—
Houdini (Himself), the World-famous Self-Liberator;
Naughton and Gold, Two Minds with One Thought,
"Laughter"; 10 Loonies, the famous Musical Comedians;
Susie Marney, the Chorus Comedienne; Four Mackwells,
Italy's Greatest Novelty Gymnasts; Zenora; Jack and
Tommie. Box Office 10 to 10 daily. Tel. 905. Please
Note: FREE LIST ENTIRELY SUSPENDED.

An advert for Houdini's show at the Palace Theatre, Hull between 22 and 27 March 1920.

Houdini on a tram in Hull, again, filming clips for 'Haldane of the Secret Service'. (*Image courtesy of John Cox http://www.wildabouthoudini.com/*)

Houdini disguised as Mr White, a persona he took on to discredit séances.

At the Hull Palace this week, Houdini presents some wonderful feats. Outstanding is his 'water torture cell' feat. In the course of this, he is suspended upside down in a glass tank full of water, his ankles being clamped into the lid, which is also padlocked from the outside. Houdini cannot, of course afford to waste any time trussed up in this position and he succeeds in liberating himself expeditiously.

Two photos show Houdini in Hull taken from scenes which appear in *Haldane of the Secret Service*. The first shows him running through the city and the second shows him on a tram. He's easy to spot in his grey suit and flat cap.

A still showing Houdini in Hull filming clips for his movie 'Haldane of the Secret Service'. (*Image courtesy of John Cox http://www. wildabouthoudini.com/*)

Will Goldston wrote about Houdini's failure in his films in his book *Sensational Tales of Mystery Men*:

To err is human, and Houdini was a human being. He did not make many mistakes during his lifetime, but it must not be supposed that his judgment was always infallible. The greatest blunder he ever made was to act for the films.

Harry had an idea that he could make a fortune on the movies. He decided to produce a film bringing in his more daring escapes and was convinced that he would be an enormous success. Pride, they say, goes before a fall.

Houdini was never cut out for film acting. Some years later he told me that his venture had cost him more than £100,000. But that was not all. Arnold de Biere, who had been persuaded to put some money into the scheme, also lost several thousands. In this manner was a long and affectionate friendship smashed beyond repair.

De Biere and Houdini were very great friends before the unhappy failure. Afterwards they became bitter enemies. De Biere's long and painful story casts very little credit on the American magician.

I remember Houdini calling on me one morning in one of his ugliest moods.

'Hello, Harry,' I said pleasantly. 'A friend of yours has just been in.'

'Oh? Who's that?'

'De Biere.'

'That b--,' cried Houdini, using an epithet that would have sounded better from the lips of a bargee. 'Does he often come in here?'

'Yes, quite often.'

'Well, if I meet him, I'll fling him down the stairs. So to save you any bother, p'raps I'd best not see him. Say, how do you switch on that light outside your door?'

'I have a switch on my desk.'

'That's O.K. When De Biere's in there with you, switch on the light. If I come up the stairs and see the light on, I'll know who's in, and come back later.'

I sighed. 'Alright, Harry,' I said. 'It's a fine idea.'

After his film failure, Houdini decided to return to vaudeville. He remembered the magical apparatus that had been stored since his failure in England, and thought the time had come when he should again present his conjuring act. Yes, he would stage a programme that America had never seen before, and call it the 'Houdini Road Show'.

Now he wanted the American Press to boost him again, and it was some time before he hit on the right scheme. At last he had an idea inspired by a number of spiritualistic lectures which Sir Arthur Conan Doyle had been giving in the States. Houdini would expose the spiritualists!

So Harry, the hero of sensational escapes, disguised himself and attended several of the séances which were being held as a direct outcome of Sir Arthur's tour. Then he declared he had discovered that Spiritualism was nothing but a gigantic fraud. He invited several pressmen to follow his lead, and find out the truth for themselves. As he had anticipated, his 'disclosures', as he called them, created a great sensation,

As a spiritualist myself, I know Houdini was not sincere in his statements. Every Jew believes through his religion that the spirit which passes out from the body at death, lives on. And Houdini was really a good Jew. On the death of his mother, he prayed that her spirit would be guarded and protected, and that she would be eternally happy. No real disbeliever would do that.

When he had the Press of the country with him, Houdini put his show on the road. His campaign against the spiritualists had met with such astounding success, that he decided to incorporate further propaganda in his programme. His performance consisted of magic and illusions, escapes (he could not entirely forget his old love) and a lecture against spiritualism, introducing apparatus which, he declared, was used by 'mediums' for faking spirit effects.

During the course of this lecture Houdini was in the habit of throwing a photograph of myself on to the screen. 'This is a friend of mine in England,' he would tell the audience. 'He is a magician, an author, and an inventor. But what astounds me more than anything else is this – he is a firm believer in Spiritualism!'

A description of Houdini was given, years later, by Edmund Wilson. Added to Will Goldston's accounts of Houdini's personality, it gives a good indication of what Houdini was really like. It read:

Houdini is a short strong stocky man with small feet and a very large head. Seen from the stage, his figure, with its short legs and its pugilist's proportions, is less impressive than at close range, where the real dignity and force of his enormous head appear. Wide-browed and aquiline-nosed, with a cleanness and fitness almost military, he suggests one of those enlarged and idealized busts of Roman generals or consuls. So it is rather the man himself than the showman, the personality of the

A description of Harry Houdini was given by Edmund Wilson in later years.

stage, who is interesting. Houdini is remarkable among magicians in having so little of the smart-aleck about him: he is a tremendous egoist, like many other very able persons, but he is not a cabotin. When he performs tricks, it is with the directness and simplicity of an expert giving a demonstration and he talks to his audience, not in his character of conjuror, but quite straightforwardly and without patter. His professional formulas – such as the 'Will wonders never cease!' with which he signalizes the end of a trick – have a quaint conventional sound as if they had been deliberately acquired as a concession to the theatre. For pre-eminently Houdini is the honest earnest craftsman which his German accent and his plain speech suggest – enthusiastic, serious-minded, thoroughgoing and intelligent.

Unfortunately, some emulators of Houdini's act ended in tragedy. In the *Nottingham Evening Post* of Saturday, 27 March 1920, a story appeared under the headline *BOY OF 14 HANGED*. It read:

At an inquest held in Lewisham yesterday on John Horatio Nelson Merrifield, a 14 year old boy of Davids Road, Forest Hill, who on Wednesday was found hanging from a clothes line stretched across the kitchen, a neighbour stated that in his opinion the lad had strangled himself while doing tricks to amuse the baby, of whom he had been left in charge. Merrifield was hanging from a slipknot.

The father said that the deceased had never threatened suicide.

When the coroner remarked that boys often saw lassoing acts at the cinema, the witness said that his boy was talking a lot recently about a film in which an actor named Houdini tied himself up in ropes.

Medical evidence showed that the death was due to suffocation by hanging and the coroner said that he would record an open verdict as there was no evidence to show how the boy was tied up.

Unfortunately, this wasn't an isolated case and there were reports of other boys hanging themselves while trying to copy Houdini.

Houdini next appeared at the Empire Theatre in Nottingham between 29 March and 3 April. Posters for the show announced, 'Houdini escapes out of an air-tight galvanised iron can, filled to the brim with water and locked with six padlocks. Everybody invited to bring padlocks.'

A critic from the *Evening Post* described the show as 'lacklustre'. The show was reviewed in advance but once the reporter had seen it, he felt compelled to issue an apology.

However, he had written:

Why on earth should Houdini imagine that any audience would be entertained by hearing a long and uncalled-for account of what he has been doing during the past six years? People go to a Vaudeville house to see a performance not to hear a diatribe on the personal pronoun worked around 'the story of my life, sir'.

The tour of 1920 pulled in Houdini's highest earnings ever and the people came not only to see him perform great escapes but also to be enthralled with stories from his life. While the reporter had not enjoyed Houdini's talk, the audience had.

From Nottingham, Houdini travelled to the Empire Theatre in Cardiff and played there between 5 and 10 April. His performance was advertised in the local newspapers but unusually, there are no reports of his shows.

When Houdini died in 1926, an obituary in the *Cardiff Western Mail* (on 2 November 1926) said that his last appearance in the city was in October 1920 and said that he was paid £400 for the week. However, the last newspaper advert for Houdini's act appears in April 1920 and none appear for October.

Houdini next appeared at the Hippodrome in Brighton between 12 and 17 April.

On 14 April, Houdini took a break from his act so that he could visit the home of Sir Arthur Conan Doyle in Sussex. As mentioned earlier, Houdini had introduced himself to Doyle by sending him his book, *The Unmasking of Robert Houdin*. He thought that Conan Doyle, a spiritualist, would be very interested in the chapter on the Davenport Brothers who were famous American nineteenth century mediums.

Over lunch the two discussed the Davenports and their alleged psychic abilities. Conan Doyle politely disagreed with Houdini, dismissing his claim that they were fakes. However, Houdini had interviewed Davenport ten years previously and he had admitted that it was all 'trickery'.

Houdini wrote about his friendship with Conan Doyle in 1924 in his book *A Magician Among the Spirits*:

The friendship of Sir Arthur and myself dates back to the time when I was playing the Brighton Hippodrome, Brighton, England. We had been corresponding and had discussed through the medium of the mail, questions regarding Spiritualism. He invited Mrs. Houdini and myself to the Doyle home in Crowborough, England, and in that way an acquaintanceship was begun which has continued ever since. Honest friendship is one of life's most precious treasures and I pride myself in thinking that we have held that treasure sacred in every respect. During all these years we have exchanged clippings which we thought might be of mutual interest and on a number of occasions have had an opportunity to discuss them in person. Our degree of friendship may be judged best from the following letter of Sir Arthur's:

'15 Buckingham Palace Mansion,
S. W. 1
March 8, 1923.

My dear Houdini:-
    For goodness' sake take care of those dangerous stunts of yours. You have done enough of them. I speak because I have just read of the death of the "Human Fly".
    Is it worth it?

(Signed)
Yours very sincerely,
A. CONAN DOYLE.'

There were many performers who called themselves the Human Fly, including Jack Lamonte and Rodman Law, but the one that Conan Doyle was referring to was Howard Young who died while scaling the Hotel Martinique, New York in 1923 when he fell from the eighth floor. At the time, his act was being filmed for a motion picture and hundreds had gathered to see him. In the crowd was his wife who fainted when the mishap occurred. From 19 until 24 April 1920, Houdini appeared at the Hippodrome in Portsmouth.

While at Portsmouth, Houdini wrote to Harry Kellar on the 20 April. His letter said, *'I had lunch with Sir Arthur Conan Doyle on Thursday and he saw my performance. He was so much impressed that there is little wonder in him believing in Spiritualism so implicitly.'*

During his 1920 tour of Britain, Houdini visited over 100 mediums with the aim of proving that they all employed fraudulent means.

The *Lincolnshire Echo* of Saturday 24 April reported:

After six years, Houdini, the Handcuff King, is back in London. In the early days of the war, he crossed the Atlantic, and though he admits that his recruiting efforts produced only 18 volunteers, he raised £20,000 for the British Red Cross by his entertainments and spent two years amusing the troops. In America, he put in some time as a 'movie star,' which, in his case, is a more than usually correct description, because his work in this connection has been done in mid-air, and for the sake of making a sensational film story has swung from one plane to another at the end of a rope. Then, after overtaking his movie-picture quest, he went through the experience of a genuine 3,000ft fall to earth and suffered no injury.

Houdini travelled to Newcastle-upon-Tyne to play at the Hippodrome between 26 April and 1 May. Posters on the tour described the showman as 'Houdini (himself)'. This was to stop confusion as Houdini movies were showing in every picture house up and down the country.

An article in the *Illustrated Chronicle* told of a reporter who had noticed a large crowd by St Nicholas' Cathedral at 12pm. Everyone was looking up at the spire of the cathedral and he asked a girl nearby what everyone was looking at. She told him that Houdini was due to be put in a box and thrown off. At 5pm, the reporter was again passing the cathedral and there were even more people there. An old man said that Houdini was due to appear at any minute. In reality, Houdini was in his dressing room at the Hippodrome preparing himself for his show. He knew nothing of the outdoor performance and the first he heard of it was when the reporter told him about it.

On 28 April Houdini visited Castle Keep in Newcastle where he hung off the Castle Parapet preparing himself for future movie stunts that he had to perform in America. While there, he was challenged to escape from a cell at the Castle Keep but, unusually, he turned the challenge down.

Also on the bill at Newcastle were Jack Shires, Les Videos, Nelson Jackson, the Great Maurice, the Sherlock Sisters and Clinton and Will Collinson.

The *Era* of Wednesday 28 April carried a story under the headline *HOUDINI RETURNS TO TOWN*:

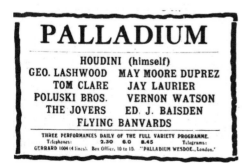

Houdini appearing at the Palladium in London between 3 and 8 May 1920.

'The Grim Game' showing at the Great Hall Cinema in Kent during December 1920.

After an absence from England of about six years, Houdini, 'the extricator,' recently returned fit and well and will open an engagement at the Palladium on Monday next. He was warmly greeted by an assembly of friends at the Victory Restaurant on Friday. Houdini has been on war work in America.

Houdini gave an interesting resume of his career, in which he declared that England was the first to recognise him. He added the description of a film 'stunt' in which he took part, when he hung to a rope suspended about 100 feet in the air, and had to wait for one of the several aeroplanes manoeuvring about to get near enough for him to transfer himself to it. Happily, he had had the inspiration to tie knots in the rope beforehand and was able to use them to stand upon.

Houdini once more played at the London Palladium between 3 May and 15 May. He was already a huge draw by the time he appeared again and the theatre was packed. On the night of the show, his name was announced and the curtains parted to show a movie of him escaping from a heavy roped trunk that had been dropped into the sea. After the movie, Houdini strolled onto the stage to much applause and charmed the audience with stories about his life.

The main part of his act was to be lowered into the Water Torture Chamber, bound and upside down. He managed to escape in 40 seconds and the audience

Houdini in front of the Houses of Parliament and Big Ben shooting scenes for 'Haldane of the Secret Service'. (*Image courtesy of John Cox http://www.wildabouthoudini.com/*)

A studio publicity photo of Will Goldston with facsimile signature.

cheered and applauded loudly. Will Goldston, who was at the show, recalled that Houdini had to beg to leave after being called back onto the stage four times.

Will Goldston remembered Houdini's performance at the Palladium in his book *Sensational Tales of Mystery Men*:

Arthur Conan Doyle and Harry Houdini outside the Automobile Club, Pall Mall, in London in 1920.

> *I can recall an amusing story of Houdini which throws an interesting sidelight on his extraordinary character. To appreciate the full point of this little yarn, it must be remembered that I am a professional magician of many years experience in performing and inventing. In addition, I was Houdini's greatest friend for a long period of years, and on many occasions he asked me to help and advise him with his illusions.*
>
> *When the American last appeared in this country, he was engaged at the London Palladium for a fortnight at the enormous salary of £900 a week.*
>
> *Before he was due to open, he informed me that he was running a 'really great show'. One trick in particular was a 'winner', and he wanted me to be in the theatre to see it. I could clearly see what the man was driving at, for I guessed he would be as pleased as Punch if he could mystify me as well as the rest of the audience.*
>
> *As I was talking to him in his dressing room before the performance, an assistant rapped on the door, and entered.*
>
> *'Well?' asked Houdini.*
>
> *'It's all right, boss,' came the answer.*
>
> *'I've fixed up those two confederates in the stalls and circle.'*
>
> *'You b-- fool,' screamed Harry jumping to his feet, his face white with rage. 'Can't you see we're not alone?'*

The assistant had inadvertently given the game away to Goldston by admitting that they had plants in the audience.

While Houdini appeared at the Palladium, Sir Arthur Conan Doyle wrote to him and asked if he would like to have luncheon at the Automobile Club, Pall Mall. Houdini accepted on behalf of his wife, her cousin and himself. He wrote back to Conan Doyle: 'If you would care to see the performance at the Palladium, please let me know how many seats you want and for which performance.'

While in London, Houdini told reporters:

If I were to die tomorrow, I could not complain. I would pass out content with the fullness of life and with the knowledge of experiences such as few men have had. I have performed every feat of magic. The largest thing, probably, was my vanishing elephant, Jenny, weighing 10,000lbs, who used to disappear systematically twice nightly, and my smallest feat, swallowing a couple of packages of needles and bringing them out threaded.

About two years ago, I decided to go into motion pictures to perpetuate my work as a magician. The next generation will be sceptical about the stories of my magic and I want handed down actual proofs. Even then, it will be difficult to convince the sceptical.

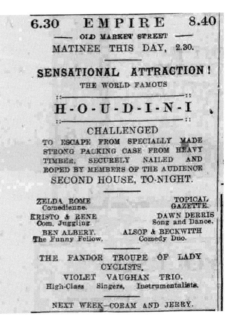

Also on the bill at the Palladium were George Lashwood, May Moore Duprez, Tom Clare, Jay Laurier, the Poluski Brothers, Vernon Watson, the Jovers, Ed J. Baisden and the Flying Banvards. Three full performances were given daily at 2.30pm, 6.00pm and 8.45pm.

Houdini's next appearance was at the Empire Theatre, Bristol between 24 and 29 May. The employees of Mr Frank Wilkins, builder and contractor of 24 Temple Back, Bristol, challenged him to escape from a strong packing case. The escape took place during the second house of Wednesday 26 May.

An advert for Houdini's show at the Empire Theatre, Bristol, where he appeared between 24 and 29 May 1920.

Houdini challenged at the Empire, Old Market Street, Bristol on 28 May 1920.

Houdini received a second challenge while at the Bristol Empire which read:

EX-POLICE CONSTABLES' CHALLENGE!
HOUDINI,
Empire Theatre Bristol. 26th May 1920

Dear Sir,
We, the undersigned Committee, having served more than 112 years between
us, in the BRISTOL POLICE DEPARTMENT, would like to know if we could
challenge you to escape out of an OBSOLETE PUNISHMENT SUIT.
  This restraint holds the prisoner from the neck down to and including the
feet; is made from extra heavy canvas, and bound with leather. Your arms to be
crossed in front and buckled behind your back. In addition, four belting straps
encircling your body, so as to make you utterly helpless. The only condition
under which we will put you to the test, is that if you accept the challenge; you
must RELEASE YOURSELF IN FULL VIEW OF THE AUDIENCE, to prove
you obtain no secret assistance.

The announcement then listed all the names of the policemen making the challenge.

  Beneath this it read: *HOUDINI ACCEPTS CHALLENGE! And it will be performed at the Second House, Friday Night, May 28th, 1920, at the Empire, Old Market St.*

  From Monday 31 May until Saturday 5 June Houdini appeared at the Glasgow Pavilion. The *Edinburgh Evening News* of Wednesday 2 June carried a story under the headline *HOUDINI STUNT BARRED*. It read:

Houdini performing on stage at the Glasgow Pavilion on 3 June 1920.

Houdini, who is at present appearing at the Glasgow Pavilion, asked the
permission of the magistrates to be lowered into the Clyde, handcuffed, in a box.
It was proposed that a collection should be taken for charity. The magistrates
refused permission yesterday on the ground that there might be danger to the
public, as the railings of the bridge might give way under pressure.

Houdini later wrote of his time in Glasgow:

My assistant is always supplied with a stop-watch; in fact for my under-water tests, I had specially made by a watchmaker in Glasgow, the largest stop-watch in the world, by means of which persons in the gallery who did not possess such watches themselves could see the second hand as it jumped around the dial, and thus share in the interest, for you should know that not every theatre-goer carried a stop-watch.

A publicity shot of Harry Houdini.

On 7 until 12 June, Houdini appeared at the New Cross Empire. An autograph from the time suggests that he was in Brighton on 14 June.

The *Folkestone, Hythe, Sandgate and Cheriton Herald* of Saturday 3, July 1920 carried the words 'Victoria Pier, Sunday – Houdini' but said no more.

The New Cross Empire appearance of Houdini is his last well-recorded show in Great Britain but there could possibly be more. Houdini was still in England on 19 June 1920, the day he wrote to Sir Arthur Conan Doyle about a séance conducted by a French medium, Eva Carrière, whose real name was Marthe Béraud. The séance was held at the Society for Psychical Research in London. Houdini felt that the act was little more than trickery while Conan Doyle disagreed. Their association continued for many years but Conan Doyle's belief in fairies, goblins and spirits, while Houdini continued to expose much of what he believed in as nonsense, eventually led to the downfall of their friendship.

Frances Griffiths and the Leaping Fairy.

Houdini's six-month tour had proved to be his most successful ever. When he left, he wouldn't have realised that this was to be his last tour of Britain. However, he now had other interests which included making movies and writing.

While appearing at the Princess Theatre in Montreal, Houdini was given several surprise blows to his abdomen by a McGill University student, J. Gordon Whitehead. The incident took place in Houdini's dressing room.

Arthur Conan Doyle was a devout believer in the Cottingley fairies. This photo shows Frances Griffiths, one of the girls who claimed to have seen the fairies.

Houdini and his wife, Bess.

Before punching him, Whitehead had asked Houdini if he believed in the miracles of the Bible and whether it was true that punches in the stomach did not hurt him.

Houdini had been able to withstand similar blows but was completely unprepared for the attack. At the time, he was reclining on a couch after breaking his ankle several days earlier.

Houdini, although in great pain, continued to perform on stage and the discomfort lasted for a further two days before he finally saw a doctor. He had a high temperature and was found to have acute appendicitis. The doctor advised him that he needed an operation. Houdini, however, decided to carry on performing and took to the stage at the Garrick Theater in Detroit, Michigan, on 24 October 1926. He passed out during the show but recovered and carried on. Afterwards he was taken to Detroit's Grace Hospital.

Houdini died several days later of peritonitis due to a ruptured appendix on 31 October 1926. The connection between the incident in the dressing room and his death was unclear. However, Houdini's insurance company took this as the cause of death.

Houdini was just 52 years old when he died and although he was nearing the end of his career, the world lost a great showman whose name would forever become synonymous with great feats of escape.

Chapter Sixteen

Timeline of Appearances and Events

1900
2 July–1 September: Alhambra Theatre, London
3 December–2 February: Alhambra Theatre, London

1901
Houdini was still at the Alhambra on 2 Feb
4–9 February: Palace Theatre, Bradford

1902
13 October–18 October: People's Palace Theatre, Halifax
20 October–25 October: Palace Theatre, Blackburn
27 October–1 November: Palace Theatre, Bradford
3 November–8 November: People's Palace Theatre, Halifax
3 November–8 November: People's Victoria Hall, Halifax (extra matinees)
10 November–15 November: Pavilion Theatre, Leicester
17 November–22 November: St. James Hall, Manchester
24 November–29 November: Palace Theatre, Blackburn
1 December–6 December: City of Varieties, Leeds
8 December–13 December: Empire Theatre of Varieties, Burnley
15 December–20 December: City of Varieties, Leeds
15 December–20 December Coliseum, Leeds (extra matinees)

1903
9 November–14 November: Pavilion Theatre, Leicester
16 November–21 November: People's Palace Halifax
30 November–5 December: Empire, Huddersfield
14 December–19 December: The Palace, Blackburn
21 December–26 December: Palace Theatre, Hull
28 December–2 January Birmingham

1904
18 January–23 January: Empire Palace, Sheffield
25 January–6 February: Empire Theatre, Liverpool
6 February: Charity appearance at the Empire Palace, Sheffield

8 February–13 February: Empire, South Shields
15 February–27 February: Empire Theatre, Birmingham
29 February–2 April: Hippodrome, London
4 April–9 April: Hippodrome, London (retained for Easter week)
18 April–23 April: Palace, Hull
25 April–30 April: Empire Palace, Sheffield
2 May–7 May: Empire, Leeds
9 May–14 May: Hippodrome, Brighton
16 May–21 May: The Empire and Hippodrome, Bristol
29 August–3 September: Empire, Leicester Square
5 September–24 September: Zoo Hippodrome, Glasgow
26 September–8 October: Regent Theatre, Salford
10 October–15 October: Empire Theatre, Bristol
17 October–29 October: Hippodrome, Liverpool
31 October–5 November: Palace Theatre, Halifax
14 November–19 November: Tivoli Theatre, Leeds
28 November– 3 December: Pavilion, Newcastle
5 December–10 December: Hippodrome, Brighton
12 December–17 December: Palace Theatre, Manchester

1905
2 January–7 January: Barnard's Theatre, Woolwich
16 January–28 January: Palace Theatre, Glasgow
January 30–4 February: Barnard's Palace of Varieties, Chatham
13 February–18 February: St Georges Hall, Bradford
20 February–25 February: Theatre Royal, Stockton
3 April–8 April: Alexandra Theatre, Sheffield
10 April–15 April: Kings Theatre, Cardiff
17 April–22 April: Lyceum Theatre, Newport
24 April–29 April: Hippodrome, Eastbourne
1 May–6 May: Empire Theatre, Oldham
8 May–13 May: The Grand Theatre, Wolverhampton
15 May–20 May: Pavilion Theatre, Leicester
22 May–27 May: Avenue Theatre, Sunderland
29 May–3 June: Argyle Theatre of Varieties, Birkenhead
5 June–10 June: Wigan
12 June–17 June: Hippodrome, Blackpool
19 June–24 June: Hippodrome, Hastings
26 June–8 July: Gaiety Theatre, Leith
Friday 25 August: The Protestant Hall, Ballymena one night only
Monday 11 September: Newry Town Hall

1907
4 May: Empire, Sheffield

1908
2 November–28 November: Oxford Music Hall, London
30 November–5 December: Euston Palace, London
7 December–12 December: Hippodrome, Liverpool
14 December–19 December: Hippodrome, Birmingham
15 December: Jumped into the reservoir at Edgbaston
21 December–26 December: Grand Theatre, Bolton
28 December–2 January: Paragon Theatre London

1909
4 January–9 January: Palace East Ham, London
11 January–16 January: Pavilion, Liverpool
18 January–23 January: Regent Theatre, Salford
25 January–30 January: Hippodrome, Belfast
1 February–13 February: Palace Theatre, Glasgow
15 February–20 February: Hulme Hippodrome, Manchester
22 February–27 February: Empire, Ashton–under–Lyne
1 March–6 March: Royal Hippodrome, Preston
8 March–13 March: Empire Theatre, Bristol
3 May–8 May: Hippodrome, Blackburn
10 May–15 May: Pavilion, Newcastle
17 May–22 May: Metropolitan, London
24 May–29 May: Hippodrome, Portsmouth
31 May–5 June: Palace Theatre, Chelsea
7 June–12 June: Hippodrome, Leeds
14 June–19 June: Empire, Wolverhampton
20 June: Jumped in Dundee Dock
21 June–26 June: King's Theatre and Hippodrome, Dundee
23 June: Jumped into the River Tay
28 June–3 July: Palace Theatre, Aberdeen
5 July–10 July: Hippodrome, Brighton
19 July–24 July: Palace, Manchester
26 July–31 July: Barrasford's Hippodrome, Sheffield
2 August–7 August: Hippodrome, Nottingham
16 August–23 August: Palace Theatre, Plymouth
30 August–4 September: Empire Theatre, Kilburn
13 September–18 September: Hippodrome, Willesden

20 September–25 September: Palace, South London
4 October–9 October: Coliseum Theatre, Glasgow
11 October–16 October: Palace, Oldham
18 October–23 October: Coliseum, Glasgow

1910
12 September–17 September: Empire Theatre, Kilburn
3 October–8 October: Hippodrome, Poplar
10 October–15 October: Hippodrome, Willesden
17 October–22 October: Harlsden
31 October–5 November: Palace, Hammersmith
7 November–12 November: Empire Theatre, Islington
14 November–19 November: Grand Theatre, Clapham
21 November–26 November: Olympia Theatre, Liverpool
28 November–3 December: Empire Theatre, Manchester
5 December–10 December: Empire Theatre, Holborn
12 December–17 December:Coliseum Theatre, Glasgow
19 December–24 December: Empire Palace Theatre, Edinburgh
26 December–31 December: Empire Theatre Newcastle

1911
2 January–7 January: Hippodrome, Bolton
9 January–14 January: Empire Theatre, Nottingham
16 January–21 January: Empire Theatre, Birmingham
23 January–28 January: Empire Theatre, Bradford
30 January–4 February: Palace Theatre, Hull
6 February–11 February: Empire Theatre Leeds
13 February–18 February: Barnard's Theatre, Chatham
20 February–25 February: Rochester
6 March–11 March: Empire Palace, Sheffield
13 March–18 March: Empire Theatre, Cardiff
27 March–1 April: Hippodrome, Southend–on–sea
3 April–8 April: Palace, Huddersfield
10 April–15 April: Hippodrome, Portsmouth
17 April–22 April: Palace, Burnley
24 April–29 April: Hippodrome, Southampton
1 May–6 May: Empire, Swansea
8 May–13 May: Empire, Hackney
15 May–20 May: Empire, Finsbury Park
22 May–27 May: New Cross Empire, London

29 May–3 June: Palace Theatre, Halifax
5 June–10 June: Empire, Shepherds Bush

1913

6 January–11 January: Empire Theatre, Cardiff
13 January–18 January: Empire Theatre, Swansea
20 January–25 January: Empire, Bradford
27 January–1 February: Palace Theatre, Hull
3 February–8 February: Empire, Leeds
5 February: Jumped into the lake at Roundhay Park
10 February–15 February: Empire and Hippodrome, Bristol
17 February–22 February: King's Theatre, Southsea
February: Palace Theatre, Oxford Street, Manchester (exact date unknown)
24 February–1 March: Empire, Finsbury Park
3 March–8 March: Empire, Newport
5 March: Jumped from Newport Bridge
12 March: Appeared in court at Newport
16 March: Opened the Magicians' Club at 2 Gray's Inn Road
17 March–22 March: Olympia, Liverpool
24 March–29 March Hippodrome, Devonport
31 March–5 April: Empire Theatre, Newcastle
1 April: Jumped from the Swing Bridge at Newcastle
7 April–12 April: Empire Theatre, Edinburgh
14 April–19 April: Glasgow, Coliseum
April: Hippodrome, Hall Craig Street, Airdrie (exact date unknown)
21 April–26 April: Empire Palace, Sheffield
28 April–3 May: Empire, Birmingham
5 May–10 May: Empire Theatre, Nottingham
12 May–17 May: New Cross Empire, London
17 July: Houdini's mother died
26 July: Hippodrome, Sheffield show cancelled because of death of mother

1914

12 January–17 January: Tivoli, Barrow in Furness
19 January–24 January: Bradford, Empire
26 January–31 January: Grand Theatre, Birmingham
1 February: Attended the first anniversary of the Magicians' Club
2 February–7 February: Sheffield, Empire
9 February–14 February: Empire Theatre, Glasgow
16 February–21 February: Empire Theatre, Leeds

23 February–28 February: New Palace, Manchester
1 March: Attended the annual dinner of the Manchester Press Club
3 March–8 March: Swansea, Empire
16 March–21 March: Empire, Newport
23 March–28 March: The Empire, Bristol
30 March–4 April: Empire, Newcastle
6 April–11 April: Empire Palace Theatre, Edinburgh
13 April–18 April: Olympia Theatre, Liverpool
20 April–25 April Palace Theatre, Oldham
26 April: Jumped from the Corporation Pier, Hull
27 April–2 May: Palace Theatre, Hull
4 May–9 May: New Cross Empire, London
25 May–30 May: Empire Theatre, Cardiff
1 June–6 June: Kings Hall, Dover
2 June: Jumped from a motor-boat into the Admiralty Harbour between the Prince of Wales and promenade piers at Dover
8 June–13 June: Empire Theatre, Nottingham

1919
19 December: London Palladium

1920
12 January–17 January: Alhambra Theatre, Bradford
26 January–31 January: Empire, Finsbury Park
 2 February–7 February: Empire Palace, Liverpool
23 February–28 February: Empire Theatre, Edinburgh
1 March–6 March: Coliseum, Glasgow
8 March–13 March: Empire, Leeds
15 March–20 March: Empire Theatre, Sheffield
22 March–27 March: Palace Theatre, Hull
29 March–3 April: Empire Theatre, Nottingham
5 April–10 April: Empire Theatre, Cardiff
12 April–17 April: Hippodrome, Brighton
19 April–24 April: Hippodrome, Portsmouth
26 April–1 May: Hippodrome, Newcastle-upon-Tyne
3 May–8 May: London Palladium
10 May–15 May: London Palladium
24 May–29 May: Empire Theatre, Bristol
31 May–5 June: Glasgow Pavilion
7 June–12 June: New Cross Empire

Acknowledgements

Thanks to John Cox whose wonderful blog Wild About Harry is a great inspiration. John has always been very helpful, friendly and supportive while I've been putting the book together and it's much appreciated. Many thanks also go out to John Connolly and Marco Pusterla who were both very kind and lent me some excellent photos and memorabilia from their collections.

Thanks also to Mick Hanzlik, Dan Robinson (Weazle Dandaw), Paul Zenon, Paul Kieve, Allan Taylor, Alison Cable (Medway Archives and Local Studies), Narinda Chadda (Birmingham Central Library), Sarah Powell (Bradford Central Library), the Community History Department (Blackburn Central Library), Lorna Basham (Plymouth Library Services), Dan Robinson, Michael Towsey (Clapham Library), Peter Hey (Hampton Library), Shona Milton (Brighton Library), Sarah Steenson (Belfast Library), Katrina Presedo (Kensington Central Library), Zoe Edwards (Hastings Library), Ken Crowe (Southend Museum), Carole Higson (Burnley Library), Shirley Nuell (Bristol Library), Stephen Hawley (Newcastle Library), Hannah Lincoln (Stockton Reference Library), Penny Rudkin (Southampton Central Library), Michael Stephens (Cumbria Archives and Local Studies Library), Aidan Flood (Holborn Library), Edith Wemyss (Aberdeen Library), Jacqueline Evans (Swansea Library), Katrina Coopey (Cardiff Library), Gary Carson (The Local and Family History Centre, Blackpool), Anne Jackson (Calderdale Library), John Wood (Sunderland Library), Julie Baker (Wigan Library), Christine Barraclough (Huddersfield Library), Lesley Openshaw (Bolton Library), Lynne Humphries (Sheffield Library), Roger Hull (Liverpool Record Office), Sarah Powell (Bradford Central Library), Helen Skilbeck (Leeds Library), Community History Department (Blackburn Central Library), Toby Evans (Southend on Sea Library), Martin Haynes (Edinburgh Library), Allie Dillon (Islington Local History Centre), Zoe Darani (Lambeth Archives), Edmund Dunne (The Manchester Room & County Record Office), United States Library of Congress and David Logan (Cardiff Library), Tina Cole, Tilly Barker and Phil Morris. Thanks to the many people who have kindly sent me stories, cuttings and photos. I apologise to anyone not mentioned.

Bibliography

Books:
The Adventurous Life of A Versatile Artist by Harry Houdini (1922)
A Magician among the Spirits by Harry Houdini (1924)
Houdini: The Untold Story by Milbourne Christopher (1969)
Houdini: A Pictorial Biography by Milbourne Christopher (1998)
The Amazing World of Sunderland by Alan Brett (1994)
Magic: A Picture History by Milbourne Christopher (1992)
The Magician Annual (1909)
The Secret Life of Houdini by William Kalush and Larry Sloman (Pocket Books 2007)
The Secrets of Houdini by J.C. Cannell (Dover Publications 1973)
Houdini by Clinton Cox (Scholastic 2001)
Looking Into The Mirror by Mick Hanzlik (2007)
Houdini's Mirror Handcuff Challenge 1904 by Mick Hanzlik (2007)
Houdini: A biography by Mick Hanzlik (2007)
Houdini and Conan Doyle: the Story of a Strange Friendship by Bernard M.L. Ernst and Hereward Carrington (1933)
Randini, The Man Who Helped Houdini by Ann Beedham (2009)
Sensational Tales of Mystery Men by Will Goldston (1928)
The London Palladium: The Story of the Theatre and Its Stars By Chris Woodward (Jeremy Mills Publishing 2009)

Newspapers:
The Aberdeen Free Press
The Aberdeen Journal
The Ballymena Observer
The Birmingham Daily Gazette
The Blackburn Standard
The Blackburn Star
The Blackpool Gazette and News
The Burnley Express
The Burnley Gazette
The Cardiff Review Western Mail

The Cardiff Western Mail
The Daily Express
The Daily Illustrated Mirror
The Daily Mirror
The Derbyshire Times and Chesterfield Herald
The Dover Express
The Dramatic Mirror
The Dundee Courier
The Dundee Evening Post
The Dundee Evening Telegraph
The Edinburgh Evening News
The Era
The Exeter Gazette
The Evening Despatch
The Fife Free Press and Kirkcaldy Guardian
The Folkestone, Hythe, Sandgate and Cheriton Herald
The Glasgow Times
The Graphic
The Halifax Evening Courier
The Halifax Guardian
The Hastings and St Leonard's Advertiser
The Hastings Observer
The Hastings Weekly Mail and Times
The Hull Daily Mail
The Illustrated Chronicle
The Lancashire Evening Post
The Leeds Mercury
The Lincolnshire Echo
The Liverpool Daily Post
The Liverpool Echo
The London Daily News
The London Evening Standard
The Manchester Courier and Lancashire General Advertiser
The Newcastle Journal
The New York Player
The Northern Daily Telegraph
The North Mail
The Nottingham Evening Post
The Oldham Chronicle
The Oldham Standard

The Performer
The Portsmouth Evening News
The Rochester Democrat and Chronicle
The Scotsman
The Sevenoaks Chronicle and Kentish Advertiser
The Sheffield and Rotherham Independent
The Sheffield Daily Telegraph
The Sheffield Evening Telegraph
The Sheffield Independent
The Shields Daily Gazette
The Stage
The Star
The Sunderland Daily Echo and Shipping Gazette
The Weekly Dispatch
The Western Daily Press
The Western Evening Herald
The Western Morning News
The Western Times
What's on in Southampton
The Yorkshire Evening Post

Recommended websites:
John Cox's website at:
http://www.houdini–lives.com/Houdini_Lives/HOME.html
John Cox's Wild About Harry blog at
http://www.wildabouthoudini.com/
Kevin Connolly's website at http://houdinihimself.com/
Marco Pusterla's blog at https://smallmagicollector.wordpress.com/
The Houdini Museum at https://houdinimuseum.wordpress.com/

Index